westlife
on tour

westlife
on tour

EDDIE ROWLEY

EBURY
PRESS

First published in Great Britain in 2001

3 5 7 9 10 8 6 4 2

Ebury Press
Random House · 20 Vauxhall Bridge Road · London SW1V 2SA

Random House Australia Pty Limited
20 Alfred Street · Milsons Point · Sydney · New South Wales 2061 · Australia

Random House New Zealand Limited
18 Poland Road · Glenfield · Auckland 10 · New Zealand

Random House (Pty) Limited
Endulini · 5A Jubilee Road · Parktown 2193 · South Africa

The Random House Group Limited Reg. No. 954009

www.randomhouse.co.uk

Papers used by Ebury Press are natural, recyclable products
made from wood grown in sustainable forests.

A CIP catalogue record for this book is available from the British Library.

ISBN 0 09 188094 7

Designed by Lovelock & Co.

Printed and bound by Clays Ltd, St.Ives plc

Front cover photograph © Philip Ollerenshaw/Idols

Researcher: Sarah Hamilton

All photographs included in the picture section © Eddie Rowley,
except where indicated

Contents

CHAPTER 1

Dancing boys and a baby shocker

The svelte dancer with the Scary Spice look and attitude flicks back her shoulders, wriggles her hips and flexes her two arms in a pumping action.

Clapping her hands, she demands in a deep, throaty voice: 'OK guys, show me what you can do. Dance as if you were in a club. Do whatever you do on a night out.'

Switching on the music of a Westlife track, Dreams Come True, the choreographer waits for her dance students to launch into their individual styles. Instead, the five handsome young men hang their heads, glance sheepishly at her and appear to be frozen rigid on the spot.

'C'mon, guys, just do what comes naturally to you!' she roars, encouraging them on.

The five statues refuse to budge. The reflections of their faces in the massive mirrored wall of the studio clearly reveal their gut-wrenching nerves. A tanned Kian Egan sucks in his cheeks. Dark, broody Shane Filan rocks his right leg back and forth. Blue-eyed Nicky Byrne fidgets with his baseball cap. Towering Bryan McFadden pulls one of his manic faces; and heavy-set

Mark Feehily's solemn look and navel-gazing gives the impression that he wishes the ground would open up and swallow him.

Clearly embarrassed and fearful of appearing foolish in front of this world-renowned choreographer, who has worked with everyone from Tina Turner and Whitney Houston to the Spice Girls and S Club 7, none of the Westlife boys is eager to make the first move.

Priscilla Samuels sighs and shakes her head. This is going to be more difficult than she'd anticipated.

It is the morning of January 9, 2001, and Westlife's first day of rehearsals in Dublin for their world tour that kicks off in just four weeks' time. Priscilla, a wiry bundle of energy with a big personality, has been drafted in to whip Westlife into shape as dancers. Even though they've created pop history by this stage, scoring SEVEN Number One hits in a row, the five Irish heart-throbs aren't like many bands of their ilk because they haven't been trained as dancers. They are a vocal group. It has never been about dance with them. With ambitious plans in place for their very first major stage production, a tour that will take them into the superleague as a live act, Westlife have a new challenge on their hands. They are pin-up idols to a generation of teens and twenty-somethings, but now need to prove themselves to be world-class entertainers. That means their performance will have to be visually exciting, energetic and like nothing the critics and fans have come to expect of them.

This morning, however, their star status seems to have been thrown out with the Christmas wrapping paper. The fired-up choreographer has yet to detect the showbiz fighting spirit that has taken them to the top of the pop world.

It's not that she's looking for the genius footwork of Michael Jackson, or the flamboyance of Michael Flatley, the Irish-American who put Riverdance on the map around the world. When world-renowned coach Priscilla signed up to choreograph their stage show, the London-based showbiz diva had known that Westlife weren't a dance act.

But she'd expected them to be able to do SOME dancing.

'C'mon, Mark, you know you can do it, give it a go,' she prods, waving her arms wildly in front of him.

'I can't,' he insists, glued to the spot and with a pained expression on his face.

Clearly, Priscilla will have to work on some confidence-building exercises. She switches off the music, and with a manic swing of her spindly arms, calls the boys to gather round her, like a football trainer.

'I have to see everybody move before I can choreograph you,' she explains, scanning their distressed faces and recognising the nervousness in their eyes. 'That's the way I work. Every group I work with is different, so I tailor the dancing and moves to suit the individuals and their music. I don't just duplicate the steps of other acts. My aim is to create a Westlife routine, one that will be instantly identifiable with each and every one of you. And it will be movement that you are comfortable with.'

An animated Priscilla now has their attention and the ice is beginning to melt. Mark is even showing the trace of a smile.

'I know it's not easy to step up cold and start dancing in front of strangers, or even friends. The only reason you don't want to dance is because you don't feel confident doing it. It doesn't mean you can't do it. Everybody is shy at first. But don't worry about looking like a prat. It's all about doing it and building up your confidence. You all have it inside you and my job is to bring it out.'

Priscilla beckons over her assistant Paula Barratt, who has been hovering in the background. In contrast to Priscilla's bubbly, in-your-face personality, the young, dark-haired Paula is quiet and reserved.

'Relax, guys, and watch us,' Priscilla says, bouncing across the room to power up the music system. Priscilla and Paula now launch into a series of dances that are poetry in motion. It's an exhilarating experience seeing the girls effortlessly strutting their stuff, and the five boys are so mesmerised by the fluency of the female dancers' movement that they forget about their own inhibitions and begin to join in.

'Yeeaah!' Priscilla roars, her face beaming with satisfaction. 'Now we're going places.'

Inspired by the performance of Priscilla and Paula, the boys step forward and tentatively prepare to do their solo spots.

'It's like being back in school all over again,' Kian quips.

'What do you think I am, some snooty school mistress?' Priscilla jokes, her laughter reverberating around the studio.

'I suppose she'll give us lines, lads, if we don't get it right,' says Bryan.

'Damn right!' Priscilla responds with a frown that indicates she just might be serious.

They all look at each other, then laugh. Bonds are beginning to form between the teacher and her students amid all the light-hearted banter.

Westlife have never worked with Priscilla before, so day one of rehearsals is also about the boys getting to know her and vice-versa. It doesn't take long for Priscilla to realise that she is dealing with a bunch of cheeky schoolboy types and she really will have to adopt a school mistress approach every now and then to keep them in order.

Priscilla turns on the music again and, with the exception of Mark, the boys begin to loosen up and attempt their individual routines. Despite his carefree image, Bryan still looks a little nervous as he jumps around.

'Bryan, you can see, is a disco person,' Priscilla remarks. 'Definitely. Put your handbag down and go for it, is that one.'

The attention moves to Shane, Kian and Nicky.

'Shane is a good dancer. He's very Greased Lightning,' she notes. 'Kian and Nicky are not bad either.'

Mark seems to be completely lost at sea. There is very little rhythm going on. He just can't seem to get into a groove.

'Relax, Mark, and let the tension out of your system,' Priscilla coaxes. 'Just do whatever comes natural to you.'

'I can't,' he pleads, as he walks around the studio, totally bewildered by the exercise. 'I can't. I can't,' he mutters again.

'Don't worry, Mark. It'll come,' Priscilla assures him.

All five are struggling with their routines. They stand back and watch Priscilla and Paula demonstrate the moves. It all looks so simple until they try to replicate them.

The boys have been used to sitting on high stools singing ballads. Now they have to extend their talents to bring an entirely new element to their performances. The new dances come at them like an avalanche. They occasionally look shell-shocked at the prospect of having to move, run around the stage and sing – all at the same time.

Dreams Come True, the opening number of the Westlife tour, is the first routine they have to master. It is also one of the most intricate in terms of movement, so it's quite demanding. At first, Priscilla works the boys to the music without the vocals, to see how they move to it.

Somebody Needs You turns out to be another big dance number from which Priscilla develops a story theme that will later become a major scene with the addition of female dancers. Whenever they can't get to grips with new routines the boys become angry and frustrated with themselves. Hand-held mics are chucked across the floor. Baseball caps go flying around the room with abandon.

'Feck!' Shane snaps when he forgets to turn in unison with the other lads during one routine.

'Shit!' Bryan growls as he stumbles over his steps.

Mark huffs and puffs so much it looks like he is experiencing a heart attack. Nicky, his face flushed and the lines of concentration etched across his forehead, has the look of a condemned man on his way to the gas chamber. He lifts his baseball cap and runs his fingers through his long locks, now matted with sweat. Kian too appears exhausted as he bravely battles to follow the moves.

Priscilla is totally supportive and encouraging. Whenever their confidence drops, she takes them aside for a morale-boosting team talk. She realises that they are working against the clock and are extremely worried that they won't master their routines before opening night in just four weeks time. Disaster is looming in their minds, so Priscilla has to keep them motivated and thinking positively.

'Guys, you're doing great. Believe me, it's happening. I'm amazed at what you've picked up so far, so don't panic. Panic is a killer. When you panic, you foul up at what you do. You need to take it a step at a time.'

Having two choreographers working with the boys ensures that even the weakest link is soon brought up to speed.

'With two people we can spread ourselves around with the five boys,' Priscilla explains. 'With five guys to watch, we can both spot things. If someone is a little slower on a number, then Paula or myself will spend time with that person getting it right, while one of us can continue working with the others.'

Four days into the intensive coaching, there is an upbeat atmosphere at Camp Westlife. Priscilla has waved her wand, woven her magic and the transformation in the boys is astonishing. Their limbs are now moving in rhythm to the music and they have mastered some impressive routines. Suddenly, it is beginning to dawn on Westlife that they are making serious progress. After completing a dance sequence for Dreams Come True without flunking a single move, the boys, who could see their performance in the mirrored studio wall before them, are totally elated.

'Yee-yesss!' they roar in unison when the music stops. Suddenly they launch into a series of hugs and high hand claps. And they jump around as if they've just scored the winning goal in the Cup Final at Wembley. They have amazed themselves.

'How does that feel now?' Priscilla inquires of Mark at the end of the set.

A smile breaks across his sweaty face.

'Great! Just great!' he pants, obviously revelling in his newly acquired skills. Michael Jackson eat your heart out!

'I had done a lot of dancing on stage in musicals, but this was much more difficult at the start,' Mark says. 'Personally I wasn't very confident when Priscilla asked us to dance freestyle; that's just a personal thing. But it's different when you are doing a routine. It's almost as if you're not responsible for the movements you are doing. You don't get embarrassed because it's not you.'

Westlife's manager, Louis Walsh, looking nothing like a major pop guru in his turned up jeans, navy-striped shirt over a T-shirt and a lived-in leather jacket, has been watching the boys' performance from the sidelines.

'This is going to be mega, mega,' the man known as 'Ireland's Peter Pan of Pop' enthuses, delighted with the progress of his protegés. 'Obviously there's a lot more work to be done, Priscilla, but I'm really surprised at what they have achieved. It looks great, it really does. It's an enormous relief to me because you don't really know what people can do until they do it. And I feel more confident now that these guys can do it.'

Priscilla is beaming from the satisfaction of honing and shaping the singers into a serious dance quintet.

'They're going to be great,' she agrees. 'Just look at Mark. He would sing his heart out, but didn't want to know about dancing. He was really holding out at the start, but now he has completely turned around and you can see he loves every minute of those dance routines.'

After the Christmas festivities, the boys are slightly out of shape and unfit. Working through their dance routines, they are using muscles they never knew existed and are struggling to keep up with the tough physical demands of the daily rehearsal regime.

'Oh, man! My body feels like it has been run over by a train,' Kian admits as he lies flat out on the bare floorboards of the studio at the end of a particularly energetic day. The other four Westlifers are also complaining of aches and pains. Mark isn't sure that he can maintain this level of physical exercise. Some of the fast and furious sets also leave Nicky, Bryan and Shane looking like they've just completed a major marathon.

'That's just normal,' Priscilla reassures them as they whinge about their stiff and sore limbs. 'Your body needs to adjust. It'll be OK by next week. You won't feel any pain then.'

As their confidence grows, the lads are eager to move on to the next routine. But when Priscilla and Paula demonstrate the intricate set of leg and arm movements that have to be perfectly synchronised, their jaws drop.

'We're not doing that!' Bryan exclaims.

'Oh yes we are,' Priscilla says, firmly.

'Jeez, you're a real Sergeant Major,' Bryan moans, a smile betraying his cheeky sense of fun.

Priscilla likes to challenge them and push them creatively. She begins by giving them the basic steps and moves and then she lifts them up level by level. They are always routines that the Westlife lads can eventually master with a little effort. She never makes it so complicated that they will lose their nerve and admit defeat. If they are struggling with a step, then she won't push them to the point where they feel incompetent. This choreographer's main priority is not to kill off their spirit. Once Priscilla senses that they have a hidden ability to perform, she uses a combination of ego massage and gentle but firm cajoling to help them develop the new skills.

'Come on guys, you're well capable of doing this. Let's not sink to simplicity. If I only give you simple moves then you'll never grow,' she says.

She stands back and scrutinises each individual during the workout to ensure that every one of them is comfortable with the routine. 'OK, did everyone enjoy that? Good. It's important that when you go out there on the night, you enjoy what you're doing. If you are not enjoying it then you are going to foul up the routine. And you can't fool an audience, they know what's fun and what isn't,' she tells them.

'This is really hard,' Shane admits. 'I've danced in musicals, like *Grease* and *Oliver Twist* and I always tried to copy Michael Jackson when I was younger. But I haven't danced in two years, so I've been trying to remember how to groove again. I'm just really worried now about remembering all the dance routines and how the five of us will work together as a unit. That's my only problem.'

Their Irish chef Denise Downey has catered for a range of visiting acts including Robbie Williams, Tracey Chapman, Moby and The Verve, as well as local heroes U2 and The Cranberries. But Westlife have already won her heart as a group of guys for whom it is a joy to serve food.

'They're actually very easy to please out of all the bands I've looked after,' she reveals. 'They all like plain, simple food. Mark is the only one who likes something different. He's into satays and dishes like that. Kian's favourite is chicken and mushroom. But none of them is fussy.

'They don't have a strict diet. In fact, they don't have any kind of diet. They eat what they want. I'm trying to keep them on low fats because it's after Christmas and some of them have gained a few pounds, like the rest of us. I'm not supposed to give them dessert, but I give it to them anyway. Instead of using cream I use milk to make a sauce. And I try not to let them eat chocolates and sweet stuff, although it's hard not to spoil them because they're such pets.'

Away from the spotlight and the glare of the media, the Westlife stars are barely recognisable as they go about their daily business in the rehearsal studios. They dress for comfort, rather than style. Bryan wears baggy, beige-coloured trousers and a T-shirt; Mark arrives unshaven and togged out in a navy tracksuit and baseball cap; Nicky throws on denim jeans, T-shirt and a black leather jacket. Kian and Shane are also prancing around in loose-fitting trousers and T-shirts.

Kian, who has just returned from a post-Christmas holiday in Miami, has allowed his hair to return to its natural dark brown colour and keeps it hidden under a baseball cap. Nicky, sporting several days' facial growth, is bemoaning the fact that he is fed up with his long tresses and is definitely going to have a new, shorter hairstyle for the tour. Meanwhile, he keeps his flowing locks tucked up in a woollen hat or baseball cap.

The Dublin headquarters for Westlife's rehearsals is located in an off-the-beaten track, stone-clad building called The Factory, situated off a grim street near the Dublin docklands. Passers-by could be forgiven for assuming that it is a warehouse. Two gleaming BMW cars, owned respectively by Kian and Nicky, look totally out of place as they sit in the compound. Yet, despite its grungey appearance, The Factory boasts some serious rock 'n' roll history. It has been a recording and rehearsal base for the likes of U2, REM, David Bowie and Van Morrison. U2 recorded a couple of their albums in the very same room where Westlife are being put through their paces. It had been curtained, draped and carpeted for the recording. Chris de Burgh, Boyzone and The Corrs also shaped their live shows within its walls.

In another life, The Factory had been a storage facility for a local flour mill called Boland's. Its association with the music industry will end when Westlife leave the premises. The building is due to be demolished and converted into flats. U2 had planned to use its facilities to rehearse for their new tour, but when they rang up to make the booking they were told that Westlife had beaten them to it, having staked their claim in August, 2000.

A steep metal staircase takes the visitor up to the first floor of The Factory where the rehearsal rooms are located. Music pumps out of every doorway along the corridor, as the premises is also home to Ireland's National Performing Arts School. Every now and then young girls slip out of their respective studios and hover in the corridor, whispering and giggling to each other, hoping to catch a glimpse of the pop idols.

Westlife's studio has a tiny kitchen. Anto Byrne, the group's genial tour manager-cum-dad and big brother on the road, is sifting through a sink full of dirty cups and cutlery.

'This place is a mess,' Anto declares as he surveys the debris from the morning's breaks. Unused tea bags are strewn around the surface. Milk and coffee granules are splattered on it like an abstract painting. It looks just like a trashed flat that has been occupied by a gang of bachelor boys.

A long table and an assortment of chairs occupy most of the space in the cramped quarters where Westlife and their crew congregate to eat. There is a small table on the opposite side which has been designated as Anto's 'office'. He sits there working his way through sheets of papers and dealing with an endless stream of mobile phone calls.

Above the table is a notice board which has pages of the group's schedule pinned to it – along with Anto's words of wisdom for the rehearsals. In block letters he has written with a marker: 'You need a little bit of luck and a large dose of determination to make your dreams into a reality. Ants.'

Anto, a small man in his thirties, is their rock and calming influence amid the stress of keeping up with the demanding schedule of a successful pop career. He has a quiet manner and his deadpan look sends out signals that here is a man not to be crossed. But it's an image that is at variance with his true personality. Anto is blessed with oodles of patience, has the capacity to soak up endless amounts of pressure, obviously has a degree in diplomacy and possesses a good sense of humour – qualities that are essential for survival in the music business.

He also guards his charges with the tenacity of a pit-bull terrier. And they feel secure in his capable hands.

Apart from ensuring the smooth running of Westlife's day-to-day career and keeping expenses under control, this on-the-road manager is also a mother hen figure to the boys. Earlier that morning Nicky had arrived at the studio from his family home. He had skipped breakfast and by 11 a.m. was complaining of being 'starving.'

'What do you want, Nicky? I'll get it for you.'

'I'd murder a rasher sandwich,' Nicky replied.

Anto slipped out of the studio and walked up the street to a café where some workers off a building site were tucking in to fry-ups. Ten minutes later, Nicky was licking his lips and munching into his bacon butty. Anto smiled.

'It's all part of the service. My job is to oversee. To make sure the boys are happy and that they've got what they want.'

Like a conscientious parent, however, he doesn't spoil his boys. Kian, Shane and Mark arrived late for rehearsals one morning earlier in the week, complaining of being hungry.

'Guys, you get breakfast in your hotel. If you don't get up in time to have it, that's your problem. Now is not the time. You have work to do. This is serious business now,' he told them.

Although they are all enjoying a rare opportunity to spend some time in Ireland, only Nicky and Bryan are staying with their families. It is impractical for Shane, Kian and Mark to make the daily trips to the town of Sligo, which would involve a three- to four-hour journey every morning and evening. Instead, they have made their home in a very plush hotel on the south side of Dublin city. Anto phones their hotel every morning before breakfast to give them a wake-up call.

'Are you up, Kian?'

'Whaa! Eh, yeeah.'

'Kian, you need to move, OK?'

Shane and Mark get the same call every morning at around 9.45 a.m. And every morning Anto finds them in a similar state...comatose. At 10.30 a.m. he calls again.

'Kian, are you on the move?'

'Eh, yeeah,' he lies.

Anto's voice drops to 'I mean business' mode.

'Kian, you have 30 minutes to get down here to the studio!'

Calls to Shane's and Mark's rooms reveal that they hadn't made any progress, either. It is the same scenario, day in and day out during the rehearsals. Anto is used to their ways. On the group's earlier promotional tours he always insisted on holding a duplicate key card for all of their hotel rooms. And there were mornings when he had to storm in and physically rouse them from their sleep in order to catch flights or turn up for breakfast shows on TV and radio.

'I have to crack the whip occasionally,' Anto admits. 'One morning I had to go into Shane's room and literally pull him out of bed by the ankles. He went down on to the floor and I threw his clothes at him. When he realised I'd gone that far, he knew I was serious. I try to be firm but fair with them and I know that the boys do respect me. I wouldn't work with them if they didn't.'

It is a couple of days before Westlife fans discover that their idols are holed up in The Factory. Anto realises their secret is out when he arrives in the morning to find a half dozen young girls staging a vigil at the entrance.

'How'ya, girls?' he nods.

'Are Westlife in there?' one teenybopper asks.

'Nah, girls, Westlife aren't here. They're in London.'

The ploy doesn't work.

An hour later, when Nicky and Bryan turn up, the little group of girl fans is still there.

'Oh my God! Oh my God! Oh my God!' they scream as they jump up and down, put their hands to their faces and pull out their hair.

'Hiya, girls,' Nicky smiles and waves.

Their deafening screams startle two builders, who almost drop their cups of takeaway coffee from the local café.

'Nicky I love ya, yer bleedin' massive,' a little blonde-haired girl screams in her thick Dublin accent, the tears running down her face.

'Are the girls still out there?' Anto asks.

'Yeah, but it's no hassle. There's only a few and it's not a problem.'

'I'll have to keep an eye on the situation,' Anto sighs. 'It's only a few now, but once they realise you're definitely here the word will spread like wildfire. Dublin is a small town. It's just a big village really.'

Anto is right. The following day there are over 50 fans waiting with cameras, pens and slips of paper.

In the afternoon, Nicky is devastated to discover that his car – his pride and joy – has been scratched while parked inside The Factory compound and will need to be completely resprayed to repair the damage. Kian had noticed a few young guys hanging around the area and had warned them to steer clear of the cars.

'They probably intended to scratch Kian's car and did mine by mistake,' Nicky sighs.

Anto contacts Westlife's security chief, Paul Higgins, a towering man in his thirties with close-cropped hair and a power-packed physique. He looks like a very large Tom Cruise.

'Paul, we need a guy to look after the cars. Nicky's BMW has been damaged outside the building. Some little gurrier just came up and scratched it for no reason other than jealousy, I presume. Nicky's fuming because the car is only three weeks old.'

'Leave it with me, Anto. I'll have a guy on the job straight away.'

Paul is no stranger to the frenetic world of pop stardom. He worked on security in Dublin clubs for years and that's where Louis Walsh first got to know him. Paul now heads a company that looks after the security of stars when they visit Ireland to do signing sessions in record stores, and because of his reputation as one of the best in the business, Louis has also signed him up as a personal minder to Westlife.

By nine o'clock that night there are a hundred fans outside the gate. Nicky, Shane and Kian, who are the first to leave, stroll over to the closed gates to sign autographs. Suddenly all hell breaks loose as the girls go wild with excitement. They surge forward, screaming, crying and roaring out the names of the boys. Hands proffering biros and scraps of paper are thrust through the bars.

'Over here, Shane!'

'Over here, Kian. You're bleedin' gorgeous!'

After ten minutes the boys return to their cars and take deep breaths as they prepare to make their exit through the manic army of young girls. Paul Higgins and Shane McHenry, who has just been employed to guard the Westlife cars from mindless vandals, help to clear a path through the human wall of kids, so that Nicky, Shane and Kian can drive their cars through. Girls swarm around the BMWs like locusts in the darkness, and Nicky's heart skips a beat.

'This is a nightmare,' he gasps as he manoeuvres the powerful car at a snail's pace through the throng. 'I'm really scared of running over somebody's foot out there.'

Eventually, after what seems him like an eternity, he is out on the open road and roaring off into the night. From then on, that manic scene is repeated nightly when the boys make their way home after rehearsals.

By the end of the first week, the Westlife boys are treating Priscilla as a friend who has always been a member of their gang. They enjoy her fighting spirit and the fact that she is totally oblivious to their superstar status.

Priscilla looks at Westlife and sees five young men, rather than five pop idols.

'People make the mistake of seeing artists as artists,' she says. 'People who work with stars sometimes forget that they're human beings just like everybody else. They grow up like everybody else and get a job. Some people are lawyers, doctors or nurses. Some people are performers. It's a job.'

Coming from ordinary family backgrounds in Dublin and Sligo, Shane, Kian, Nicky, Bryan and Mark respect down-to-earth people like Priscilla. They laugh when she announces, 'I don't count no stars as stars. Stars are twinkles in the sky and none of you fly above my head like that.'

'Whad'ya mean we're not stars? Hey guys, Priscilla doesn't believe we're stars!' Bryan mocks.

'If you were really stars you wouldn't be coming to me to learn something,' Priscilla blasts back.

And they all laugh.

It is a constant battle, though, for Priscilla to exert her authority and maintain discipline in the group. Westlife can be like an unruly bunch of schoolboys sometimes. Now that they have started mastering their routines, they occasionally become a little complacent and lazy. Getting them motivated in the morning is always a tough task. They huddle together in the massive room, chatting and laughing like kids in a schoolyard.

'Don't you guys see enough of each other?' Priscilla bellows. 'This is not a pub, you're all here to work. Let's get cracking.'

As the boys continue to dally, Priscilla bounces up and down on the wooden floor with frustration.

'Get the f*** over here now!' she bawls.

'Ooh, look at you. What's wrong with you?' Bryan teases.

'Guys, we're here to work. There's a bloody show in three weeks time. Now move.'

Realising that they are pushing their luck and that Priscilla is in no mood for fun and games, they instantly take up their positions to begin the day's regime.

'When you get them to shut up they are good listeners,' Priscilla said later. 'If I can't get their attention I usually swear. That's the way I do it and it works. They aren't used to this kind of discipline or being taught in this way. I have to put my foot down and show them who is boss from the start. Every job has a boss. I am here to do this job, so I have to be the boss.

'When I started swearing around the place at first, they thought it was funny. Now they know when I am angry and serious. Their attention span is very weak. They want to have fun among themselves, so I have to be strict or everything will fall apart. I think they now realise that.'

Priscilla and Paula also had to quickly get to grips with Westlife's laddish behaviour, particularly their anti-social habits like frequently breaking wind. This display of irreverence started after the first couple of days. Bryan, in particular, is quite proud of his ability to let off really loud ones.

'Aaahh! That feels much better,' he would sigh with a cheeky grin after dropping a bombshell. Then he'd coyly glance at the girls to judge their reaction.

'I've never seen a bunch of guys fart so much,' Priscilla once declared in exasperation. 'It must be something in the food.'

Delighted that they were getting a response to their shelling, the Westlifers increased their explosions. Priscilla shook her head and laughed.

'Boys will be boys!'she smiled, resigned to the fact that she would have to put up with their idiosyncrasies.

While chatting over lunch mid-week, Mark discovers that Paula has an interesting background. She grew up the daughter of a famous dad.

'I remember him!' Mark exclaims excitedly when Paula reveals that her father is the eighties pop star Shakin' Stevens, who had appeared on *Top Of The Pops* at least 50 times. Nicky's ears also prick up. Shakin' Stevens was a legend in Nicky's musical history as well.

'What were his big hits? Don't tell me...yeah...I've got them – This Ole House and Green Door...that's it. My dad and myself used to do those on our karaoke nights,' he says.

'I remember seeing him on *Top Of The Pops* when I was a kid. He was really cool,' Kian adds.

'I'd love to meet your dad. I was a real fan, too,' Bryan chips in.

Shaky, as he was known to his fans, had four Number One hits, including Oh Julie and Merry Christmas Everyone. He was known for his trademark denims and white shoes, as well as his salmon pink jacket with black shirt and trousers, in addition to a distinctive dancing style.

'So did your dad not try to talk you out of going into showbusiness?' Bryan enquires.

'No,' says Paula. 'It's what I've always wanted to do. I've been dancing since the age of nine. There was no stopping me. But dad was happy for me to do it anyway. He's been very supportive.'

Priscilla, meanwhile, waxes lyrical about her idol Tina Turner, whom she had the thrill of working with.

'I've never seen anyone strut so much as Tina,' says Priscilla. 'I felt tired just watching her. She really put me through my paces when I danced with her and she enjoyed watching me struggle. She turned to me on the stage and threw me a look as if to say, "C'mon, girl, keep up". The amazing thing is that she also does those dance moves in her stiletto heels! Tina could be your grandmother, and if she can still do it then you guys can.'

Every day, including the weekend, is a work day for Westlife. But they still stay out late at night, going for drinks, catching a movie at the cinema or going bowling with friends. It seems like an eternity since they've been home for a long stretch, so they are determined to make the most of it. The Sligo boys check out the Dublin social scene, while the two homeboys, Nicky and Bryan, have the added bonus of sleeping in beds they'd grown up in, as well as enjoying their mothers' home cooking.

Whenever Louis drops in to see them, he warns them not to be partying or keeping late nights.

'Lads, this is serious. There'll be plenty of time for clubbing when you've mastered the show. This is the big one, you've got to give it everything. You've a long way to go and a lot to learn. If you stay out at night your minds will be tired and you won't be able to concentrate. It will take you longer to pick up on everything and time is not a luxury that you have to play around with.'

They nod their heads in agreement. The boys are painfully aware that the clock is ticking away to opening night. But they fight a frequently lost battle to maintain a military-style existence that confines them to camp.

They can't resist going for the occasional drink, and they really cut loose at weekends.

'It's great to be able to chill out in our own home town every night,' Bryan says. 'One of the things I really look forward to doing at the end of the day is playing snooker with me mates. We play a game called "killer" and we're all hooked on it. We all get really competitive and it's great fun.'

Bryan's close pal, Mark Murphy – 'he's going to be my best man when I marry Kerry' – is a DJ in a local venue called the Buda Bar at Blanchardstown outside the city. Some nights when he leaves The Factory, Bryan jumps into his BMW and heads for the Budda Bar to join Mark on the decks.

At the end of the first week, Priscilla calls the Westlife boys to attention for their appraisal. The five lads sit in a circle on the bare wooden floor of the studio and fidget nervously, not knowing what to expect. They crack jokes among themselves and burst into fits of laughter to break the tension.

'OK, guys, listen up!' Priscilla says loudly. 'We're making great progress here. The most important thing I see in you is that you all have the desire to dance. If you didn't have the desire to do it you would never do it. So you're winning, although there is still a long way to go.'

'Is there a star pupil, teacher?' Bryan jokes.

Priscilla laughs. 'No,' she says, 'but I'm pleased that you've all got your own different styles. This is not about five guys looking the same and dancing the same. I want you to have unique individual styles.'

Like school kids released into a playground for lunch break, Kian, Shane, Bryan, Mark and Nicky made a dash for some of the city's trendy clubs at the weekend. There are several top hot spots to choose from, including the POD, Spy Bar, Renards and Lillie's Bordello.

Nicky is accompanied by his long-time girlfriend, Georgina Aherne, daughter of the Irish Prime Minister, Bertie Aherne, while Bryan escorts his fiancée Kerry Katona around town.

On the Sunday, all five look the worse for wear as they crawl into work at one o'clock in the afternoon. Priscilla, who has also hit the town but still looks like she's spent a week on a health farm, shows them no mercy.

'Let's do some warm-up exercises,' she announces.

Her demand is greeted by a chorus of groans.

'Ah, Priscilla, give us a break,' Kian pleads.

'C'mon, guys, this isn't a holiday camp. There's work to be done.'

'Slave driver!' Bryan admonishes her.

Reluctantly, they drag their feet across the floor and line up in front of the mirror.

'Liam Gallagher, eat your heart out!' Kian remarks as he cops his bloodshot eyes in the mirror, the effects of his boozing and partying into the early hours of the morning.

Priscilla struggles to keep their attention span throughout the afternoon.

Bryan wanders all over the room, stepping in the path of the other guys and knocking them out of their stride. Kian's eyes occasionally glaze over as his mind wanders far from the confines of the dance studio. Mark yawns so much his jaw looks in serious jeopardy of locking in that position. Shane is dead on his feet and Nicky has to sit down every five minutes.

Priscilla realises that she is fighting a losing battle to whip them into shape today and eventually decides to put the boys out of their misery.

'OK, guys, I'll let you off early. But no partying tonight, right! It's business as usual tomorrow.'

'Are we really free to go?' Bryan asks, like an excited schoolboy.

'Well, you're no good for anything else,' Priscilla quips.

'Yeaahh!' the boys roar.

'OK, lets go to the Chocolate Bar,' someone suggests.

'Guys, no drinking today. I want you in feeling fresh in the morning,' Priscilla warns.

Faces drop all round.

'This week,' Priscilla announces, 'I'll be taking you to the next stage, when you begin working with the dancers, and Kim will be in to introduce you to the demands of the set.

Englishman Kim Gavin, who has been hired as Westlife's show producer and stage director, already has a formidable reputation in the pop world. After moving up through the ranks of TV, where he choreographed sketches for shows such as the Russ Abbot series, Kim made his mark in pop with Take That. He created the moves for their very first hit, It Only Takes A Minute, and went on to spend four years with the famous boy band before working with Eternal, 911, Five, Steps and B*Witched. He had previously been asked to work with Westlife's Irish predecessors, Boyzone, but the timing was never right, as he had always been involved with other projects when they called.

Kim had only ever seen Westlife on TV before he received a request to produce their first tour. It is a personal challenge for him as he has never created and directed a fully fledged live pop concert for any of his previous illustrious clients.

'This is my first rock 'n' roll experience, going on tour, doing arenas and making a show that will play to up to 15,000 people,' he reveals.

He initially met up with Westlife in October, 2000 and presented them with his concept for their tour. Sitting around a massive boardroom table at a London production office that day, Kian, Shane, Nicky, Mark and Bryan were like excited kids on Christmas morning as they waited for the description of their first Westlife production. For once, they were stunned into silence as Kim snapped open the locks on his leather briefcase and shuffled sheets of paper on to the polished surface of the mahogany table. Kim inhaled deeply, stood up from his chair and rested his hands on the table.

'Guys we are going to stage a big theatrical Westlife production. It won't be just you guys up there singing and dancing. There will be lots of stuff going on and it'll be a real extravaganza of sound and vision. Even though it's your first major production, we're lucky to have the financial resources to play with, which is good 'cos it means we can reach a very high standard in terms of production. This is the first impression you're going to make on audiences, so it's important to get it right. Together we'll make it an unforgettable experience for your fans, night after night.'

All five nodded and smiled.

'I've taken the theme of "life" and the idea is that when the show starts you are dormant and then life kicks in. We've planned a dramatic opening; a huge build-up to you coming on stage. The big introduction will be enacted through video footage on a massive screen out front. There will be lots of alien characters in it and a spooky doctor. Westlife will start off as lifeless individuals and then these aliens will administer electric shocks to bring you to life. It will be really dramatic for the kids who are watching. Then the show begins.'

Turning to a set of architect's drawings pinned to a wooden display board behind him, Kim announced, 'This is the set you'll be working around.'

Bryan looked perplexed, not quite knowing what to make of the series of sketches. Kim, sensing that the Westlifers weren't overly excited by the drawings which seemed dull and lifeless in comparison to the jaw-dropping experience they had envisaged, jumped in with a detailed description.

'The set is basically a series of boxes that move. Now that may not sound very exciting, but when you see it in reality and in operation it'll be impressive. When the boxes turn in one direction they become a screen and then they turn the other way around and give you different levels to work from. It'll be like a playground with steps and ladders and a bridge. We can also rotate the boxes and take them off and then the band comes forward and it's like a traditional stage. So it will be constantly changing and moving and visually interesting to watch.'

The blank stares of the Famous Five indicated that they weren't sure how to interpret Kim's vision for the first Westlife tour. They had their own ideas that they were quick to put forward. Kian, Shane, Bryan, Mark and Nicky had been to see many shows by some of the biggest names in pop and they'd picked up all kinds of big ideas for their first live production. Kim listened as they offered a variety of suggestions and then made detailed notes.

In the weeks leading up to Christmas 2000, Kim kept in frequent contact with Westlife, updating them on changes and new additions to the show. There were now going to be travelators on the stage as well – moving sections on the floor, allowing the boys to give the impression of walking and gliding.

Sorting out which songs fitted the bill for Kim's production was another headache. The hits were obvious choices, but how would Kim decide the rest of the repertoire from two Number One albums?

'To the band, every song is a hit, but when I look at the range, there are tunes that direct me in a certain way and give me ideas to build the show around. Some are up-tempo so they're going to make it exciting. I've taken the hits that I know I have to do and come up with ideas to portray those.

'Then I looked at other songs to see how they could fit in with what's happening and I'll blend the show together like that.'

Kim explained to Westlife that he had created a lot of images, like a video backdrop of seasons changing for Seasons In The Sun, to bring the ballads to life on stage.

'I want to add extra zest to the ballads and put something behind you that is visually spectacular without you having to move and do things. It has to be a stage that is quite dynamic and can constantly change.'

Kim later tweaked the opening to change it from a theme of life to a dream, incorporating the track, Dreams Come True. The whole set was now beginning to take shape in the boys' minds and they were getting more and more enthusiastic with each passing day.

'Westlife themselves have come up with lots of new suggestions and that's great because anything that helps to portray the songs and make them exciting is good for the over-all show,' says Kim, pleased with the boys' constructive input.

There is a frisson of excitement in The Factory at the beginning of the second week of rehearsals with the arrival of a stunning group of young women. These are the Westlife dancers who have been hired for the tour. Priscilla and Paula had decided to work with the boys on their own for a week to build up their confidence before bringing in the girls.

'Artists who haven't danced before often find it an extra anxiety to work with professional dancers when they're starting off. It can be embarrassing as they don't want people watching them struggle. So to avoid that pressure

I gave them a week on their own,' Priscilla confides. 'Female dancers are quick to pick up and, anyway, they're not involved in the whole show.'

The dancers turn up in the building half an hour before the Westlife boys on their first morning, and are greeted by Anto.

'Just make yourselves at home here, girls. It's not posh, but you'll get used to it in no time. Anyone for coffee? I'll stick on the kettle,' he says in the one breath.

The girls slink out of the kitchen area and into the main studio to inspect their new workplace. They congregate in one corner, dropping their bags on the floor and giggling with nervous excitement. Anto sticks his head around the corner.

'OK, girls, coffee's up.'

'Are you looking forward to this, girls?' Anto asks, as they sip from their hot mugs.

'Yeeaah!' they all reply at once.

'The boys are great lads. You'll find them very easy to get along with. They enjoy a bit of slagging, but don't worry, you'll get used to them,' Anto assures them.

With that the door bursts open and Bryan's large frame appears.

'How'ya, girls! Alright?' he bellows. 'Have you made the coffee already? Great!'

The girls look at each other as if they've just spotted an alien from another planet. Bryan flashes them one of his cheeky grins and walks off.

'Don't worry, girls, you'll get used to him,' Anto says, reassuringly.

Within minutes, Nicky, Shane, Kian and Mark arrive for work. The dancers nervously shuffle around in their company.

'Hi, girls, alright?' Nicky says, looking a little bashful. 'I hope you know how to dance because we're experts now,' Kian jokes.

The girls laugh. Lene Godfrey, Karen Holley, Jessica Forsman, Jodi Leigh and Marilena Nicolaou had briefly met Westlife before Christmas, during one of the planning meetings with Kim. Naturally, the boys had seen it as an ideal opportunity to cop a look at the girls.

'Boys being boys, they wanted to see what they looked like; were they pretty, tall or short or whatever?' Priscilla says.

As they would be spending months performing on stage and touring with the dancers, the Westlife stars were also anxious to ensure that there were no personality clashes. The girls obviously came through the test with flying colours. They were all around three to four years older than the guys, but although they'd worked on pop videos, TV and fashion shows, they'd never been on a proper pop tour with any of the major groups like Take That, Boyzone or Five.

'They're fresh and different,' Kian points out. 'The whole idea behind our show is that it's not going to be like anything people have seen before. Most groups go for typical blonde dancers who wear hot pants and jump around. We have a totally different vision as to how the girls will help bring our show to life.'

During the first day of rehearsals at The Factory the boys are uncharacteristically coy around the new girls on the block. During breaks they drift away from the dancers to their own corner, huddling together deep in conversation, occasionally casting sly glances in the direction of the stunning females.

Bryan is the first to break down the barriers and build up friendships between the two camps. Being an extrovert and secure in his personal life with Kerry, he is soon larking about and sending the girls into fits of giggles with his jokes.

'Do you know which bees wear bras?' he asks them.

'No,' replies Lene.

'Boobies!'

The dancers giggle, some rolling their eyes towards the heavens in response.

On the second day, the chemistry between the boys and their female dancers is noticeably more relaxed. The Westlifers are back on their normal laddish form, cracking jokes, breaking wind and slagging Priscilla at every opportunity. If the girls had been in awe of Westlife's star status when they arrived for work the previous morning, all their illusions were now being stripped away.

Although the female dancers only have a week working with the boys in Dublin, Priscilla reckons it will be sufficient for them to master their routines. Firstly, the girls are professional and very quick to learn. But Priscilla has also carefully constructed a series of dance routines that involves only a minimum of interaction with Westlife. This is to ensure that the fans are not going to be offended when they see the girls getting up close to their pin-up idols.

As she tucks into one of the healthy dishes prepared for Westlife and their entourage by Denise Downey (in this case a low-fat Irish stew), Priscilla tells how she has learned from the experience of working with other male groups that female fans are very possessive of their idols.

'I've been in situations where fans have been evil to dancers on a stage,' she reveals. 'Females with their boy bands are very tricky. They don't want to see the guys constantly holding up a girl on stage. I've seen fingers come up from the crowd and thought, that's not a wave, I know what that means.

'I learned from those experiences, so when it came to the Westlife show I didn't take any chances of offending the girls. I made sure there wasn't too much going on between the boys and the girls to reduce the risk of getting the female fans jealous.'

Priscilla sees her role as also including a responsibility to the boys' fans.

'In a lot of ways the audience is my priority,' she says. 'I have to take into account what entertains them, how they are feeling and what they want to see. It's the fans who are paying the money to come and see the show, so I have to focus on what they expect. Sometimes in this show the girls will be around the boys, but they won't be looking at them in any sort of sexual way.'

During the week, Bryan organises a night out bowling with his mates and invites the girls. Lene tries to cry off, despite the fact that an army of female fans would have killed for the chance to spend a night in his company.

'Don't be boring,' Bryan chides. 'It's just me and a bunch of my buddies.'

But Lene can't be persuaded.

'They are really friendly guys and have invited us out several nights. They go, "Please come out." And I'm saying "No, no, no." Then I think, God I'm the envy of half the girl population. But I don't look at it like that. It's a job.'

The boys enjoy the thrill of cruising around the city in their dream cars whenever they get the opportunity. As soon as they heard that the girls needed to go shopping, they promptly offered their services as chauffeurs. It all contributed to the 'getting-to-know-you' process and gradually a real team spirit began to develop.

'They kept to themselves to themselves the first day, now slowly but surely they're coming out,' Jodi says. 'Nicky has been the last one to come out, but that's just shyness. I was probably the last one to come out as well.

Nicky was saying the other night that he was really, really embarrassed to be dancing in front of us at first because we're professional dancers. But I was embarrassed to dance in front of THEM, so it works both ways.'

The dancers are relieved to discover that the boys aren't pretentious or bigheaded.

'I thought they would be five really pop-starry guys and smooth operators,' Lene admits. 'But as I've got to know them I'm like, "They are really nice boys; they are five guys who sing for a job." Maybe it's the fact that they are Irish, but they are so laid back and not at all arrogant.'

There is a lot of bawdy but good-natured banter between the boys as the week progresses. Lene arrives in one morning wearing white trousers that leave little to the imagination. As if directed by radar, all male heads swivel in her direction. Then the slagging starts.

'I'm used to it now,' Lene says later. 'It's just fun and games. They like to wind you up. At first I found their sense of humour quite hard because I didn't know them very well. But now I realise it's just harmless fun with them. They have their own Irish slang for female parts that I haven't figured out yet. There is also a special word they use when your pants are showing; they've told me what that one is, but I've been sworn not to tell anyone.'

Jodi admits all the dancers got a big surprise when they first arrived at the Westlife rehearsals.

'When we told people that we were going to Ireland to work with Westlife, everyone was saying, "But Westlife can't dance. All their songs are ballads. What are you going to do?" But when we got to rehearsals and saw them dancing, we said, "Wicked. They're all great. They can all actually dance." '

In addition to the girls, there is another new face in The Factory studio on day one of the second week. Vocal expert Dave Tench has been drafted in by Kim Gavin to give the boys training on how to cope with the demands of an all-action performance. He has also created a showpiece medley of mainly Motown songs for the concert, which he is going to teach the five Westlifers.

Dave has some immediate concerns upon his arrival. The slightly-built 23-year-old with the boyish looks is just two years older than the oldest boys in the group, and is worried about gaining their confidence and respect. Will he be able to control and marshal them for the intensive rehearsals that have to be completed to a very tight deadline?

There is one ace card up Dave's sleeve. His expertise will help Westlife cope with a full-on singing and dancing show that spans over 90 minutes. His tuition will also lift their singing to a standard that is required for a concert in the super league of pop. It is in their interest to knuckle down to the serious business of work with their vocal trainer. That's the message he will deliver if things started to go horribly wrong.

After a couple of hours of dancing that morning, the boys take a break.

Priscilla stays behind to drill the dancers for a spectacular martial arts-type dance section which they'll perform in the show while the boys are backstage doing a costume change. Westlife go to a small room off the dance studio, where there are chairs and a piano. Dave is already there, waiting like a patient schoolmaster. The boys sit and listen as he explains how he has devised a ten-minute set of songs to hold their audiences spellbound with a really big scene.

'I've had a look at legendary American groups like The Four Tops and The Temptations and I've come up with a few tunes that I think will work really well,' he informs them.

Westlife are all ears. Dave fills them in about a medley that will eventually kick off in the show with More Than Words, which had been a hit for a group called Xtreme. It will then lead in to the Motown classics My Girl, Can't Get Next To You, Ain't Too Proud To Beg, Baby I Need Your Lovin' and What Becomes Of The Broken Hearted?

'They'll all be mixed together to make a big party vibe,' Dave enthuses.

The boys are genuinely excited and enthusiastic at the prospect of tackling some new numbers and learning a different routine. Suddenly they are wildly babbling together, tossing the ideas around and fantasising about being on stage and performing the songs.

Dave seems pleasantly surprised by their passion and desire to take on new challenges. But getting them to settle down and concentrate on their class is a different story. They are all having different conversations among themselves. Some are laughing at private jokes. All seem to be oblivious to their new mentor.

'Guys, let's try to concentrate!' Dave pleads in a desperate bid to gain some control over the situation.

Bryan is still cracking jokes. Shane is doing a hilarious impression of Boyzone's Stephen Gately.

'Guys!' Dave begs again. And they all settle down.

One of Dave's first priorities taking on Westlife is to teach them techniques that will help them to protect and maintain their vocal chords.

'The first thing we're going to practise is a system called siren. Have you ever done it before?'

'No,' they all reply, sitting back in their chairs.

'It's a vocal warm-up and a way of accessing what notes are available to your voice on a particular day.'

Dave then puts the boys through their paces and their voices sound great.

'You are in good shape at the moment,' he says. 'Any notes that you siren when you go all the way from the bottom of your range to the top is your voice and you can do any of that. However, you will often notice problems when you get tired. What happens is, when you reach around the top of the range, to the parts that you often use, scratchiness will occur and the vocals stop vibrating together. It's something you should be aware of, so as not to panic. It just means that you are tired.'

Because the new Westlife show is going to be a major theatrical production, Kim has hired Dave for his background in theatre.

Dave has been musical director on productions such as *Oh What A Night* and *The Rocky Horror Show*. He understands the demands of such a performance, particularly one that is going to be as energetic and as long running as the planned Westlife extravaganza. He now coaches the boys on how to sing and dance without damaging their vocal chords.

'I always have concern for singers in this kind of show where singing is accompanied by dance,' Dave says. 'If you are not grounded and not supported and not breathing properly then you could damage your vocal chords. When singing you have to have your feet connected to the floor and anchored. The problem with this gig is you can't do that. So that's an area where we have to concentrate on reducing the risk.'

During the first couple of days working with the boys, Dave isn't sure that he has gained their respect. They are giddy and bold and loud and funny and he doesn't feel connected to them.

'The five of them are a very tight-knit family and they don't let you in,' he says. 'Maybe it's to do with being in a major band that they mistrust people. They know each other so well and there are a lot of in-jokes. I'm not interested in those anyway because I'm here to make them sound good.'

It is nothing personal, as Dave discovers when Nicky comes to him and proclaims, 'You're teaching me a lot this week.' He is reflecting the general view of the guys in Westlife. They are thrilled with their new tutor and his crash course in vocal warm-ups and singing techniques. They love the arrangement on the

Motown set and the work he is doing with them on the harmonies.

At the end of the day, Dave feels more confident that he can have a good working relationship with the boys in the lead-up to opening night.

'I got really concerned earlier because I thought we were never going to get anywhere. Anything will distract them, but I just have to be strong with them and say, "Look, let's get on with it otherwise we are never going to get this done on time." That seems to work.'

Dave isn't used to working with bands. In fact, this is the first time he has coached and trained a pop group. He had been aware of Westlife's music from their hits on radio and TV, but wasn't familiar with them as individuals before he arrived in Dublin for the rehearsals.

'When I was booked to do the job I got my head down and learned all the songs that are going to be in the tour,' he says. 'I got their albums, but it was still very difficult for me to figure out who did what just from listening to the records. I couldn't put their voices to their names. But now, after meeting them, everything makes sense.'

Apart from the Motown medley, Dave takes Westlife through the show song by song to make sure that all the harmonies are in the right places and to assist them through any problems that crop up during the singing and dancing.

'They quite often use a lot of vocal techniques that are tiring. There is a lot of air that goes up with their vocal chords, which is something they do to make sounds the fans want to hear. A lot of young men singing this style do it and it's really good, but it's hard to sustain because the muscles get really tired. So I have to work on that.'

There were days when Dave was at his wits' end trying to work within a time limit. While rehearsing Seasons In The Sun, the boys suddenly ignore Dave and start a conversation among themselves on how it should be performed, where they should be standing and what clothes they should wear.

'Easy, guys, let's move on,' Dave says, raising his voice above the din.

'They are always getting distracted and talking about things other than what I should be doing with them at that moment,' he sighs. 'It's good in the sense that they all have their own ideas about how things should be in the show. It's the first time they've been given the chance to do something like this, so they're excited and on edge. But it doesn't make my job any easier.'

While working on Swear It Again with just a piano, they decide that it sounded so good they would do that version of their first Number One hit, rather than the heavily produced format of their CD.

By the end of the week, Dave has got to grips with the individual talents of each Westlifer. He is pleasantly surprised to discover that every one of them has an impressive singing voice. It's no secret that not every member of every boy band can sing, but that's not the case with Westlife – they certainly have the tools at their disposal.

Here is Dave's appraisal.

Shane Filan: 'A really strong singer. The one thing I particularly like about Shane is that his phrasing is really natural. On this tour he is going to be quite exciting because he's really coming in to his own. More than the others he has a rocky edge; it's such a strong lead – I call it a Bryan Adams sound. But on the other hand, his range is still limited to about an A, where he stops. As he works and as he grows, he will be able to stretch that up.'

Kian Egan: 'Sings a lot of the bass parts because he is one of the few who has a quality that works down there. With most of the guys there is a lot of air that goes up with the vocal chords, so there is not a lot of projection at the bottom, whereas Kian has that.'

Bryan McFadden: 'He is the belter; the one that makes a lot of noise. He projects himself very well. A good solid member of the group.'

Nicky Byrne: 'Capable of a lot of different things. He doesn't fall into a category. He changes all the time to suit whatever is going on. If he wants to be cool he lets lots of air out and sings quietly. If he wants to burn it up, he can be a belter like Bryan. The fact that he has versatility means I can get him to try different things.'

Mark Feehily: 'The one I call "No Fear." He has a very big voice and he has never put a limit on it. Whatever line you give him it doesn't matter. He will find a way to make it work. I think everyone knows that from the records because he does all the ad-libs and they sound great. Where I worry about Mark is on the fast tunes in the show, like When You're Looking Like That and Dreams Come True, because he has really long, extended high lines to accompany difficult steps. So when he is moving and stepping he's not grounded. But he makes great sounds and he's always the really nice cherry on top in harmonies.'

Dave takes time with Mark to stress the importance of being supported on the ground during his vocal acrobatics. At one point he gets Mark to lean back on him. Dave takes all Mark's weight when he sings. As Dave held Mark, he could sense him tensing as he got higher in range.

'A lot of singers use their legs and thighs and start tensing them. People don't normally think about the whole body being affected by the singing voice, but it totally is. And really it's about grounding,' Dave explains. 'The higher you go the more you need support. A lot of the big notes Mark has in the show take so much belt that support is needed in that situation.

'Also, in harmonies he hangs around in the lower part of things and then when he goes to do some high stuff it is sometimes a bit of a shock to the system. But once he is aware of all of that, everything will be fine.'

Dave is raving about Nicky's input into the Motown section. 'Before I came to work with the boys, I associated Nicky with soft tone. But he is capable of doing a lot of the stuff that Bryan does in that style. Quite often he is underused, so I decided to turn that around and get him to really grab it by the balls and go for it. And he has done. I have given him a lot to do in the Motown spot and he goes for it. He can give it real volume and he's enjoying it.'

Bryan has a smile on his face. He's the happiest young guy in the world right now. It has nothing to do with the thrill of Westlife's first world tour about to kick off. Or the excitement over the fact that all the concerts around the globe have sold out. A weight has been lifted from his shoulders in his personal life. Bryan was plunged into an emotional rollercoaster just before Christmas when his girlfriend, Kerry Katona of Atomic Kitten, discovered that she was pregnant.

It had been unplanned, but the hopelessly romantic couple were ecstatic over the news that they were going to have a little baby. They were going to be Mum and Dad.

His joy, however, was tempered by his concern over how the 'bombshell' would be greeted in the Westlife camp. Bryan had already been through an unhappy and turbulent period in his personal dealings with their manager, Louis. There were personality clashes and a lot of conflict between the pair. But in recent times they were both developing respect and admiration for each other. Now Bryan was about to confront Louis with a major issue for Westlife. It was a tense period for the young performer as he had no idea how the manager would react.

'Me and Louis had a bad relationship all through the band,' Bryan reveals. 'We didn't see eye to eye on a lot of things. I was just getting my relationship together with Louis, although we still weren't great friends.'

Bryan and Kerry broke the news to his parents and her mum as soon as the pregnancy was confirmed. They had also told 'a handful of friends.' But finding the right moment to inform Louis and the rest of Westlife was Bryan's biggest difficulty.

It was a stressful time.

Shortly before the start of rehearsals, Bryan decided to test the waters with Nicky. He asked him to come for a drive. Nicky had no inkling of the shock that lay in store.

'Me and Kerry are going to have a baby, Nicky. She's pregnant,' Bryan blurted out.

'Wha-aat! Oh God!' Nicky went into instant shock. 'This is going to throw a spanner in the works,' he said after pausing for what seemed to Bryan like an eternity.

'Don't breathe a word to anyone. I want to find the right moment to tell Louis myself.'

'Yeah, absolutely, no problem. Oh God!' Nicky was still in shock.

The chance to tell Mark came around a few days later when they both went into the recording studio to do some work in London with the big-time pop producer Steve Mac.

'Mark, listen mate, I have something to tell you.'

Mark swung around looking concerned by the tone of Bryan's voice. He wasn't his usual jovial self.

'I'm going to be a dad,' Bryan continued, fixing his gaze on

Mark for a reaction. In an instant, Mark grabbed Bryan and hugged him with delight.

Mark was all excited over the fact that he was about to become 'a kind of an uncle'. Again, Bryan swore Mark to secrecy until he plucked up the courage to tell Louis.

Bryan finally picked his moment one day when the manager and all of Westlife had gathered for a business meeting. But before he could make the big announcement fate, or rather *The Sun* newspaper, intervened. Bryan was in the loo when Nicky came running in, out of breath.

'Bryan, *The Sun* are on the phone to Louis. I just overheard the conversation. Someone has obviously leaked the news. They've heard about the pregnancy and they've contacted Louis to see if it's true. He's on the way in to you.'

'Oh, shit!'

Louis arrived with Kian, Shane and Mark.

'Are you having a baby?' Louis asked in a surprised tone.

'Yeah.'

Shane and Kian nearly collapsed with the shock.

'Oh my God!' they both blurted out.

Nicky and Mark decided they'd better feign shock and surprise as well.

'Oh my God!' they both said.

There were a couple of minutes of confusion among Louis, Shane and Kian while they tried to grasp the implications. Then, suddenly Louis started hopping around the place with a glint in his eye and a smile from ear to ear. He was giggling as he suddenly plucked a mobile phone from a pocket of his leather jacket.

'This is great! This is great!' he said, getting all excited. 'Got a great story for you. Bryan is going to be a dad. Kerry is expecting,' Louis told the person on the other end of the line.

As soon as he finished the call, Louis was on the line to another media contact. 'Big story! Big story! Bryan is going to be a dad!'

The next day Bryan and Kerry are dominating the front pages of all the tabloids. And he's on the telly chatting with Ireland's TV3 showbiz reporter Lorraine Keane.

'I loved Louis for that,' Bryan says. 'He couldn't have been more supportive and since then we're the best of friends. I talk to him every day on the phone.'

Now that it was all out in the open, Bryan and Kerry could really celebrate their impending parenthood. They gathered family and friends around for a proper knees-up, with Kerry suddenly becoming very responsible by swapping hard booze for healthy mineral water.

The young couple were beaming with delight, with Bryan constantly hugging the little blonde beauty who had captured his heart from the moment they first met at a *TV Hits* roadshow in July, 1999, just a few months after the launch of Westlife.

It was Liz from Atomic Kitten who had spotted Bryan in the foyer of their hotel. Liz was all excited as she was already a fan of Westlife. But Kerry had no idea who he was at the time.

'It's Bryan from Westlife!' Liz drooled as she saw the hunk strolling through the hotel.

'Who?' Kerry asked.

'Bryan McFadden from Westlife. They're brilliant!'

'Well, go and say hello to him,' Kerry said.

'No, no. I'd be too embarrassed,' Liz giggled.

'Well, if you won't, I will,' Kerry suddenly announced as she raced after Bryan.

'Excuse me!'

Bryan turned and looked down to see the most perfect girl he'd ever laid eyes on.

'I'm Kerry from the new band Atomic Kitten!'

'Hi,' Bryan replied. Atomic Kitten? He'd never heard of them. But, God, she was gorgeous!

On the roadshow they constantly made eyes at each other. With the booze flowing on the final night, the couple veered towards each other and became lost in conversation. Their mutual physical attraction was obvious to everybody by this stage and they were surprisingly comfortable in each other's company. During the evening Bryan admitted that he already had a girlfriend, but before they parted that night they kissed and exchanged phone numbers.

Atomic Kitten were jetting off to Japan the following morning and Westlife were also heading off on a non-stop round of promotion. Initially there was no contact between the couple, as Bryan had given Kerry a wrong phone number by mistake and he had mislaid the slip of paper on which she had written hers. Eventually he made contact when Westlife were on a promotional visit to Asia and he was totally smitten. He immediately ended his three-month relationship with another English girl and in November, 1999, Kerry Katona of Atomic Kitten became his secret girlfriend.

It was only a matter of weeks before he proposed to Kerry in a scene straight out of the pages of Mills and Boon. On December 28, 1999, after Kerry arrived in Ireland to spend time with him, Bryan drove her from Dublin to a remote spot in County Donegal on the north-west coast of Ireland and stopped outside a local castle.

Kerry looked shocked as he suddenly got down on one knee.

'Do you know why I've brought you here?' he asked on that frosty afternoon.

She stared at him, speechless.

'My grandad proposed to my nana at this very spot.' Bryan then nervously produced a ring from his pocket.

'Will you marry me?' he asked.

Kerry's eyes welled up as the significance of the moment began to sink in.

'Yes,' she said, finally.

Unknown to Kerry, he had also followed tradition by phoning her mum to ask her permission before he popped the question.

Kerry's background couldn't be more different to Bryan's idyllic upbringing. While he came from a happy, stable background, Kerry, from Warrington, grew up in a series of foster homes as her mother Sue was unable to cope at the time, although they eventually established a loving relationship.

Initially, Bryan and Kerry had tried to keep their romance under wraps because it was feared that fans might react angrily to the news. For months they tried to be discreet, even refusing room service when they were staying in hotels together, in case hotel staff went running to the tabloids with the story.

Eventually they were snapped together in a loving embrace by a member of the paparazzi and Westlife Bryan's lover was 'exposed'. Contrary to the fears of the management of both groups, the fans were very supportive and through the internet and teen magazines they expressed their delight that the couple had found true love and happiness together.

When the January, 2001 issue of *Hello!* magazine hit the news-stands it contained an interview with the couple in which they announced for the first time that they'd become secretly engaged. Just when fans were getting over the surprise, days later came the news that they were also to become parents.

Amidst the daily demands of rehearsals, Bryan is now busy trying to find their dream home. The glamorous pair have decided to settle in Ireland and are sifting through the property pages of the national and local newspapers. Eventually they come across an idyllic seven-bed residence set among woods and rolling hills in picturesque County Wicklow. Bryan makes contact and says he's interested in buying the house.

One morning just before the start of rehearsals his mobile phone rings at The Factory.

'Are ya mad or whaa-at!' he laughs down the line. 'A million and a half?

That's got to be a joke!'

By now he has an audience in the kitchen.

'One point four million? No way, you've lost the plot!'

He looks all wide-eyed at Anto, Kian and Nicky as he points to the mobile phone with his index finger.

'One point three million!' he laughs again. He takes the phone away from his ear, holds it up in the air and guffaws, clearly enjoying the thrill of the bartering.

'One point two million!' he says, leaving the room. A couple of minutes later, he arrives back with a smug grin on his face. 'I just knocked £300,000 off the price of me house,' he announces. 'That's not a bad morning's work.

Kian, the Westlifer with the reputation of being a shrewd businessman, isn't impressed.

'Anyone who pays over a million pounds for a house is mad,' he sniffs.

Stylist Dave Thomas arrives with his satchel of costume drawings, prompting Kian to discard the guitar on which he's been strumming More Than Words while he passes the time before dance classes.

'Wow! Look at these, guys,' Kian roars, as the rest of Westlife suddenly appear from all directions.

They are awe-struck as they pore over all the images that Dave flashes before them.

'This is very Star Trek,' Bryan pipes up as he examines the sketches of the space suits.

'They're fantastic,' Shane gushes.

Then Dave pulls out a series of concepts for the girls' outfits. The eyes nearly pop out of Kian's head.

'These are really skimpy outfits! God love them having to go out on stage and dance in them,' he laughs.

The final weekend of rehearsals in Dublin sees the guys in a laconic mood, mainly due to tiredness. They have taken on a huge volume of new work with Priscilla, Kim and Dave, and are confident that they have mastered everything that has been thrown at them. All they now want to do is relax and enjoy some quality time at home before moving on to the next stage of rehearsals in the UK.

But being the supreme perfectionist, Priscilla is adamant that they still need to tighten up their act. Dance classes will continue until her standards have been achieved.

Kim is also still working with the boys, preparing them for the demands of the set. Large rectangular pieces of wood had been installed in the rehearsal room that week to simulate the set. This allows Westlife to become familiar with the layout and movement of the stage that awaits them in London at the final rehearsals. Kim is explaining how at one point the set will open in the centre for the dancers to step through and join them on stage.

'Imagine it opening like the crack of an arse,' Kim tells them, as he slowly opens the two rectangles.

'Would that be my arse or Nicky's arse, 'cos there's a big difference,' Bryan quips to howls of laughter.

Bryan is totally at home in the environment of the dance studio, as he is on stage in a live setting. He has learned his craft from the tender age of three when his parents enrolled him at Ireland's famous Billie Barry Stage School. There he became a close buddy of another Billie Barry kid, Samantha Mumba. Growing up in that environment allowed his natural abilities as an entertainer to flourish and it gave him stacks of confidence.

Always in a playful mood, he wanders around the studio and slyly scribbles graffiti on the back of the rectangles, 'The dancers are crap,' it reads.

'Bryan, pay attention!' Priscilla shouts across the room

'Sorry!' he answers with a wicked grin.

Priscilla then runs them through Somebody Needs You, but their concentration has gone out the window and the performance is sloppy and disjointed.

'Guys, this is the last day you'll be working in front of a mirror and you're bluffing...badly!' Priscilla snaps. 'Now let's try again and this time I want to see some enthusiasm.'

She's bouncing around the place as they swing into the routine.

'It's a hip-hop move and you have to get into the groove of it,' she shouts.

Afterwards, Priscilla is full of praise for the boys.

'They're tired now, so it's more difficult to keep them motivated. They have done it constantly for two weeks and that's hard work for anybody. But they've shown a lot of discipline and drive, apart from the odd moment or two. And they've done extremely well for a non-dance act to learn what they have learned in two weeks. They have impressed me in the way they've picked it up because the average dance act wouldn't learn what they've learned in such a short period. Even with the ballads they're moving differently than they did before.

'They're not the Westlife people knew before and I hope that fans will be surprised. When it goes to stage it will look easy to the audience, but it's a lot more difficult than people think. Not a lot of artists can sing and dance at the same time. It's quite a challenge and it's only the greatest and the best ones in the world that people remember for their singing and dancing, artists like Tina Turner and Lionel Richie.'

Kim is also satisfied with their progress over the two weeks.

'There was a lot to do as they hadn't danced till now, so they didn't have seven routines in the bag from all their singles. But I think they pick up easily. They were also starting from a disadvantage in that they have never toured before and never sung every night for months and months, so they have no understanding of the physical demands of a tour. It has been much harder to instruct them on what to do because they don't have that experience. From now on it will be a lot easier.'

It is Monday morning, January 22, 2001. Dark clouds cast an air of gloom over Dublin and torrential rain bounces off the streets as the boys arrive for work in their sleek BMWs. Mark, the only star without a car, hitches a daily ride to The Factory with Kian and Shane. Despite the grey day, the Westlifers are in upbeat form. Their dance routines are in place; all that is now required is some polishing. It feels good. Two weeks earlier, it had all been so different. Like most people's first day at work, they had been very apprehensive starting out with Priscilla.

'I wasn't as worried as the rest of them that day,' Bryan claims. 'I knew Nicky couldn't dance because he'd never danced in his life. So at least he would make me look good.'

Now, as they power through the routines on the last day, all five have a smile from ear to ear. By six o'clock in the evening they have run through the dances six times.

As they leave the building for the last time, their elation is tinged with sadness. They have grown accustomed to their daily routine; but it's time for Westlife to move on to the next stage.

Not before all the packing is done, however. Kian, Shane and Mark have a nightmare facing them back at their posh hotel. Having spent a couple of weeks in the same room, their clothes and laundry are strewn all over the place. Kian casts his eyes over the room that resembles a garbage tip.

'This is one of the worst parts of travel...packing,' he admits. 'I'll never get used to it. Clothes just seem to grow and multiply as soon as you take them out of the suitcase. It takes forever to get everything back in.'

Three hours later he is still cramming in the final bits and pieces after checking under the bed and in the bottom of the wardrobe to make sure he has scooped up all the dirty laundry and odds 'n' sods. Exhausted, he turns in for an early night.

CHAPTER 2

Uptown people and the race against time

Flying over London, Bryan is convinced that the impressive old rambling pile down below is Buckingham Palace.

'I don't think we fly over the palace on this flight,' Kian informs him.

'It's probably Charlie's gaff, then,' Bryan laughs.

'Charlie's gaff.'

It's been a running joke in the Westlife camp ever since last year's Royal Variety Performance and Bryan's cheeky banter with Prince Charles. Prior to the Prince coming backstage to meet the performers, a palace aide had given Westlife a crash course in royal etiquette.

'If his Royal Highness speaks to you, you may respond,' the stuffy geezer had told them.

Bryan had made a face behind his back and Nicky almost exploded trying to hold back a fit of laughing.

The Prince, of course, was very informal upon his arrival. Dressed in his smart dinner jacket with bow tie, Charles, who was smaller than they had imagined, was warm, friendly and full of laughter.

Bryan, who'd had a couple of drinks, was in a giddy mood. Shane, Kian, Nicky and Mark held their breath, fearing that he was going to land them in an embarrassing stew.

'Thank you ever so much. You were wonderful,' the Prince said.

'Thank you,' Shane bowed politely.

Bryan was jigging on the spot like a hen on a hot griddle.

'Charles, do you mind if I ask you something?' he piped up.

There was a sharp intake of breath from the other four, as well as the palace aide, who almost fainted on the spot.

'No, no, not at all old boy,' the bemused Prince responded.

There was a deadly silence for a second.

'Is there any chance we could come over and see your gaff sometime?' Bryan asked, a big grin cracking his face.

By this stage the palace aide looked like he needed urgent mouth-to-mouth resuscitation.

'Oh, I'm sure that can be arranged,' Prince Charles smiled.

Then, as the Prince started to move on, Bryan added, 'Don't worry, we'll bring our own drink.'

The aide's jaw hit the floor.

'Oh, yes, yes...' Charles stuttered and swiftly left the scene.

It had been the second year in a row that Bryan had breached royal etiquette at the Royal Variety Performance in the Royal Albert Hall. The previous year he had hit the headlines when he insulted the Queen. Her Majesty had worn a colourfully designed dress to the gala concert. Bryan had not been slow to pass comment:

'She looks like she's been in *Joseph And His Amazing*

Technicolour Dreamcoat,' he whispered, sending the other boys into a fit of giggles.

Westlife had performed I Have A Dream on the show earlier in the evening.

'That was a wonderful song. Who wrote it?' her Majesty asked Westlife when she was escorted backstage to meet the artists.

'It was Abba, ma'am,' Shane informed her, being very proper.

'Ma'am, may I just say I think your dress is lovely?' Bryan suddenly announced.

'Oh, thank you,' her Majesty smiled sweetly.

'It looks like a Quality Street wrapper,' Bryan added.

You could hear a pin drop.

'Thank you,' her Majesty finally responded, accepting the observation as a compliment.

'Ah, lads, I don't think she's the full shilling,' Bryan said later.

After their journey from the airport today, Bryan jumps out of the car, eager to check out Westlife's strange new surroundings.

'It doesn't look great, does it?' he quips, raising an eyebrow.

The others are frantically pulling their fleeces tightly to their bodies as a gust of ice-cold wind sweeps the forecourt.

'Never judge the book by the cover,' Mark sings.

As they retrieve their rucksacks from the rear of the wagon, you can sense that the boys are edgy this morning. This is their first day working with their new bunch of musicians. It's like moving school and having to build friendships with a whole gang of people you've never known before. You can almost read their minds. Are these guys going to like us? Will we get on with them? Are they going to be snobbish about our songs?

A maze of roads on a bleak industrial landscape in south-east London had taken Westlife to this building that looks for all the world like a barn.

There are no paparazzi with superlenses hovering in the vicinity, ready to pounce on the stars coming and going at the rehearsal headquarters. The building's location and the nature of the activities inside its four walls are unknown to the fans and the media.

Hanging out with Westlife soon strips away any notions about their day-to-day lives being steeped in glamour and glitz. This pile looks as inviting as a cold empty house on a winter's night. Inside, Westlife are greeted by a hive of activity as musicians fly around like busy bees, setting up their gear, strumming guitars, tickling keyboards and beating the hell out of drum kits.

Westlife have booked two massive production rooms here to rehearse with their new band and dancers. There's another famous figure wandering through the corridors. He's the highly respected guitarist Jeff Beck, a former member of sixties British R&B group, The Yardbirds. The sounds of his vast repertoire are going to be reverberating around the building as well, as he is limbering up for a tour, too.

'Who's yer man?' Bryan asks, as Beck shuffles past.

'Beats me,' says Nicky.

'Ah, he's been around since long before you were born,' Anto adds helpfully, filling them in on the history of this old rock 'n' roll legend.

Westlife aren't the only ones who've been anxiously anticipating this morning's encounter. The musicians have also been making regular trips to the loo. The familiar figures of Shane, Kian, Mark, Bryan and Nicky eventually swing through the doors like a tornado. Led by tour manager Anto, they look like a bunch of boisterous young boys heading to a birthday party. They are loud, laughing and joking among themselves, and there's a lot of horse-play as they push and shove each other around good-naturedly.

The musicians exchange glances, as if to say, 'Are these guys going to be a bunch of spoilt brats?'

Westlife had been used to performing live to their well produced, pristinely polished music booming out from mini-disc machines. Now they are going to hear a more organic sound coming from real people with real musical instruments.

'I can't wait to see the band in action,' Kian admits. 'I know I'm just going to love working with a live group. It's what it's all about for me and the rest of the lads.'

Shane Filan is in equally upbeat mood as he struts around the studio, looking for a spot to drop his rucksack.

'I've been dreaming about standing out front singing with amazing live musicians behind me. That's going to be such a buzz,' he enthuses.

The band had spent the previous week learning the Westlife tunes while the boys were doing their drills at The Factory in Dublin. Not having been part of Westlife world until now, they'd never played them before. So they had over 20 Westlife songs to master before linking up with the boys.

The musicians are a motley crew headed up by Richard Taylor, a clean-cut gentle giant with a baby face. He used to work with Boyzone. Apart from being the musical director of the band, he is also a top-notch keyboard player.

Then there's guitarist Milton McDonald, a gangly figure with a pony-tail, who could pass as a double for Francis Rossi of golden-oldie guitar outfit, Status Quo.

With his chubby cheeks, goatee beard and blonde highlights, guitarist Tim Maple is no stranger to the boy band scene either – he is also a former Boyzone musician.

Tall, dark and handsome Malcolm Moore, the bass player and youngest member of the band, shows serious potential as a pin-up idol himself, with his Tim Henman appeal and charming, easy-going manner.

Silver-haired drummer Niall Power, a lean, handsome, forty-something who has worked with such rock glitterati as Hazel O'Connor and Bob Geldof – he's still an official member of Geldof's band – is the only musician who comes from Ireland; the remainder all being from the UK. Niall, who is quietly spoken and grows herbs in his spare time, reveals how a chance meeting with his old friend Louis Walsh in an Aer Lingus lounge at Heathrow Airport led to him joining Westlife for this first tour.

'I was sitting in the airport waiting for my flight to be called when Louis arrived. I was delighted to see him, as we were friends going back 25 years. We started out in the Irish music business at the same time, Louis as an agent and me as a drummer. His achievements in the last ten years had been fantastic since he turned Boyzone into a supergroup and became one of the most successful pop managers in the world. "Niall, you're just the man I want to see," he said to me that day. "I'm putting together a band called Westlife. Do you fancy the gig?" I didn't have to think twice. "Yes!" I said on the spot.'

Finally the musicians take their places on the makeshift stage and a hush falls over the little Westlife gang. Suddenly all eyes and ears are directed towards the five guys on the podium as they crank up the music.

Westlife can hardly believe their ears as the band fires up and starts playing Dreams Come True.

They look at each other and then at the five members of the band who are producing sounds they have only ever heard on record up till this moment. It is the dawn of a new era for the pop superstars.

Watching their faces it is obvious that they're amazed and excited to reach a stage where there are five musicians playing their music and it's THEIR band.

Kian, who has been mesmerised by the virtuosity of the guitarists, nudges Shane with his elbow.

'Is this weird or what? Remember the dream in Sligo when we started. This is it. We're here. This is really happening. It's SO happening.'

Shane is totally engrossed in the music, barely taking his eyes away from the band for a split second. Watching him it is obvious that his fantasy has become a reality.

'It's so cool to hear them playing our music because we've never had this before,' Kian says. 'They're playing pretty much as the record, but it's playing live instead of us listening to tapes and stuff. It's fantastic.'

The boys sit and soak it up for a while, marvelling at the live sounds of songs that are etched in their brains and in their hearts. Soon they are singing along and really getting into it. Shane is the first to burst into song as they huddle together.

After drinking in the atmosphere and becoming intoxicated by the dynamism of the live sound, one by one the boys stroll up to sing with their band. A work routine has been set out for them, whereby each song is rehearsed until it is perfected. They start off with Dreams Come True and soon singers and musicians are gelling together in a marriage made in heaven.

Westlife have just one day to become familiar with the workings of their live band before they are dragged away for another series of commitments. It is a trend that will follow the boy band through their tour.

First on their itinerary the next day is the video shoot of the taped introduction to their live show. This is a scene where they are in a state of sleep and then a weird doctor (played by their costume designer, Dave, who has had his hair dyed blond especially for his starring role) arrives with his alien crew (the Westlife dancers) and kick-starts them to life with shock pads.

It's a fun day for the boys as they have very little to do except hang around until they are called into action. They have no lines, so they don't have the pressure of frantically learning a script. But best of all, it gives the boys the chance to enjoy a riotous laugh at the expense of their lovely dancers, Lene, Jodi, Karen, Marilena and Jessica, who have to parade around the space-age set in figure-hugging catsuits that cover their entire bodies. Only their eyes peep out from two little slots.

The things you have to do in showbiz!

The following day, in a diner near London's King's Cross tube station, Westlife are once again surrounding by movie cameras, lights and lots of arty types shouting out orders like, 'Quiet on set!' and 'Action!'

They may be the superstars of pop right now and pin-up idols to millions of girls around the globe, but today all eyes are on a stunning blonde woman whose legs seem to reach the sky. Every male on the set is in serious danger of suffering a severe case of whiplash as they all frantically stretch and twist their necks to catch her every move.

With perfect features and a smile that lights up a room, Claudia Schiffer cuts a striking pose as she wanders around the video set in her red stilettos, black coat and gloves and a blue hat that has a net covering her face. This is one of the world's most beautiful women.

She's a supermodel.

Westlife are about to live every young guy's dream by spending an entire day in her company. If ever there was a moment that the singers thanked their lucky stars that they hit the major league in pop, then this is it. Claudia Schiffer, one of the most successful models in the world, has agreed to perform with them in a video for Comic Relief.

The German-born beauty is taking over the role of Uptown Girl, originally performed by American model Christie Brinkley when Billy Joel scored a hit with his self-penned song back in 1983. In fact, Brinkley later became his wife.

Unfortunately for the single guys in Westlife, Claudia isn't a free woman, so there's no chance of one of them becoming her 'toy boy'. The catwalk queen, who has earned a £19-million fortune, is dating Matthew Vaughn, producer of the hit movie, *Snatch*. But who's complaining? It's not every day a young guy gets to rub shoulders with a supermodel.

'We're very lucky with the women we get to work with,' Nicky acknowledges, reflecting on how they lived out another fantasy when they got to spend a couple of days on the gorgeous, sun-drenched isle of Capri with American superstar Mariah Carey while shooting their video for a cover of the Phil Collins song, Against All Odds.

They thought they'd died and gone to heaven, but today is even more special for Mark.

'This is a weird one for me because I used to have Claudia Schiffer's poster on my bedroom wall at home in Sligo before I got into Westlife,' he reveals. 'Now I'm meeting Claudia in the flesh. Sometimes things like this are just hard to take in because you never expect them to happen. It's my bedroom poster coming to life.'

Kian suggests, 'Maybe you should take her for a drink when we're finished and chance your arm.'

Mark laughs at his pal's ribbing. 'Stranger things have happened,' he quips.

Shane is also reflecting on an amazing coincidence involving the Uptown Girl song. 'When I was seven years old my Mam gave me a tape of Uptown Girl and said, "Here's a song, learn that." She thought that I had a good voice because I was always singing along to songs on the radio in the house or on journeys in the car. I didn't pay any heed to it at the time. But she got me to learn Uptown Girl and from then on I had to sing it for all the relations when they came home from Manchester or Cardiff for Christmas or some other occasion. I'd have to get up in the middle of the sitting room and sing it for everybody. I wasn't very confident at first. I was very shy when I was young. I was afraid people would think I was bad. But after I got lots of good responses I started getting a bit of confidence and I just loved it.

'Then Michael Jackson took over for me totally. He was a real inspiration. But it's just so strange that Uptown Girl is the song chosen for this year's Comic Relief and I'm getting to record it after all these years.'

Ace screenwriter Richard Curtis, whose hits include *Four Weddings And A Funeral*, *Notting Hill* and *Bridget Jones's Diary*, is also the chief mover behind the Comic Relief charitable organisation. He'd suggested the idea of Westlife doing Uptown Girl and had even asked their opinion on who should play the lead female role. Several supermodel names had been bandied about, but it quickly emerged that Claudia Schiffer was one of the favourites with all of the boys.

'Everybody eventually opted for Claudia. As luck would have it, Richard said that he knew Claudia quite well and was friendly with her agent,' Shane reveals. 'So Richard phoned her and she said she'd love to do it.'

There had been no sign of Claudia during the first few hours here in the diner at King's Cross when the actors were recording their speaking parts. Things were moving slowly at first. With everybody performing for free and fitting the shoot into their already hectic schedules, it seemed there had been no advance preparation as lines were constantly fluffed.

There are also some real actors in the video, including Crispian Bonham-Carter (from TV's *Game On*), Tim McInnerney from the movie *Notting Hill, Cold Feet's* Robert Bathurst and *102 Dalmatians'* star Ioan Gruffudd.

Shane is telling them how he felt totally at home in the environs of the diner. 'My folks have a restaurant back home in Ireland and I've always worked there. I've even served up coke and chips to the fans since I joined Westlife, although I never get the chance to do that these days,' he reveals.

Bryan is equally at home on the set. 'This reminds me of the time I worked in McDonald's back home in Dublin. I used to sweep the floor there as well; it was my least favourite job.'

Now it's Claudia's turn and there is a flurry of activity. Claudia is quiet at first as the director fills her in on the shooting schedule. But as she becomes familiar with her surroundings and the people she's working with, her personality emerges.

During a break, the gorgeous blonde hangs out with Westlife and says how she is under orders to secure their autograph before she leaves.

'My nieces are really big fans of you guys,' Claudia tells them. 'When they heard I was going to be doing a video with you they insisted, "Oh you must get their autographs for us." It will be such a thrill for them.'

Claudia is the essence of charm. There is no sign of the tantrums, bitchiness and aloofness that is so often associated with some of the big names of the modelling world. Instead, she oozes warmth and has an easy smile.

Shane can't take his eyes off her during the shoot. At one stage, Claudia catches him staring at her, his jaw touching the ground, and he quickly glances away with embarrassment.

Shooting videos is a long, tedious process because there are so many technical things that can go wrong. It takes off, then comes to a grinding halt. Just one day has been scheduled for the shoot, so they've got to stay on until everything is perfect. With a break for meals and time out to meet the media to promote Red Nose Day thrown in, the day soon turns into night.

By eleven o'clock, Claudia's part is all wrapped up, but before she leaves she kisses each of the besotted Westlifers on the cheek.

'Claudia is very nice and very down to earth,' Kian says, his face still flushed. 'She now has five new big-time fans.'

Shane is walking on air. This has been a key moment in his life. But he's having a little cringe in a quiet corner.

'I was so embarrassed when she caught me staring at her like some kind of freak,' he admits. 'But I couldn't help myself, she's so gorgeous.'

After the other performers leave, the boys stay behind to work on the video's main singing performances. In the end, it is three o'clock in the morning by the time Uptown Girl is completed and their presence is no longer required. Then it's straight back to the hotel to get some shut-eye, as they are definitely feeling like downtown boys by this stage.

It won't be long before their alarm clocks go off like a bad nightmare at seven o'clock, to wake them for an early-morning flight to Germany.

Shane can't stop smiling, though. The Uptown Girl video and recording is going to be one of the memorable moments of his career. He's clutching a little parcel under his arm on the way to the hotel.

'It's the shirt I wore in the diner,' he reveals. 'I'm going to put the date on it and frame it for myself. This is one souvenir that really does mean a lot to me.'

Next morning the boys are shattered. As soon as they get on the plane and settle into their seats they instantly drop into a deep sleep until they touch down in Germany.

Although exhausted, Westlife put on their chirpy front as they launch into a round of non-stop radio and TV interviews with

German stations. Several strong cups of coffee later they are all buzzing with personality as they wax lyrical about their meteoric rise to superstardom.

Later in the afternoon they perform at a *Guinness Book Of Records* show in Germany. All kinds of record breakers are among the studio guests and Westlife have earned their place by notching up SEVEN Number One singles in a row, beating the Beatles in the process.

A private plane is on stand-by for Westlife, waiting to whisk them home for a quickie visit to Dublin. They are to be the star attraction at a major Irish charity pop concert called Childline. It is late in the evening by the time they finish their spot on the German show. Then it's a mad rush to the airport for the flight to Ireland.

As soon as the boys board the plane they collapse back into their seats and settle in for a quick snooze on the journey. As the minutes tick away, there is no sign of the plane moving from its holding bay. The boys glance at each other ominously, sensing that something is wrong. Then the bombshell comes through from the pilot. The flight is being aborted due to severe weather conditions. The ground is like a skating rink from an Arctic frost and it's too dangerous to fly. All the planes are being grounded.

'There goes our lie-in in the morning,' Kian groans, as he struggles out of his seat and back into a chilly night air that feels like the North Pole.

There is a sombre mood among the gang on the way to the hotel, with everyone upset at the thought of another early morning alarm call coming up.

By morning, spirits in the Westlife camp are high again. The weather has dramatically improved, the white blanket of frost that was on the ground has now been spirited away and their plane is being allowed to make the trip to Dublin.

The prospect of performing in front of a home crowd energises the five guys. It has been a long time since they've been on a stage in Ireland, lapping up the attention and adoration from a live audience at home. And with Sunday being an official day off, they can even party that night and sleep late the following day.

The Westlife plane touches down at Dublin Airport in the afternoon and they head straight into rehearsals at the Point Depot concert venue out in the docklands. Backstage, Childline is like a Who's Who of the pop world. A1, Atomic Kitten, Vanessa Amorosi, Louise, Billie Piper, Girl Thing, Stephen Gately, Keith Duffy, Shane Lynch, Samantha Mumba and Reel are all dropping in and out as they sound check for the show.

Outside, hundreds of fans are staging a vigil, screaming for Westlife and going into a state of apoplexy every time a limousine with blacked-out windows enters the compound.

'Westlife! Westlife! Westlife!' the chant rings out around the area from early morning, leaving no-one in doubt about the most popular act on the bill.

The Westlife boys bump into Australian pop princess Vanessa Amorosi, a small dark-haired girl with a friendly disposition, in a corridor backstage.

She's here to sing her current smash hit, Absolutely

Everybody, and they're surprised to learn that she is sleeping in her swag outdoors on the balcony of her Dublin hotel, despite the fact that the temperature has dropped to freezing point.

'I prefer the outdoors,' Vanessa tells them. 'I slept on the balcony outside my hotel in Germany two nights ago.'

'Outdoors in sunny Australia is fine, but freezing Dublin?' Kian asks, incredulously.

'I'm just an outdoors kind of girl,' Vanessa laughs. 'I like fishing, too. I've brought my fishing rod with me. When I went to the river in Germany it was frozen over. It was the first time I'd seen ice.'

The boys stare at her open-mouthed. You can read their thoughts. Is this girl for real?

Finally it's showtime and when Westlife appear on stage, they regret not having left their ear-drums in the dressing room as 6,000 young fans scream their heads off.

Tonight they do their ballads-and-stools regime, keeping the new routines under wraps until the launch of the tour.

The frenzied reaction of the crowd seems to catch Westlife off-guard for a few seconds.

'The noise of the audience was actually frightening when we went out there,' Kian admits when he arrives off-stage. 'When you're not doing live stuff at home you sort of forget what the reaction is like. We're counting the weeks to bringing our own tour to this venue. That is going to be so sweet for us.'

Shane is also buzzing from the adrenaline rush of the performance.

'The crowd just went absolutely ballistic. There were so many banners with our names on them and they were all so colourful. The fans will do anything to get noticed. They just love to come out in their colours.'

After the concert, which has been televised live all around Ireland, the performers hit the city's nightclubs and Westlife have a really late night, happy in the knowledge that they can sleep right through the following day.

Monday morning it's business as usual, starting off with a flight to London to pick up where they left off at rehearsals. It's now obvious that there is a very good rapport between the Westlifers and their musicians, with a mutual respect. The musicians aren't looking down their noses at the boy band and, likewise, Westlife don't see the band as second class to their big star status.

'They are really enthusiastic and you can see that they want to make this work as quickly as possible. So they've really got into it,' drummer Niall observes during a break.

'Obviously it sounds a bit different than singing with the record all the time. But they're having no problems. It's still the same songs that they've always been performing, and they just get up and sing them. It's us, the musicians, who've had to do more work because we didn't know the tunes starting out. But so far it has been pretty easy 'cos the guys are so up for it.'

As the days go on, the songs are tweaked and changed from the album versions to adapt to the demands of the show. The opening number, Dreams Come True, now has a big dance break, so the band has to accommodate that; and other tracks are getting a different treatment as well.

'We're changing as we're going along because the songs have to revolve around the production,' Niall explains. 'We learned the original versions of the songs and the boys have rehearsed those with us. But now some things have to be made longer for the show and other bits taken out to fit what's happening on stage.'

Shane glances over his shoulder and winks at drummer Niall during the upbeat and exciting Motown medley of songs. It is a signal that he is thoroughly enjoying the full-on singing that the set demands. Vocal coach Dave Tench's face lights up with delight. This is his 'baby,' his arrangement and it is shaping up to be a real show stealer.

'I think this is very good for them because it gives them a chance to really go for it, singing-wise, more than they normally do,' he comments as he watches the performance. 'I felt that they had this in them. It really stretches them vocally and shows everyone what they're capable of.'

While the boys are rehearsing with the band, the girls are in a studio next door, being put through their paces by Sgt Major Samuels, aka Priscilla. By this stage they look so sharp they could cut through a steel fence.

Every day a special teacher also arrives to coach the dancers for a novel feature of the show. The girls have been asked to perform I Have A Dream with sign language as an opening sequence to the song. This has a dual purpose. It takes the attention away from the fact that the boys aren't on stage at that moment – they'll be doing a quick change of costume – and it will also add a heart-warming dimension to the performance.

After the third day, it's time for all three sections of the show to join forces and knit together like a proper team. Suddenly, the studio resembles one massive school-room with 15 students under tuition, between the band, the boys and the dancers. Kim, Priscilla and Dave are all shouting out instructions, making adjustments, coaxing and cajoling as they blend the show together with all the ingredients mixed in. Everyone is diligently working hard to get it right as fast as possible. They have a terrifyingly tight deadline of one week before moving on to the final stage of the pre-show preparations.

With all the elements of the concert now combined and songs constantly changing to fit around the routines, progress is slow some days. In Dublin, the boys had been used to learning their stagecraft in front of a mirrored wall. Now they have to get to grips with performing 'blind,' moving around on stage without knocking into each other, or the dancers, during the routines. Priscilla and Paula occasionally become their mirrored wall, stepping out front and doing the dance routines while the boys follow their actions behind.

Some sections of the performance are more difficult to coordinate than others and rehearsals occasionally drop to a snail's pace as everyone struggles to get it right. This creates nervous tension as the Westlife boys are worried about getting everything perfect in time for opening night.

'How does it look to you, Priscilla? Are we getting there?' Kian asks, his expression showing deep concern, after an alarming series of false starts.

'Don't worry, Kian, this is just normal. It's nothing I haven't seen before. Sure it would be great to have more time. But that's life and it's nothing we can't handle,' she reassures him.

The days are long and hard, starting around ten o'clock in the morning and running till nine or ten at night. With so much to learn there is no time for partying in the evenings after work. They relax by watching TV and nibble on snacks before collapsing into bed exhausted.

Friday is a short day, wrapping up at five o'clock in the evening, as all the band's equipment, including guitars, drums, amplifiers and mixing desks, has to be loaded up and transported by trucks on to the new Westlife headquarters at Bray outside London. There, the set that has been created for their tour is being assembled for their impending arrival.

While the removal activity is in progress, Kian, Shane, Mark, Bryan and Nicky head off for abseiling lessons. It isn't that they have suddenly turned all sporty; there is a much more practical reason. They have to prepare for the demands of their show opener during which they've planned to surprise the audience by swinging towards them on ropes from the top of four-metre high towers. But they've been warned that unless they take proper training they will have to abandon the stunt as their insurance company won't cover them against injury.

After the pressure of the rehearsals, the abseiling course provides some light relief and a few laughs as the lads clown around doing their Tarzan impressions.

On the Saturday evening Westlife chill out and watch the latest developments in *Popstars,* the British TV quest to select a supergroup for world domination. It proves to be totally compelling TV, particularly for five young Irish guys who've lived through a similar experience in real life, albeit out of the glare of the public eye.

All five Westlifers had battled for THEIR places in the Irish boy band and the chance of fame and fortune when pop mogul Louis Walsh held auditions for his follow-up to Boyzone. Now they are reliving those terrifying yet thrilling experiences all over again through *Popstars.*

Nicky shudders as he turns to Bryan and says, 'Jeez, Bryan, remember the torture we went through?'

Bryan nods.

The pair were both fighting for last place in Westlife at the end of the auditions in Dublin's Red Box venue back in June, 1998.

'I wasn't even going to turn up. I thought you were in,' Bryan laughs.

It had been a talented but raw Sligo-based pop group called IOU, which included Shane, Kian and Mark and three pals, that was the foundation for today's Westlife.

In the incredibly cruel world of pop, which is littered with the corpses of would-be stars, two of the original members, Derek and Graham, were the first casualties in the reconstruction of the outfit for world domination. And the debonair RCA record company talent guru Simon Cowell wanted Shane kicked out in the initial stages.

When Louis organised the auditions for the new-look IOU he was only seeking ONE new member. In the end it was a tension-fuelled battle between two blonds – Nicky and Bryan. Eventually, they both made it into the group and it was decided that Michael had to go.

When talent-spotter Cowell, the man who signed up Five and Robson & Jerome, came back to check out the new line-up, he was dead impressed. Simon even liked the 'new' blond bloke...SHANE FILAN. Louis had been so convinced of Shane's star quality he pulled a master stroke by changing the colour of his hair to make him look like new blood.

'I'm glad we had to go through that kind of nightmare because if you come out the other end on top, it really makes you appreciate your success,' Nicky says.

Westlife now live every heart-stopping, tear-jerking moment with the young wannabes on *Popstars*.

'This is totally addictive. I've been watching every show. I've even watched the repeats,' Kian admits.

Unlike most of the TV viewers, Kian already knows the identity of the young hopefuls who have made it into the group. But he is fascinated by the often tear-jerking recruiting process that is acted out on TV in front of 'Nasty Nigel' and co.

'We actually met the band just before Christmas. They were

chosen last October, even though it's only being shown now on TV. They were a nice bunch of people, but when it all takes off they won't know what has hit them. There'll be so much media and so much work, it's going to be a real shock until they get used to it.'

Kian then admits that he wouldn't have chosen Danny. He feels that Kevin, 'the blondie guy',was a better fit for the 'look' of the group and had an equally good voice.

The boys are up bright and early Sunday morning, all excited at the prospect of seeing the new Westlife set for the first time. It's an hour-long drive to yet another big warehouse and their pulses race and hearts pound with nervous anticipation as they stop outside their destination.

Inside, people are running around with bits and pieces of machinery and various chunks of material as they battle with the obviously very complex task of building the massive construction. Westlife stand back and watch, clearly disappointed by the anti-climax. The huge set they had envisaged still hasn't taken shape. It is like a jig-saw puzzle being pieced together, slowly and laboriously. All they can do is loll around helplessly as the army of workers gets on with the job.

As the hours slip by the boys grow more and more dejected. Crucial rehearsal time is being lost and their first show is coming up on Friday. By late afternoon it is obvious that the stage won't be ready for a rehearsal that day, so Westlife troop back to their hotel with a dark cloud hanging over them.

They all spring out of their beds early the next morning, scoff their breakfast in record time and shoot out the door of the hotel, eager to launch straight into rehearsals.

But when they arrive at the venue, there is more bad news. There is going to be a delay while some technical problems are sorted out. So Westlife watch with glum faces as the moving parts of the set start and stop, and then move forward and get stuck once again.

There is also another row brewing. Some of the boys aren't happy with the opening stunt. It has been refined from a bungee jump into the audience to a scaled-down swinging movement on to the stage.

Bryan is furious.

'It's meant to be bungee ropes and getting shot forward into the crowd.' he insists.

Westlife are told that their initial idea has been turned down on the grounds that it is too risky.

The Safety Council won't allow it to be performed and the insurance company won't cover it. On reflection, the boys see the merits of the argument.

'It's not as dramatic now as we had wanted. It's still good, but we wanted more hair-raising stuff. That's the way it goes,' Bryan says, philosophically.

It is four o'clock in the afternoon before the boys finally get on to their stage for the first time. By this point they have exhausted the use of the F-word. There is a lot of nervous tension in the air as they suddenly realise their moment of truth is getting closer. They are now on their own enormous stage with a whole range of moving parts. It all seemed so much simpler back at The Factory in Dublin. Now they have to worry about things like not bumping into the towers, tripping over each other or sending the dancers flying off the stage and into the pit below.

Among the many gems of advice that Priscilla has passed on to them is to treat the stage with respect. 'Never disrespect the stage,' she says 'You go up there and you bless it. This is going to be your home for the next five months.'

By the time everyone gets set up, become familiar with their new work station and sort out their routines – where they come on and where they exit off the stage – they only manage to run through four songs before calling it a night. But Priscilla is encouraging. 'You're adapting very professionally to it,' she assures them.

The tension is now mounting and nerves are becoming frayed by the minute.

Two days allocated to stage rehearsals have been wasted, apart from four songs that have been roughly rehearsed. There are no rehearsals tomorrow, Tuesday, because the whole set is being dismantled again. The production is being shifted from the base outside London to the Newcastle Arena in preparation for opening night. The gigantic stage has to be loaded into nine huge trucks before the convoy sets off.

The Westlife roadshow is on the move...it's just a shame that the boys still haven't their routines all polished up and ready for the big blast-off on Friday night.

Westlife have a rare lie-in next morning before catching an afternoon flight to Newcastle for rehearsals. But when they arrive at the Newcastle Telewest Arena there is yet another body blow waiting for them. The stage isn't in place.

The boys stroll around the massive empty arena, hands in pockets, watching the work in progress as the crew assembles the enormous jig-saw. The sound of hammering and drilling echoes around the vast empty interior as Westlife soak up the atmosphere. Their disappointment at not being able to rehearse is tempered by the excitement of seeing their stage being built in the venue for their first ever arena concert.

The dream is closer to becoming a reality.

With time on their hands, Westlife now have an opportunity to whip up some new hairdos for the tour. They consult their stylist, Ben, who has worked with them from the early stages of their career. Nicky and Mark are going for radical new looks. Nicky, who has sported long tresses for months, wants the inches lopped off. Mark is going for a close cropped marines image because he can't be bothered styling his hair after showering.

Meanwhile, Shane, Kian and Bryan are pondering over their subtle changes.

They don't want any major surgery.

Ben, a jovial, shaven-headed Londoner, was initially drafted in by the BMG record company to define the 'look' of Westlife when they were being groomed for the super league.

'It was all very business-like way back then. I remember a big boardroom meeting to discuss their hairstyles. Getting the right image in place was a deadly serious undertaking. A lot of careful thought went into it. For inspiration, we looked around at who were the popular teen boy idols at the time. Guys like David Beckham and Leonardo DiCaprio were the sort of people in vogue. So we looked at their styles and we thought, "OK, Bryan can be our Leonardo and Kian can be our Beckham." It was that sort of thing; what's in, who looks good and who should we steer them towards. So it was me and the marketing people at the record company who came up with their image.'

From then on, hairstyles have been developed by the boys themselves, in consultation with Ben.

'As time has gone on the boys have been a lot more involved in how they look and what they want. I might see something in a magazine and take it to them and they make suggestions themselves.'

Some Westlifers are more concerned about their appearance than others.

'Mark and Bryan are pretty easy going,' Ben reveals. 'Kian and Nicky are a lot more particular and Shane is somewhere in the middle. They all want to look good ultimately, but they're not hours and hours in front of the mirror, although some take a few more minutes than others.'

It's difficult for guys not to be self-conscious about their appearance when they're constantly confronted with images of themselves in magazines, newspapers and on TV.

'You do become very vain,' Nicky admits. 'You can't avoid it.

You see so many pictures of yourself. You come across pictures of yourself with long hair and short hair or no hair. It's like looking at old photos in an album. At the time you probably thought you had a really cool hairstyle and were wearing really fashionable clothes. But when you look back, sometimes you think, "God I looked crap then." We can never get away from that. Being in a pop band is not just about the music, it's about image and fashion.'

Ben also doubles as a make-up artist, applying it when the need arises.

'Usually it's when they haven't been sleeping at night and they've got big bags under their eyes that I have a little clean-up job to do.'

On Wednesday morning they head straight for the concert arena again, arriving in at nine o'clock. The smiles on their faces are quickly replaced by grim looks as they discover the technical crew still working on the set.

'Eh, it's not quite ready yet. It's nearly there. Just a few technical things that have to be ironed out.'

The towers aren't working.

Westlife can't believe what they are hearing.

'This is not good. This is not good at all,' Kian mutters.

Anto is on the case, stressing that show night is literally upon them and rehearsals just have to be done...NOW!

If looks could kill.

Top tour agent John Giddings, who has sold out all their gigs, is astonished by the hold-ups. He has worked with the likes of Céline Dion, Phil Collins and The Rolling Stones. He's saying that none of those acts would tolerate the situation; jobs would be lost. So why should Westlife have to put up with it. He warns that people will have to get their act together.

Several hours later and after much frantic activity, during which Westlife hang around and slowly slip into a deep depression, they get the green light. Rehearsals can now begin. It is decided to run through the finale first, because that involves a dramatic scene in which the boys will literally fly over the heads of the audience, attached to a metal grid which travels across the ceiling. Being a spectacular closing number, it has the potential to blow up into a major disaster if the grid fails to move or gets stuck in mid-performance. This is practised over and over until everyone is happy with its safety and performance.

Afterwards, it is decided to run through all the songs again before doing the proper stage routines. By the time the singing is rehearsed, it's getting on for midnight. The complete run-through of the show will have to wait until tomorrow. Shattered, the boys go straight to bed when they arrive back at their hotel. Thursday – the day before the show – is now a crucial one for Westlife. They have planned proper dress rehearsals on the eve of the concert. By now they are so far behind schedule it's scary. It is unprecedented for a pop supergroup starting a major arena tour to find themselves in this precarious position. They urgently need to test-drive the entire performance to make sure that there are going to be no embarrassing hiccups on the first night.

To their horror they arrive to find more technical problems with the set and they can't go on stage until it's sorted. While they wait, Priscilla does some warm-up routines with them.

But the boys are unable to concentrate; at this point they are suffering anxiety attacks from the worry of not being properly rehearsed.

The hours drag on and eventually their worry explodes into rage as a war of words erupts between the band and the individuals responsible for the set. Westlife insist on holding an emergency meeting right there, right then to express their views. Bryan sums up the feelings of the group in an impassioned speech when he tells how Westlife have spent almost three years of non-stop promotion to reach a point where they can finally sell a major tour. Now that dream is in jeopardy because the set isn't working properly.

'We have spent a lot of money on the staging of this show and it's a complete shambles. It's an absolute mess. We're not getting what we paid for and we wanted it sorted NOW!' he steams. 'At the end of the day, it's our reputation and our career that's on the line here.'

Despite their protestations, it's 10.30 on Thursday night before the stage is ready for Westlife to begin working on their routines. Three songs into the run, disaster strikes again when one of the moving towers breaks down. A mixture of fury and fear is etched on the faces of the famous five when they are told that it isn't going to be fixed until the morning.

Kian snaps, 'We're doing a show tomorrow night and we've

never run it. We need to rehearse NOW! What do you propose we do?'

They are told that the rehearsals can begin at seven o'clock the following morning. This will allow them to do one dress rehearsal and then break for three hours before doing a second run in the lead-up to the show.

Westlife look at each other in disbelief. How can things be going so horribly wrong at this crucial moment in their career?

There is some respite when a crew member comes in and announces that the technical hitch has been resolved and they can start the dress rehearsal again if they wish. It is now 11.30 p.m. Despite being tired and deflated, they need to run the show. But with all the upset and distractions, their concentration levels are out of kilter.

The run reveals that their timing needs to be really tightened up. They are too slow doing costume changes and late getting back on to the stage between numbers. Instead of coming across as the super-slick pop supergroup that everyone expects, they looked more like a bunch of novice popsters.

'That was a disaster,' Kian exclaims at the end of the run.

It is now one one o'clock in the morning.

As they change back into their casual clothing, grab their bags and head back to their hotel the boys are in a pensive mood. Tomorrow night they are going to be exposed to the world when the curtain comes up on their first major tour. How they wish they had more time to get their act together. But it's not to be. It is going to be difficult to get some sleep tonight.

Bryan is still fuming over the technical hitches. Referring to their earlier outburst, he says: 'It's not that we're an aggressive bunch, but we can speak our minds. A lot of other pop bands might sit back and let someone else take control, but we're very hands-on. We like to be in control of everything. All the things that have gone wrong have just made us really angry and uptight. It's just like, if you bought a car and the gears didn't work the first day; then the next day the steering wheel didn't work – you'd get pissed off.'

The next morning, despite the fact that they have worked into the early hours, everyone is awake early. For once, Anto doesn't have to go through the regular rigmarole of phoning their individual rooms several times to get them up and going. Nerves have kicked in and everyone is on tenterhooks.

There is so much preparation to be done before opening time. Their hearts are thumping as they arrive at the arena. What disaster awaits them this morning?

'Morning guys,' Kim greets them with a smile.

'Everything OK, Kim?' Kian asks apprehensively.

'Everything seems to be functioning. Let's hope there are no hiccups.'

All hands are on deck this morning with the rehearsals down to the wire.

Various elements of the show are worked on in sections during the first few hours. Then at 1.20 p.m. everyone is ready to perform the extravaganza that fans will see for the first time when it kicks off at nine o'clock tonight.

Kian, ready for lift-off

△ RED ALERT: Anto displays a
warning card for his Westlife boys

△ Nicky preparing for
the show in Wembley

◁ Nicky signing
autographs in Oslo

△ Louis giving advice
on the Westlife coach
before Wembley

▽ Anto the passport minder

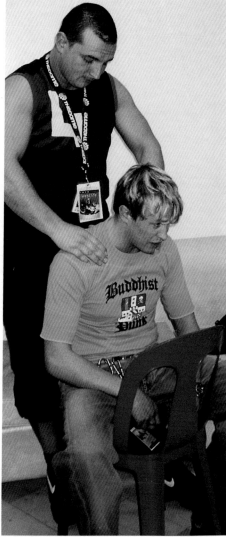

△ Kian gets a
massage from minder
Paul Higgins

△ Meeting the fans at Wembley

▽ CARTEL: Bryan with Darragh and Tim – his first group. The Point,
Dublin March 2001

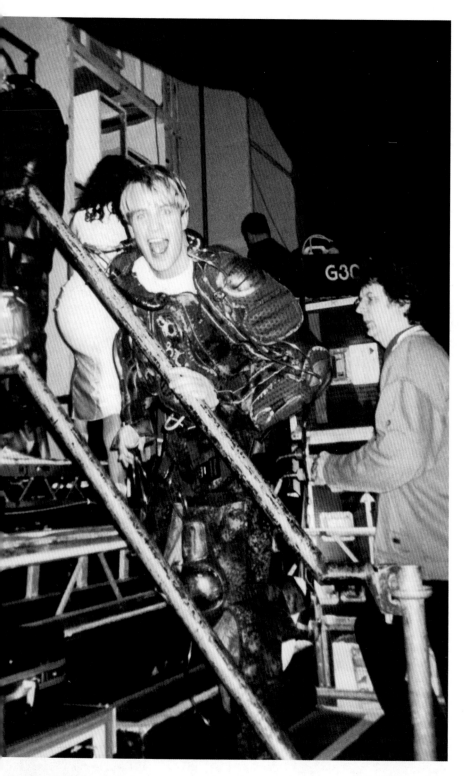

Kian backstage in Oslo

△ FAMILY TIME: Shane at The Point, Dublin with his family, including parents Mae and Peter, and Louis

△ The lounge on Westlife's coach with videos, Playstation and TV

◁ BUNKING DOWN: Nicky in the Westlife Sleeping Section on the coach

'Stand by, this is going to be our only run-through,' a voice booms around the empty auditorium.

Kim sits in the middle of the arena in front of the mixing desk with a notebook at the ready to assess the performance. Vocal coach Dave Tench is close by and Priscilla is also sitting out front.

The lights go down, the screen lights up and the videotaped introduction kicks in. Dreams Come True, the dramatic opening scene, works like...a dream. Towers turn when they are supposed to, and the boys abseil on to the stage, launching into the upbeat dance routine like seasoned performers.

During the run, the individual members of Westlife occasionally shout out requests and comments.

'We only have a tiny little light up here. We need more light on the stage,' Kian roars when the lights are dimmed during the intro to one of the songs.

Instead of singing Swear It Again, Kian whistles his way through the number. After Fool Again, Shane shouts 'We messed up on that one. We need to do it again.'

Various technical shortcomings are noted. 'That black-out needs to be quicker,' someone shouts at the end of another song as the boys disappear off the stage.

Kian appears to be unhappy with his costume during Seasons In The Sun. Mark, sweating profusely, is annoyed because his ear-set isn't working. And Bryan fluffs some of his moves.

But for their first full dress rehearsal it's an impressive effort. Although they hold back on their vocal delivery, saving their voices for the main event this evening, there is a communal sigh of relief at the end. Apart from minor work on some of the routines, they have proven to themselves and everyone associated with the show that they have the ability to pull off a major-league event. Just as well, they are going to be doing it for real a few hours later. Talk about living dangerously!

Kian is as excited as a Lottery winner. 'I feel a lot more relaxed after that one. There are three or four things that need to be cleaned up, but they'll only take five minutes to clean. They say in this business, "A bad rehearsal, a good show," although I don't believe it. Last night we were terrible, but that seemed to run a lot faster. Everybody appeared to be a lot more spirited. We ourselves didn't give it our all on a performance level. We were holding back in here without the audience to conserve our voices and our energy. You've got to hold it.

'If you've ever been in a fight you'll notice that because you're so nervous you lose your energy after five minutes. And that's what happens after you get on that stage. When you hear 10,000 people screaming at you, you get a huge adrenaline rush and you've got to pace yourself. I think we're all ready for the show now. There have been a lot of arguments in the lead up over things going wrong or not living up to our expectations. Everybody was getting nervous and uptight. But it's all fine now.'

Priscilla's face is also beaming.

'Seeing them in their costumes out there has made me glow. The Adidas trainers and baseball caps have been replaced by those great outfits and now they really look like artists in a band. When they did the If I Let You Go routine (the third song) I was like, "Yes, they can do this!" It was perfect and they were really in time with each other. Their facial expressions in that number showed that they were so into it and it was really giving them a lot of confidence. They were sticking their thumbs in the air, going "Yeeahh!"

'Another thing I was happy to see was them sweating after the second number. I thought, "Fantastic. The band is sweating. I love it." To me, that means they are working. If you're not sweating you're not working as far as I'm concerned. I wanted them to smell of sweat by the fifth number and they did.

'But I also have to tell them to pace themselves because I don't want to hear them panting into the microphones after the fourth number. They are not a bunch of extremely fit boys. They don't take any physical exercise other than what they do performing. They sit on their bums a lot. So this is pushing them physically.

' I guarantee that at the end of the five months these boys will be fitter than they've ever been in their lives. Lean, mean, fighting machines. At the moment they're just leaning on the machine,' she laughs.

After a chat with the boys, Priscilla adds: 'I think it has hit home mentally that show time is here. Yesterday they were going, "Oh my God! Tomorrow is Friday and we're doing our first show. It's here after all this time." They had been thinking starting out that they had all the time in the world to get it right; now there is no time. But I think now they're more excited than scared. It's exciting them now that tonight they get the chance to really show off.'

The Malmaison, a modern, stylish yet unpretentious hotel set in the heart of Newcastle's quayside – the northern English city's regenerated and lively waterfront – is Westlife's home-from-home during their five concerts at the local arena. By Friday afternoon the Irish invasion of the hotel is underway as family and friends of various Westlifers begin arriving for the show.

Bryan has the largest gang. They include his fiancée, Kerry; parents, Brendan and Mairead, sister, Susan, and five of his mates, including best pal Mark Murphy, who is set to be his best man when he ties the knot with Kerry.

'These guys are a mad lot,' Bryan announces over introductions in the hotel bar when he arrives back from the dress rehearsal.

Two of his pals, Brian 'Kraner' Krane, who is a dead ringer for the late British comedian Les Dawson, and Gary 'Sosy' Nolan, a chubby, jovial character, soon emerge as the life and soul of the party, constantly cracking jokes and telling hilarious tales.

'Do you know how Sosy got his name?' Bryan asks, before answering the question himself. 'They used to call him sausage at school because he had a sausage head!'

Sosy tells Bryan how he almost got thrown off the flight on the way over from Dublin that morning after walking up the aisle of the plane while pretending to smoke a cigarette and chat on a mobile phone at the same time.

Bryan's parents, Brendan and Mairead, enjoy a great relationship with his buddies. Obviously considered to be totally 'cool', they're absorbed into the gang. The McFadden home back in Dublin had been an open house to Bryan's mates down through the years, so strong bonds were formed with Ma and Da McFadden.

'It's so quiet since Bryan's gone,' Mairead admits. 'I really miss him around the house. There was always something happening while he was there.'

By contrast to Bryan's strapping six-foot tall frame, dad Brendan, a sales rep, is small in stature. Similarly, whereas Bryan is a whirlwind in company, dominating a room with his banter when he enters, his father is quiet by nature. But they have a rock-solid relationship.

'Bryan is a great lad. He never gave us any hassle growing up,' Brendan reveals. 'As parents, we've been very lucky with both of our children.'

He glances over at his son, who is throwing his head back and laughing in the midst of his group of friends. 'He's got a great personality,' Brendan says. 'I think he really stands out in Westlife.'

Brendan then reveals how he played a role in Bryan's rise to pop stardom with Westlife. 'I drove him to the auditions for Westlife,' he says with an obvious sense of pride. 'Bryan wasn't going to go, but I encouraged him to go for it. He even wore one of my old shirts that day.'

Since Westlife shot to stardom, Brendan admits he's become a dedicated follower of pop. 'I now watch all the Saturday morning pop shows on TV. I'd never miss Ant and Dec on CD:UK. My friends are the same. They read all the teen magazines and they tell me things abut Westlife that I don't know. It's great to see them all taking such a big interest in them. It's all new to us, I suppose. We've never had anything like this before.'

Bryan is now obviously determined that his parents and sister, Susan, get to enjoy some of the fun and excitement surrounding his success. 'He rang us and invited us over for the shows here in Newcastle,' Brendan says. 'We might as well enjoy it while its happening.'

Kerry arrives down from the hotel bedroom, a vision of beauty dressed in baggy pants and a loose fitting top. There are hugs and kisses all round as she's greeted by Bryan's family and pals.

'They're two happy young kids and I think Kerry is very good for Bryan. It's great to see him making a life of his own. His mother and myself were delighted when they told us about the baby,' Brendan reveals. And he adds: 'I think he was more concerned about telling Louis because of the effect it might have on the band. But, as it turned out, Louis was very supportive.'

Kerry is telling the boys that she has now left Atomic Kitten. 'I can't be a pop star and a mum. I know some people can do both, but I'm going to concentrate on being a mum,' she says.

Newcastle Arena at 6.30 p.m. and the fans are streaming into the venue, excitedly babbling with the anticipation of seeing their idols in the flesh for the first time, on stage in their home town. From twenty-somethings and teens to tiny tots accompanied by mums and grandmas, the colourful Westlife army of followers converges on the concert arena from north, south, east and west in all modes of transport.

Backstage, Westlife are a bundle of nerves. Priscilla is with them, encouraging them to relax and chill out. 'Two hours before the show you shouldn't do anything,' she says.

At 7.30 p.m. the show blasts off with Masai, the first of the support acts. Seats are still filling up and the venue is resembling a birthday cake from a mass of red strobe lights that fans have purchased on the way in. A new UK group called Fixate is next up, trying to win over the Westlife fans.

Bryan's girlfriend Kerry wanders out to the front wing and young fans go wild when they spot her. Kerry notices the fuss she's causing and gives them a wave. Several young girls immediately rush over to the barrier looking for her autograph. She had been hoping to join the fans out front when Westlife came on, but now realises that this is impossible. She'd literally be mobbed.

Fellow Irish popsters Reel, who'd won Best New Tour Act on the *Smash Hits* Roadshow 2000, are the last 'warm-up' act before the main attractions. The mums who've tagged along with their little Westlife fans love Reel's song, Come On Eileen, which has everyone jumping up and down. The older members of the audience remember when it was a hit for Dexy's Midnight Runners.

It's now eight o'clock and the final countdown has started to Westlife's performance. In their dressingroom, Priscilla is giving Shane, Kian, Bryan, Mark and Nicky some warm-up exercises.

'Jump up and down like mad things and just let go,' she says.

'You need to get the adrenaline pumping beforehand. If you wait till you go on stage you'll suddenly get an adrenaline rush when you hear all the screaming girls and it'll create nervous anxiety. You'll be sweating before you even start the show.'

At 8.30 p.m., Priscilla makes the boys sit down and relax. 'You don't do any steps at least half an hour before the show,' she says. 'It's like doing an exam; what's the point in doing the last half hour when you should have done it all beforehand? The last half hour you don't need to go saying, 'What's that here? What's that there?' Just be confident that you know. Go for it in your own head, but don't question anything. Just relax.'

As the minutes tick away, the toilets have never been busier. One by one the boys slip away to do their business. There's nothing like first-night nerves to get the waterworks flowing. Soon it's time to get kitted out in the wardrobe department. Wardrobe assistants Karen and Fiona are on tenterhooks as they wait for the Fab Five to arrive. Apart from the fact that one of the original assistants has dropped out at the final hour, the two ladies are not familiar with the boys. To make sure that they give the right outfit to the right Westlifer, they've labelled everything. They spend their time checking and double checking their chart to make sure that each guy has a costume. The fact that they'd only had one dress rehearsal has them on edge as well.

Karen reveals that a staggering £70,000 has been spent on clothes for the show.

The boys arrive and each individual strips down to his jocks. He's kitted out with a body mic and then slips on his 'alien suit.' Karen and Fiona then help the guys into the space suits, or 'cockroaches' as they call them. Why Karen? 'Because they look like cockroaches.'

As he gets kitted out, Shane launches into bursts of vocal warm-ups. Mark and Bryan are singing their heads off in another corner.

'OK lads, give it everything out there tonight. This is the big one. Keep it simple and keep it tight. Concentrate on what you're doing. Just remember what we've all learned and stick with the routines.'

'Why are you shouting?' Kian asks. 'You're making me nervous.'

'I'm shouting because I'M nervous,' Shane laughs.

Then they march out to the backstage area and wait, admitting to feeling weak at the knees as they get ready to take up their positions on the stage.

The moment of truth is here. Priscilla is giving them a last-minute confidence-building pep talk.

'Just go out there and enjoy yourselves,' she says. 'Even if things go wrong, don't worry. It's the first time. The important thing is that every fan out there wants to see Westlife enjoying themselves.'

The boys huddle together and then launch into their pre-show Irish mantra,

'Háon, dó, a trí…Westlife!'

Shane says, 'C'mon, lets go, lets do it! We can't turn back now. They're waiting.'

It's 8.55 p.m. as the boys climb the steps up to the stage to take up their positions. Kian, Shane, Bryan and Mark are strapped to a harness on top of the four-metre towers. Nicky is standing on a metal grid in the centre of them, also secured by his harness. The sound from the crowd going crazy out front is deafening. By this stage the audience is watching Westlife being energised on a massive screen beamed on to the towers which are locked together to make a wall. They can see the famous figures prowling through a corridor, getting closer and closer. The screen splinters and suddenly the set starts to move as the towers turn to reveal the boys.

There's a thunderous roar from the crowd as they begin to glimpse the boys in the flesh. But disaster strikes. Kian's tower is stuck. Crew members rush on behind the scenes to quickly shift it manually. The boys are momentarily thrown by the hiccup, but the technical glitch is totally missed by the fans. They've gone into raptures at the sight of their idols and don't even notice this blip in the performance. The boys sway from side to side to the weird and dramatic opening music, like monkeys in a zoo enclosure, threatening to leap forward. They glance at each other. Something is not quite right. The intro music has all kinds of weird sounds that shouldn't be there. No time to think about it. Suddenly they're airborne, and they free-fall to the floor.

Landing safely on the stage, they power up the action as their first song, Dreams Come True, kicks off in an all-singing and all-dancing performance.

The 'No Stools Tour' is finally under way and the fans are on the edge of their seats as they realise from the off that this is going to be a Westlife show like they've never seen before.

No No is next and the five aliens, aka the Westlife dancers, help the boys remove their 'cockroaches' to reveal the white body suits with reflective striping underneath. The 'aliens' arrive back at the quick-change area and drop the space gear into tubs.

Out front Kian is speaking. By now there's hardly any need to inform the crowd that Westlife is no longer a group who dress in black and sit on stools, but he does it anyway.

'There'll be none of that tonight,' he assures them, as he welcomes everyone to 'the first ever Westlife concert.

Nicky tells the audience how Westlife have 'dreamed of this night all our lives.'

Then the crowd very quickly spots the comedian in Westlife as Bryan announces that it's the end of the show.

'Kian has diarrhoea and we can't do any more than two songs a night,' he jokes with a deadpan expression.

The girls return with white leather coats and slip them on the boys before they perform If I Let You Go, which leads on to what Nicky tells the audience is 'a very special song to us'. It's Swear It Again, their first number one hit.

Nicky recalls how the group first played in Newcastle on the *Smash Hits* Roadshow when they were then called Westside.

'We were voted Best New Tour Act on that show and Swear It Again went straight in at Number One. It's all down to you guys, so thanks very much,' he adds.

The audience goes wild as Swear It Again strikes up. It's a spine-tingling moment in the show. Somebody Needs You lifts the tempo again and there's more action as the dancers interact with the boys for this number.

Then it's time for Seasons In The Sun. This is a scary moment as it's their first real costume change. They've got to race off the stage, slip out of the alien gear and into a new set of clothing. They literally only have seconds to do this. The longest changeover allowed in the show is 1 minute, 38 seconds.

There's a mad panic in the quick-change area as they trip over themselves trying to remove their sweat-soaked opening costumes. The more they rush, the longer it seems to take. Every second seems like an hour when there's an audience out front waiting patiently. Black trousers, coloured tops and winter coats are being tugged and pulled as the boys jump into them. Shane almost topples over as he puts his right leg into the pants. Mark and Bryan are the slowest and now everyone is assisting them. They're just a split second behind Shane, Kian and Nicky as they head out on to the stage, but Bryan hasn't noticed that his flies are still undone.

As soon as they arrive back on stage the boys discover that there's another mechanical failure. The travelators, which are like flat escalators that move and allow the boys to give the impression of walking, have stalled. It completely throws the guys as they do their strip, peeling off their layers of clothing to indicate the changing seasons. Everyone is now removing items at different times and they appear frustrated. But the crowd doesn't notice what's happening.

Bryan discovers that his flies are open and, ever the showman, in true he pretends to remove his pants, to an excited burst of applause and collective gasps. Such a tease!

After I Have A Dream and You Make Me Feel, the screen shows some dressingroom activity...it's the girls changing into their sexy outfits for the When You're Looking Like That routine. It takes the female audience a few seconds to realise what's transpiring on the screen. When they discover it's the girls who are changing, they're not impressed, judging by the way they go silent.

Westlife's manager, Louis Walsh, realises the mistake. 'That doesn't work. The fans don't want to see the girls in that situation. The girls are also too good looking. The fans don't like it. But it's too late to change it now,' he says.

This is a red-hot routine for the dads and boyfriends in the audience as the dancers parade across the stage in their sizzling attire. Marilena is a showgirl in her purple leotard with big purple plumes. Karen is Flamenco girl in her long, red dress and red cape. Jodi is every man's dream in her figure-hugging catsuit. Jessica is Cowgirl and Lene is Miss Leotard in her dress. The song is one of the highlights of the show.

After My Love there's another panic as the boys arrive backstage to change into their Dolce and Gabbana outfits for the Motown medley. While all this is happening the dancers are back on stage entertaining the audience with their martial arts-style dance routine. Kian is first dressed and he rushes back on stage to stall the crowd while the other boys get ready.

Hugging a guitar he tells the fans, 'I have some bad news for you. While the girls were out here doing their karate chops, we had a row backstage and the other four have gone home and left me to do the rest of the show. So I'm going to play the guitar and do some rock 'n' roll.'

Kian then launches into a version of the song, Wild Thing, to wild applause.

'Only joking,' he says, as the rest of the boys arrive back to perform the big Motown showpiece, which kicks off with Westlife's version of the Xtreme hit, More Than Words and segues into My Girl, Can't Get Next To You, Ain't Too Proud To Beg, Baby I Need Your Lovin' and What Becomes Of The Broken Hearted?.

After Fool Again, the song that gave Westlife their fifth Number One in a row, it's time for another big costume change. Karen and Fiona are waiting to help the boys into red boiler suits which have reflective strips and their names emblazoned in crystal on the back.

'They've been complaining all night about their trousers falling off them on stage because they're too big,' Karen reveals. 'Nobody realised when they did their initial fitting that by the time they went on stage they'd have lost weight from all the rehearsals.'

As the audience is distracted by the set for Uptown Girl, which has lots of garage sounds like welding and air hoses, the boys are slipping into the boiler suits. When they reappear Mark is missing, oops! Here he comes, late again. Visually, Uptown Girl is a fantastic showpiece. Dancer Karen fills in the role of Claudia Schiffer as she emerges from the boot of a Fifties American car.

What Makes A Man is the final song before the encore and it finishes in a blaze of glory with fireworks lighting up the venue and a blast of sound almost lifting the roof.

But it's not over yet. Backstage, Westlife are making their final costume change as they peel off their boiler suits, which are now dripping with body perspiration. There are just two more songs to do, Lay My Love On You and the big finale, Flying Without Wings. The boys change into long white silk trousers with long white silk jackets for the closing numbers. After Lay My Love On You they disappear. The sounds of a massive thunderstorm rage through the venue and lightning flashes across the video screen. Backstage, the grid that Nicky had started the show on is going into action again, this time with all the boys strapped on to it. As the towers open and the grid rolls across the skyline, it's a jaw-dropping moment for the audience. There are uncontrollable tears as they look up to see their idols almost within touching distance. The girls wave, scream, cry and blow kisses up to the guys as they travel into the heart of the arena. Then the grid slowly moves back to the stage and disappears behind the towers.

The screen reads DREAM OVER...but it's just begun for the boys.

Within seconds of being released from the grid Westlife are racing down corridors and out into the backstage enclosure where Trevor, their driver, has the coach running. Still wearing their silk outfits and with towels around their heads, looking every inch members of the Ku Klux Klan, the boys race on to the coach and plonk down in the upper chamber.

'My ears are ringing from so much music in them,' Shane announces.

'Mine are the same,' Bryan says.

'What did you say?' asks Kian.

'I said mine are the same,' Bryan replies.

'What did you say?' Kian asks again.

'Messer!' Bryan snaps, realising he is having his leg pulled.

Their manager is last on and as he joins the boys they nervously wait for his reaction. There is an awkward silence before Shane finally asks, 'So what did you think?'

'Guys, it was OK for a first night,' Louis replies.

'Just OK?' Kian asks incredulously.

'Yeah, it was like a good dress rehearsal,' Louis responds. 'There are still a lot of areas which need to be improved. The dancing has to be tighter. The links (chat between songs) weren't great.'

'What do we have to do to get a compliment?' Bryan asks.

'Seriously, there is still lots of room for improvement. You know that yourselves.'

On the post-show journey back to their hotel, Shane relives the concert.

'That was amazing. That was a really, really big reaction. It was kind of what we expected. We wanted to get a really good reaction tonight, but it was actually more than what we expected. We were all nervous for the last ten or 15 minutes before we went on. Once we got into the towers it was really nerve-racking. When Kian's tower didn't turn we were worried about that. We didn't know what was happening. But once the towers turned that was it. It was then a case of get out there and do your best. Coming down off the tower felt great, but I was worried that I would swing back and hit it. Once my feet touched the ground it was a relief.

'I looked out at the audience and they were going ballistic. I was going, "Oh my God!" The first song was really nerve-racking. Taking off the harness clip, then taking off our suits and going into a dance routine with the girls was all a bit worrying as we had never done it in front of a crowd before. So it was all kind of scary at the start.

'I don't really remember No No and If I Let You Go, but Swear It Again was kind of mellow and Somebody Needs You was brilliant, I thought. That's one song I thought went really well. When the back track (travelator) didn't work for Seasons In The Sun I thought, "Oh, my God! We're all taking off our clothes at different times." But it all looked good and the fans loved it. They didn't know exactly what had happened.

'The highlights for me were Somebody Needs You. That was brilliant, I thought. One of the best parts of the show was definitely the Motown piece.

'Uptown Girl was another personal favourite. I was so looking forward all night to singing that song in front of a big crowd. I thought Lay My Love On You could have been better. My long coat kept getting caught during that number and it sort of threw me.

'Even though I say it myself, the ending is fantastic. Even if the whole show went bad, it ended on a good note. It's an amazing feeling up there.

'You feel like you're flying. You see everybody's heads thrown back, watching you as you go by them. It has left everyone with a really good impression of Westlife.

'I'm really up about some parts of the show and down about others. The technical stuff going wrong is obviously annoying. We messed up a couple of dance routines ourselves. It wasn't so bad that the fans would notice, but we knew it and we're our biggest critics. If we sing one bum note in the whole show we'll be thinking about it for a week afterwards. It's just the way we are. If I sing a bad note on a lead vocal I feel terrible. We always want to do better.'

Upon arrival at the hotel, the boys all disappear to their respective rooms to recover from the physical demands of the show.

'I'm knackered,' Shane admits as he goes up in the lift.

In the aftermath of the show, Kim breathes a sigh of relief.

'It took a while to get all the bits together and we did have a few setbacks, but when I looked at the opening and how it all moved into shape, that's how I always imagined it would be. You create something in your mind that you think is achievable. But there are always problems to be ironed out when you build it. I always thought the towers would move faster, so we've had to adapt to that late in the day.

'What I've found in shows is that after 45 minutes to an hour you want something else to happen, but there is always something happening in this show because there are four or five different stage sets. It gives loads of different variations. When the boys go off stage it's normally a low moment, but I've done videotape inserts to cover their changes and the girl dancers are doing routines and its keeping something happening all the time. It means that the audience isn't sitting in darkness for a minute and a half or two minutes and the boys are back on before they realise they've been gone.'

The Westlifers chilled out for half an hour, had a shower and then resurfaced to party over a few beers and discuss the show with family and friends.

With the exception of Bryan. He had an early night with Kerry.

At three o'clock in the morning, Shane and Kian are still partying in a private room at the hotel. They're all wound up from the excitement of the concert and reluctant to retire.

As Priscilla says, 'There's no stopping this band. I wish I could take them off the stage and lock them in the hold of the bus or put them to bed myself with a chain; lay them there, shut their eyes and wake them up in the morning.'

But she's beaming with pride in the aftermath of the show. 'No one knew that Westlife could dance. I am proud to be the person to bring that out in them. It's nice to be able to do that for a band.'

Snowflakes are falling over Newcastle in the morning, but there's no sign of Westlife around the foyer of the hotel. Newspapers sitting on a coffee table have banner headlines raving about last night's performance. WEST IS BEST FOR THOUSANDS OF FANS, says one, describing how Westlife 'wowed thousands of North-East fans last night as they kicked off their first ever live concert tour' and are 'the first band to perform five nights on one visit' in Newcastle.

Now, with no commitments in the early part of the day, they're enjoying a late lie-in. The first one to rise is Bryan.

'I've been up since seven o'clock,' he announces with a sense of pride, looking fit and refreshed. Kerry is by his side.

'Since she got pregnant, Kerry has to eat as soon as she wakes up. So I get her breakfast. It's the same every morning,' Bryan reveals.

Although the snow has now turned to rain, the couple decide to go shopping for baby stuff in Mothercare at Newcastle's Eldon Square. Bryan rings his pals' room – three of the lads are sharing the same bedroom! – and he invites them along on the shopping expedition. After what seems like an eternity, the bleary-eyed and dishevelled looking gang, Kraner, Sosy and Mark, arrive down.

'I'm bleedin' wrecked,' Kraner announces.

'We had a mad night on the tiles,' Sosy admits.

'OK guys, lets go,' Bryan shouts.

There are a small group of fans outside the hotel, sheltering under colourful umbrellas from the torrential downpour, as Bryan, Kerry and his mates head out into taxis. He stops to sign autographs for the excited young girls before jumping into the car to avoid being soaked to the skin.

Down in Eldon Square the city has obviously come to life as people are shooting around on a Saturday shopping spree. With his giant frame and blond mop, Bryan stands out in the crowd and quickly gets noticed. Sosy, Kraner and Mark are clowning around, pulling their hoods over their heads and pretending to be his bodyguards.

Inside Mothercare Bryan's stopped every two seconds by autograph hunters as he and Kerry check through a range of baby clothes and prams. The store is filling up with young girls.

'Bryan and Kerry are here! Bryan is here! Get here quick!' a young fan is excitedly telling a pal on her mobile phone.

As Bryan, Kerry and pals enter a lift, loads of young girls try to cram in around them. The girls are screaming and all getting a bit frantic. Bryan laughs, taking all the attention in his stride. Moving through the store he signs his name on hands and arms that are thrust in his direction. The mall outside is now choc-a-bloc with hundreds fans. They're surging forward, roaring his name and crying with the excitement of getting up close to their idol. It's just a normal morning in the life of a pop star, but Bryan is beginning to look concerned. Fearing that the situation is getting out of control and worried that someone may get hurt in the crush, he asks the security guys if there's a back way out of the store. They escort the Westlifer and his entourage through a rear exit and away from the madness.

It takes several minutes for the fans to realise that Bryan has left the building. Slowly they drift apart in different directions, determined to continue scouring the city in the hope of another sighting.

It's six o'clock on Saturday evening and a taxi drops off a middle-aged couple outside Newcastle arena. Peter and Mae Filan have arrived in from Ireland to see their son Shane's performance in the first Westlife tour.

'I told the taxi driver, "You know, if it wasn't for this woman there'd be no show here tonight. She's responsible for all of this,"' Peter says.

He was right. Westlife's concert is the realisation of Mae Filan's dream for her son's pop group. She contacted Boyzone's manager in 1998 and told him all about Shane's band, then known as IOU. Although they didn't know each other, Mae and Louis had grown up in the same sleepy backwater Irish town of Kiltimagh in County Mayo. After sparking off his interest in IOU through her phone call, Louis checked them out and spotted their potential.

He immediately got his friend, Irish promoter Peter Aiken, to give them the support slot to the Backstreet Boys in Dublin a couple of weeks later. It was their first glimpse of Louis' pop power. Suddenly, from performing to crowds of 200 people in their home town of Sligo, the boys found themselves entertaining 6,000 screaming kids at a Backstreet Boys gig. Although the line-up of IOU would change along with the name, with only Shane, Kian and Mark remaining from the original formation, it was the start of Westlife's rise into the super league.

Mae Filan stops to watch the crowd gathering outside Newcastle's Telewest Arena. And her smile betrays her personal delight at the role she's played in this momentous event in the life of Westlife and her youngest child.

The boys are backstage gearing up for their second show. They are about to begin a routine that will continue throughout the tour. One of the pre-show highlights is a trip to 'catering' to sample some of the food of the day prepared by their own chefs on the road.

The menu today reads like one from a very exclusive restaurant: Minestrone soup. Beef chili with taco shells (and all the bits). Chicken mayo and salad baguettes; Vegetable quesadillas. Roasted vegetable tart. Tomato mozzarella salad. Chicken and spinach salad. Cheeseboard. Cakes.

'It's one of our favourite parts of the day. The people who cook our food do amazing dishes,' Shane says.

At 7.30 p.m. the boys have a 'meet-and-greet.' This is where fans, who've won competitions through the media, get the chance to meet Westlife in person. About 50 young girls, many accompanied by parents, wait nervously in a room upstairs in the Newcastle Arena venue. They are clutching autographs books, cameras, posters, books and CD covers, and their heads swivel in unison every time the door opens.

Finally, Anto arrives in with Shane, Kian, Bryan, Mark and Nicky in tow.

The girls shriek with excitement and jig up and down before

Anto and genial security chief Paul form them into an orderly queue. Soon cameras are snapping and autographs are being dished out as a dream comes true for the lucky fans.

'Did someone just fart?' Bryan asks mischievously.

The girls and their parents giggle uncomfortably.

'I can't believe you just farted, Kian. It's all those beans you've been eating again,' he adds.

Kian pretends to be hurt by the accusation. 'Don't mind him,' he tells the fans.

Tonight they also meet special guests before the show, eight-year-old Peter Hope and his mum and dad from Newcastle. It's a heart-breaking scene, and the boys are choking with emotion as the parents battle to hold back tears when Peter is introduced to them. The boys are already aware of the tragic background to this meeting.

Peter's older brother, David, aged ten, had been a big fan of Westlife and for Christmas he'd been thrilled to receive tickets to their concert in Newcastle and a copy of their new album, Coast To Coast. David loved the album and played it non-stop in his bedroom, particularly his favourite track, My Love.

Just a few days after Christmas, every parent's worst nightmare happened when the little boy was knocked down by a car outside his home. David was rushed to hospital, but nothing could be done to save his life. When his distraught mum and dad returned from the hospital they heard music coming from David's bedroom. Going to investigate they discovered how David had been playing his Westlife album before he went out on to the street that day.

And his top Westlife song, My Love, was still running on repeat.

When the boys meet Peter before the show they invite him to join them on stage later to sing My Love.

'We were gutted when we heard about this tragedy,' Bryan says as he prepares for the stage. 'We hear those kinds of stories all the time and it really breaks your heart.'

Before the boys go on stage they're told that there's another technical fault and the travelators aren't working.

'This is so annoying,' Kian admits.

Ten minutes later there's good news. Everything is OK. They're working again. The guys look at each other, shake their heads and laugh.

Out front the Newcastle crowd seems even more manic than the previous night. There are no heart-stopping moments for the boys starting off, as this time all the towers turn when the dream begins all over again.

Tonight they seem to be enjoying their performance all the more, now that they know after last night's show that they can pull it off.

When My Love comes around, little Peter Hope joins Westlife on stage.

'Our next song is dedicated to David Hope, a special friend who we lost a couple of weeks ago,' Bryan tells the audience. 'This is David's little brother, Peter.' During the performance, Bryan takes off his jacket and belt and puts them on Peter; then he kneels down beside the little boy and encourages him to sing the chorus. The crowd cheers him on. Although they're unaware of the background to Peter's performance, the fans are touched by the gentle nature that Bryan displays while taking care of the boy on stage.

Back at the Malmaison hotel after the show, Bryan's dad is on a high from the excitement of a rock 'n' roll experience. Bryan had arranged personal transport to the concert arena for Brendan and his mum, Mairead.

'We went into the venue in a car with blacked-out windows. We could hear the kids screaming and they were taking photographs. We felt like stars ourselves, it was all very exciting,' he says.

As he chats in the foyer of the hotel, Brendan is treated to another very rock 'n' roll experience. A group of girl fans have been pressing their faces against the window outside, trying to catch a glimpse of the Westlife boys.

Suddenly they spot Bryan as he chats to his dad, and one of them lifts her top to reveal her naked breasts in a desperate attempt to catch his attention.

Bryan's dad just happened to be glancing in her direction at that very moment.

'That's not something I see very often,' Brendan remarks, as he saunters off with blood rushing to his cheeks.

Bryan giggles uncontrollably.

Minder Paul, meanwhile, has a security nightmare to deal with. He's organised a piano bar across the road from the hotel for their after-show party, but several of the Westlifers want to go clubbing. Newcastle on a Saturday night is throbbing with revellers and Paul realises it's going to be virtually impossible to look after the boys. Bryan insists that he wants to go out partying with his pals who're over from Dublin. Despite Paul's protestations he's refusing to take no for an answer.

'I'm going out with my mates and that's it,' Bryan insists.

Paul shakes his head with frustration. 'I'm responsible for your safety. You're not going anywhere until I check out the clubs and assess them.'

As Paul heads off to do a recce on the city's hot spots, Bryan storms down to his parents.

'What's wrong, Bryan?' mum Mairead asks.

'I want to go out with me mates and bloody Paul won't let me,' he fumes.

'Why don't you have a couple of drinks here?' dad Brendan suggests.

'C'mon dad, it's boring here. We want to go out.'

Paul eventually returns with some bad news. The clubs are hopping with people and it's not possible for Westlife to slip in unnoticed.

'I don't care what you say, Paul, I'm going,' Bryan insists.

'Bryan,' Paul replies sternly, 'I can't look after everyone in that situation. Someone will get hurt.'

Bryan storms off to his mates. But after a couple of drinks they're all having a laugh as Kraner entertains everyone with his jokes and monologues.

When he cools down, Bryan goes over and apologises to Paul.

'Sorry, Paul. I know you were doing your job,' he says.

Later, as Paul reflects on the incident, he admits that sometimes the life of a pop star can be frustrating. 'There are times when they feel trapped. When you're told that you can't walk down a street or go into a club, it makes you feel like a prisoner.'

But the life of a security man is not an easy one either.

'It can be horrendously stressful,' Paul admits. 'My job is the safety of the group at all times. You go to your hotel bedroom and your head is scrunched up like a prune from constantly watching, watching, watching them. There are only two of us looking after them, so if one has to go to the toilet in a club, one of us has to go with him while the other looks after the other four.

'Now, some people might ask, why does a star take a minder to the toilet? It is a necessity. There is always danger about, particularly in clubs where people are drinking. A boyfriend might get jealous because his girl is looking at them. And then there are girls who just want a piece of them. None of the band wants me to go to the toilet with them, but they would never get back to where they are sitting if I wasn't there. They don't want to be rude to people along the way, so I have to be there to make sure that things don't get out of control.'

Bryan admits that Anto, Paul and Fran are 'the backbone of Westlife'. He acknowledges that without them running the show, it wouldn't work.

'We do listen to them. There are a lot of pop star wankers who think that they are the boss. At the end of the day, we are the boss, but we respect what Anto, Paul and Fran say to us. When they tell us not to go here or here we do listen to them. We do have a lot of respect for them.'

Just a couple of days into the tour it's obvious that Bryan is a fast food addict. In particular, he appears to have a constant craving for McDonald's.

Most stars avoid going to public areas where they're easy targets for fans. Not so Bryan. He still acts like a regular guy. In Newcastle on Sunday afternoon, Bryan, Kerry and his pal, Ray, leave the Malmaison and set off to McDonald's.

The humming sound from assorted groups of families and friends in the busy restaurant suddenly goes silent. Young girls gape open-mouthed in the direction of the Westlife idol as he takes his place in the queue. It seems to take several minutes before people's brains click into gear after the shock of the apparition. Then the murmuring starts. 'It's Bryan McFadden and Kerry!'

Bryan doesn't seem to notice the fuss he's creating. He orders his burgers and chips and joins Kerry and Ray who've found a table. Then the fun starts. One young girl plucks up the courage to approach the star for his autograph. Like a dam bursting, there's suddenly a wave of people behind her. It isn't long before the line is stretching out the door of McDonald's. Bryan just sits there signing everything that's put in front of him. By this stage it looks like people are assuming it's an official signing session by a member of Westlife as they keep on joining the queue outside the entrance.

Bryan looks down at the human line, shrugs his shoulders and laughs.

Sharing a burger with a hundred fans is all in a day's work for a Westlifer.

CHAPTER 3

A crash, attacks, and concert highs

In the lively heart of Glasgow near Blytheswood Square the local Malmaison Hotel with its traditional French Brasserie bar, built around a former church, has gathered a massive crowd of 'pilgrims' outside its main entrance.

They've come in search of their young pop gods, hoping to catch a glimpse of the icons, touch them even, as they enter and leave the building. An industrious young crew of pristinely attired hotel staff has been dispatched to set up crowd control barriers to fend off the early morning invasion. This is not an ordinary day in the life of the plush hotel.

It's the day that Westlife is due in town.

Their pop circus has now left the north of England and its huge convoy of articulated trucks and buses has crept into Scotland on the next stage of their world tour.

The reaction the boys generated in Newcastle now seems tame by comparison to the antics of the wild Scottish fans who are chanting the band's name outside the Malmaison. There are hundreds of young girls working themselves into a state of euphoria, jumping up and down, holding their heads and screaming like mad witches casting a spell. As Westlife's tour bus comes into view, the excitement spills over into a frenzy. The scenes are reminiscent of TV images from the heyday of The Beatles. Girls are screaming and crying. Dozens of banners and messages of love are flailing amidst the mêlée. And this is just the hotel! What will the concert be like?

With Westlife mania spreading like wildfire throughout Glasgow, security supremos Paul and Fran have a nightmare on their hands.

'Glasgow fans are nuts,' Bryan exclaims.

'They're just crazy,' Kian agrees.

'We always get this kind of reaction in Scotland. I don't know why that is. Maybe it's because they like the Irish,' Shane adds, seemingly bemused by the hysteria Westlife are generating in this neck of the woods.

Inside, with the roars of the fans still ringing in his ears, Nicky drops his suitcase and looks around the spacious room with its gigantic bed, which is covered in a yellow and bottle green striped quilt with matching pillows. The green and lime walls are decorated with little works of art and entertainment accessories that include satellite TV and CD player.

'Nice gaff,' he remarks.

If progress can be judged by the standard of their hotel accommodation these days, then Westlife are doing exceptionally well.

'At least we all have our own rooms now, not like in the

beginning when we used to share two to a room,' Nicky reveals, as he relaxes on a comfy couch.

The tone in his voice indicates that he didn't relish having another band member occupying his personal space. 'Some people would snore. Some people's feet smelled,' he admits. 'I started off sharing with Shane and then I shared with Bryan. Shane had dodgy feet alright.'

With five members in the group, there was always a single room going begging. This was initially rotated between the boys until they eventually gave in to Mark's pleading to have a room to himself.

'Mark is a very private person,' Nicky reveals. 'At the start he was more of a shy type, although he has changed a lot. I think if it came to it now he'd have no problem sharing.'

After a few months, every member of Westlife was craving some privacy.

Spending 24 hours cooped up together was grating on their nerves and creating unnecessary tension. They were a successful pop band with a Number One hit, Swear It Again, yet they were still being forced to live within a strict budget.

'The record company wouldn't pay for single rooms until we had sold a million albums. The day we hit that figure we rang up and said, "Right, single rooms, please!" But there are times when we still occasionally have to share and it's not a problem. We haven't gone all starry and precious. There have been incidents in America where we arrived in cities to find that there's been a mix-up over the number of rooms booked and we'd end up sharing. It's only four or five hours sleep, so what's the problem, lie down and go to sleep.'

Nicky shudders as he recalls a nightmare experience sleeping on airport benches in Chicago on a promotional tour of the States during the previous summer of 2000. The weary and bedraggled Westlife group arrived at the local airport at 1.00 a.m., only to discover that their connecting flight had been cancelled. No amount of pleading by tour manager Anto could get them out of the airport on any other airline. It didn't matter that they were WESTLIFE.

'The lady on the desk had never heard of Westlife, so there was no chance of getting priority. Anto was stressing how important it was for us to get to our next destination as we were going to miss a big TV show. But all his pleading fell on deaf ears. She was like Anne Robinson on *The Weakest Link*.

"Flight is cancelled. Goodbye."

'Anto frantically rang around trying to get us into a hotel until the morning. But there was a massive thunderstorm and they were all booked up.

By this stage we were sick from tiredness and the stress of the saga. We bedded down on the floor and on benches.

'But it didn't end there. At 4.00 a.m. somebody in the airport that Anto had been dealing with, woke him up and said there was a hotel free about 20 miles outside of town. So we got two taxis and headed off into the night. By this stage we looked like we'd just escaped from a mental institution. We arrived at the place and it was like something out of the American films where you see people on the run pulling into, a maze of one-storey rooms in the middle of nowhere with cars parked outside them. To make it worse, it was a huge complex and we were all split up. I was in room 21 and Anto was in room 98 on the other side of the compound. I closed the door behind me and I was completely on my own. It was the scariest night of my life. I felt totally isolated. Even my mobile wasn't working. It was a night when I would have had no problem sharing.'

The sound of fans howling Westlife's name outside the Malmaison jolts him back to the present.

'At least I'm not alone here,' Nicky smiles.

When the boys leave the hotel, the girls go frantic. When they return to the Malmaison the girls are still there and going frantic.

'Shane! Shane!' they chant.

'Kian we love you!'

'Bryan, you're a hunk!'

On the Friday evening as Westlife launch into their first performance in the city, there's enough electricity coming from the throng at Glasgow's SECC to run the show, if not every house and factory in the vicinity. It's almost impossible to hear the boys singing above the screams. Westlife feed off the excitement level.

Earlier in the day, Anto had been out shopping and picked up a couple of sexy little numbers for the boys – a set of Scottish kilts. When they appear on stage in the outfits during Seasons In

The Sun it sends the crowd into even more hysterics. Bryan, ever the showman, has besotted females swirling with excitement when he suggestively lifts his kilt and threatens to reveal what's underneath. But, to their disappointment, he refrains from going beyond the bounds of decency. This man is fast earning a reputation as 'Mr Tease'.

At the end of the performance and before the audience realises it's all over, the boys are on their way backstage to cars that have their engines running.

'Nicky! Kian! Into this one. Quick! Quick!,' minder Paul roars.

'Mark! Bryan! You go in that one.'

'Shane! In here, fast.'

'Go! Go! Go!'

Then it's a mad dash to beat the traffic and avoid getting caught up in the thousands who are spilling out of the venue.

Back at the hotel, the boys chill out and wind down for a couple of hours over drinks. With so much adrenaline pumping through their bodies, there are no thoughts of sleep in the aftermath of a high-powered, all-action live performance.

'It's strange when you come off stage,' Kian reflects. 'You're not wrecked. You're still on a high. It's a weird situation to cope with. One minute you're on stage in front of 10,000 screaming fans and the next you're back in your hotel room and you're on your own. It's just me and a TV and a telephone. I've talked with the crew about it. They've worked with all kinds of groups and they say it's the same for everyone.'

By the time they retire to their beds they're so knackered a bomb wouldn't disturb their sleep. And just as well. Outside it seems the girls are only starting to come to life. They're singing Westlife songs. All the Westlife songs. And it seems the performance is going to go on all night long.

As six o'clock in the morning comes around the residents – those who managed to get some sleep through the unofficial concert that's been raging outside their windows – are waking up to...Westlife songs. The girls are still singing. Westlife have only released two albums, but it seems there are enough songs to keep the show going 24/7.

And with their heart-throbs in town, who needs sleep!

'WESTLIFE ARE OUT OF THIS WORLD' reads the headline in the local *Daily Record* newspaper as the boys wake up to a rave review of their first Glasgow concert.

Kian is thrilled. 'As the tour goes on we're definitely improving all the time,' he says.

'Every time we do a gig to a big crowd my confidence is getting better in every respect,' Mark reveals.

Sunday brings the news that a VIP has requested to meet them. It's none other than the British Prime Minister Tony Blair. The Labour Party is in town, holding its own annual shindig in a venue right next door to the arena where the Westlife concerts are being staged. Westlife are no strangers to Prime Ministers. After all, Nicky is dating the daughter of Ireland's PM (or

Taoiseach, as the lofty position is known in his country), Bertie Aherne.

There's no mistaking the toothy smile and receding hairline among the army of dark suits. Tony Blair is affable and friendly.

'Hello guys,' he says, giving each Westlifer a hearty handshake.

'Which one of you is going out with Bertie's daughter?' he asks.

All heads turn to Nicky, who is now going red in the cheeks.

'Bertie is a very good friend of mine. I was talking to him during the week and when I told him I was going to be meeting Westlife he said his daughter is going out with you. He told me to be sure to say hello.'

Nicky shuffles uncomfortably as the Prime Minister focuses his attention him.

'We work together very hard on Northern Ireland and it's paying off. Bertie is a great man. He's very down to earth,' Mr Blair says.

Then he turns to all the Westlifers and adds, 'My daughter is a big fan of Westlife and she'll kill me if I don't go home with your autographs for her.'

The boys laugh as Anto gives them a selection of posters and picture cards to sign for the Prime Minister.

Afterwards, Nicky is beaming. 'Tony Blair is very nice. He himself seems tobe very down to earth for such a powerful person.

'He was cool.'

The days are busy in Glasgow. Westlife are recording a single for South America and Spain...in Spanish! As the boys don't speak the language, they've drafted in an expert, Joel Numa from Miami, to work with them.

'I'm here producing Westlife for Rudy Perez,' Joel says. 'Rudy is a producer for Bullseye Productions and I'm his right hand man. He did Christina Aguilera's songs in Spanish and that's how Westlife got in touch with us.'

The boys are doing I Lay My Love On You, now called En Tide Je Mi Amor in Spanish.

'We got hold of the song a couple of months ago and Rudy Perez adapted it and created our guide vocal which we sent back to them,' Joel reveals.

'Basically it's the same song, but in Spanish we have a new adaptation. We did the track and sent it over to the guys to get acquainted with it and get comfortable with it. Now I've come over to work in the studio with them.'

In the studio the boys are taught the lyrics phonetically. The track is recorded in little bits, line by line and phrase by phrase. Sometimes a whole verse is recorded and then they go back and fix lines or words that weren't perfect.

'There's nothing I can do to make somebody sing without an accent. That is something I can't teach or coach, it's up to the individual to pick it up,'

Joel says. 'It's a nice surprise for me that they are picking it up so well. Mark is really good with languages. He speaks French sometimes, so that helps him out a lot. What I've found with

Bryan is that he's very good at mimicking, so that helps him. Shane has turned out to be a natural, so it's a pleasure working with him. Kian is really good; he's very serious and very focused. Nicky is just so easy going and no problem.

'They are excellent and sound very fluent on it. They are also responding well under pressure and they have great drive. They are eager to do it and they're so into it and those are all the elements you need. They are as good as anybody I've every worked with. The one thing that's really, really outstanding is that they are nice guys; they are down to earth and have a great disposition.'

Westlife can't move in Glasgow without being shadowed by a gang of fans.

One young girl falls in her excitement to catch a glimpse of the boys disappearing inside a building.

There's blood everywhere. Anto is on the scene and people are quickly attending to the girl who has cracked her head off a kerb, causing a horrendous facial injury. The skin has literally peeled down from her forehead and is hanging over her face. Anto calls Bryan on the phone and the Westlife star immediately rushes to the scene.

Despite the shock of her accident, the girl is clearly thrilled to see Bryan. She appears to be totally oblivious to the gaping wound on her face. Her main concern is that she's getting blood all over her Westlife T-shirt.

Bryan, who has been cuddling her, is also covered in her

blood. An ambulance arrives on the scene and the fan is rushed to hospital.

'It's terrible when something like this happens,' Bryan says, clearly shaken by the experience. 'Even though it's outside your control, you feel like you're responsible for it.'

Two days later, Westlife are visiting the fan in hospital, where she's recovering after having about 40 stitches inserted in her injury. With her favourite group hovering around her bed, the girl just can't stop smiling, despite her shocking ordeal.

As the tour moves on to Manchester on Friday, February 23, there is more insanity. Westlife are now juggling their nightly shows with trips to London to rehearse for The Brits at Earl's Court. But their first night at the massive arena is a huge thrill for the lads. The venue holds 17,000 people and it's sold out.

'It's an amazing feeling to perform in front of an audience this size,' Kian says. 'We used to watch videos of Take That playing this arena and Boyzone did a video here as well. Now it's Westlife's turn and, believe me, we don't take it for granted. We do stop and look back at the time we watched those videos and think, I can't believe it has happened for us.'

The review in the morning paper after the concert perfectly captures the atmosphere: 'The noise was deafening as the undisputed champions of the boy bands appeared before a screaming crowd at the Manchester Evening News Arena. Hysteria reached a peak as Westlife were shown being resuscitated in a futuristic surgery on a huge video screen. If they had taken any longer the same treatment would have been required in the stalls. But relief was at hand as a stunning stage opened to reveal the fabulous five to the excitement of the adoring mass.'

Their hotel in Manchester seems to have been completely taken over by fans.

'There's a hundred fans in the bar waiting for us,' Kian announces.

'They've all checked in to the hotel. We were trying to get family members booked in recently, but it was completely booked out because of the fans. I've had letters posted under my door and presents left outside the door.'

The following night after the performance, Westlife travel overnight by road to London for The Brits rehearsals. The sleeper coach arrives at the venue in the middle of the night and parks until the morning, with everyone asleep on board.

At nine o'clock the boys are up and about, as they have rehearsals at 11 a.m. Arriving at Earl's Court they're told that there's going to be a delay as Robbie Williams' set has got stuck. Now where have they heard that before?

Eventually Westlife and 56 trumpet-wielding dancers get the chance to run through their routine on their very impressive set.

'It has cost £185,000 to stage this song for just four minutes,' Anto reveals as he examines the big production.

But Westlife reckon it's worth every penny as they're determined to make a major impression on one of the biggest pop showcases of the year. This is an opportunity to show the music industry that they're not a boring group who sit on stools singing ballads. They really can do that Michael Jackson thing.

After the rehearsal, it's back to Manchester where there's another show in the evening. When that's over they return to the coach and bunk down for the night while they're whisked back to London.

On Sunday, after a couple of hours of rehearsals, they return to Manchester for that evening's performance – then travel back to London overnight.

'This is nothing compared to some of the stuff we do,' Kian says, matter-of-factly.

Monday morning, Westlife wake up to Brits day and you can sense the tension in the camp. It's six o'clock in the morning and they're itching to get going. After all, their performance is going to be one of the big showpieces of the night. At eight o'clock, after they've had some breakfast, they have a date with stylist Ben who snips their hair into shape.

By eleven o'clock they're backstage at Earl's Court where they discover that Sonique and Robbie Williams are next door, while Craig David is just across the hall. Robbie and Geri Halliwell are among the stars who knock on Westlife's dressingroom door to say hello.

'A couple of years ago we would have been going "Aaaahh! I can't believe who I've just met!" But it's strange how this becomes so normal to us these days,' Shane observes.

But there is a major thrill in store for Westlife out in the arena. Their heroes, rock supergroup U2, are doing a live rehearsal in the auditorium and the boys get to sit in on it.

'I can't believe I'm sitting here with just 70 people, including the gorgeous Destiny's Child, watching U2 perform,' Kian sighs.

Before they know it, it's showtime. With all the bigwigs of the UK and international music industry sitting out front, they're naturally a little nervous. But you wouldn't know it once they hit the stage. The boys begin a low-key performance on stools in their old ballad-style before EastEnders hard man Phil Mitchell (Steve McFadden) appears on massive screens and orders them:

'Hey Westlife! Get up and rock 'n' roll.'

Suddenly their bar stools explode, and when the Fab Five turn around massive fireworks unveil their new all singing, all-dancing performance, complete with 56 'uptown girls' in black dresses and hats.

Westlife show the industry big-wigs and the critics that they've got another side, and the boys are exhilarated as they come off stage. But there's more excitement ahead of them. They've been asked to stay backstage, which can only mean one thing – they've won an award.

Westlife glance at each other and their excitement is palpable. Their award turns out to be Best Pop Act Of The Year. Despite their crazy schedule in the last couple of days, the lads are determined to go out and party afterwards. Their record company has organised a big hooley in their honour at the very trendy Home House club, where 400 revellers are waiting to greet them as the sound of ambient dance music sets the mood. The venue is thronged with stunning girls, sipping cocktails and trying desperately to catch the eye of a Westlife boy. There are Page Three models in skimpy outfits sashaying around the ornate rooms of this very grand house with its olde-worlde atmosphere and high ceilings. Wonderbra model-turned-pop-star Caprice arrives looking for the Irish party.

'You guys always throw the best ligs,' she says.

Stunning Samantha Mumba, wearing a very revealing dress, is chatting in a corner with her childhood pal Bryan and his fiancée Kerry.

Shane is sitting on the arm of a couch, deep in conversation with former Take That star Mark Owen. 'I was a big fan of Take That when I was younger, so to meet anyone from Take That is kind of an honour for me,' he later reveals.

Andrea Corr wanders over to congratulate the boys. With her striking dark looks and bee-stung lips, the Corrs' singer stands out among the beautiful people in the room. Andrea is small and petite like a china doll, but despite her own massive fame she's not at all starry.

'Andrea is very friendly,' Shane remarks, as he watches her mingle with the crowd. 'She always comes over and says hello. I don't really know the other three that much. But I've met Andrea a few times and she comes across as a really nice girl.'

It's the early hours of the morning and Westlife are still in full flight.Shane has several vodkas and tonic sitting in front of him. He's too busy to drink, as he's entertaining a group of friends, including Kian, Mark and little Craig from Big Brother, with his impressions of other celebrities.

Westlife have barely hit their pillows when it's time to get up, as they're on the move again. There's a show in Nottingham Arena in the evening. The boys are wrecked, but the euphoria of winning a Brit award and doing a sensational performance keeps them going.

'I do think we made a big impression on The Brits last night,' Shane says, the dark shades concealing his red eyes. 'We were a band renowned for ballads and to come out and do something that wasn't expected made people sit on the edge of their seats. We knew it would be full of critics waiting to knock us. But we went out, sang live against a big production with loads of "uptown girls" and I think we made the right impact.'

There's no rest on Wednesday either, as they record a *Top Of The Pops* performance of Uptown Girl in the morning, followed by two-and-a-half hours of interviews with numerous TV stations to promote the single, which hits the shops the following Monday. There's another Nottingham concert in the evening and a flight to Italy ahead of them in the morning.

It's Thursday afternoon and the boys are in San Remo where they're appearing at a major pop festival on an all-star bill that includes one of Kian's favourite groups, Bon Jovi, and American power-house singer Anastasia. This is a hit-and-run job for

Westlife. After their rehearsals and performance, they head straight back to their private plane for a three-and-a-half hour flight to Birmingham.

On Friday night after their concert in Birmingham the boys hop on their sleeper coach and head for London for an appearance on the CD:UK television show with Ant and Dec and Cat Deeley. When that's over, they return to the coach and make the same journey back to Birmingham for a show in the evening.

'Sometimes they're at the end of their tether,' Anto admits. 'But they always say it's worth going for it because they know if they don't they won't get their rewards. I do have to perk them up every now and then.

'I've said to them, "Look at Take That, they never gave up. For the last two years you wanted to do this and here you are now. It's hard work, but we gotta keep going at it. If you don't go at it you'll let down the fans who've supported you for the last couple of years. If you don't turn up because you're tired, or if you don't put on a good show it's the fans who are going to suffer. And remember, they bought the tickets to your show a year ago. That's how much they think of YOU."'

Among the string of laminated passes that dangle on Anto's chest are two bearing the colours red and yellow. The tour manager has employed a soccer referee's method of maintaining law and order in the group.

So does he ever have to flash them?

'Occasionally,' Anto admits.

In what circumstances?

'They can party a bit too much at times, or they're late for engagements, stuff like that.'

However, Anto does admit he's been fighting a losing battle to instil discipline into the five boys. 'They've never had a proper job where you clock in and if you're not in by 9 a.m. you get docked money. They will never learn discipline now because it's too late. They will always do what they want to do. If they want to have an extra ten minutes in bed or say, "I'm not going to be the first down today," that's what they'll do.

'It's not because they're playing at being stars, it's just because that's what they want to do and nobody is going to tell them to, "Get out of bed or you're fired!" Who is going to fire them? They are their own bosses.

'I've worked with the likes of Van Morrison, Brian Kennedy, Andrew Strong (The Commitments), jumping from one band to the other in Ireland. Whenever I said to those groups, "The bus will be outside the hotel at nine in the morning," I'd come down to check the hotel bill and everybody would be checked out and on the bus. If Westlife are leaving at nine, I have to tell them that we are leaving at 8.30. Then I call them at 7.45, eight o'clock, 8.15 and by 8.30 they still wouldn't be out of bed. We might get away at 9.40, if we're very, very lucky.'

Despite their lack of punctuality, there has only ever been one occasion when a Westlifer missed a flight.

'There was an incident in America with Mark,' Anto reveals. 'We were travelling from Florida to Dallas and then on to

Springfield in Missouri and we were actually in the airport in Orlando. Mark is always wandering. It's always a case of "Where is Mark?" As we were going towards the gate, we spotted him having a cup of tea in a bar.

'I said, "Mark, the flight is boarding now. You'd better hurry up." And we all went ahead, with him saying, "I'll catch up with you." So I'm sitting on the plane and I have my phone still on because there's no sign of Mark. They've now closed the door of the plane and it's being pushed back. My phone rings and he's going in a panic, "Anto, they won't let me on the plane." I said, "That's right because we're now moving."

'Before I switched my phone off I got our travel agent to ring Mark and re-route him. We got to our destination at two o'clock and Mark didn't get there until eight, so while we were having a nice relaxing day, he was running around changing terminals. Did it teach him a lesson? No! He's still last on the plane. He still wanders.'

Bryan reveals how Anto used to impose fines for misdemeanours, but had to drop that as a form of punishment because the boys refused to pay them.

'He's like a proper daddy to us,' Bryan says. 'If we curse and swear during interviews he'll tell us to stop. We do have arguments with him and actually treat him like a daddy.'

The aftermath of their first night in Sheffield should be grounds for a red card. There are severely hungover Westlifers in every corner, despite the fact that Sky Box Office are trailing them, filming an Access All Areas feature on the group.

Last night is a bit of a blur. There are visions of Bryan and Kian jumping on a table and doing a strip to the Robbie Williams track Rock DJ. There are recollections of an anxious moment when Shane, who's full of the joys of whatever he's been imbibing, falls on a glass and slashes his arm. It was one of those let's-go-for-it nights that ends just before breakfast. Now they're paying the 'entertainment tax' – they're hungover – and knocking back cans of Red Bull in a desperate bid to lift their energy levels.

After the series of concerts in Sheffield comes Wembley Arena, a major milestone in their short but eventful career. It isn't the biggest venue in the world. But it's London and one of the most prestigious. All the legends have trod the boards at Wembley. From Prince to Take That. It's a symbol of a major level of success when you get there. And now Westlife are wending their way to the famous arena on this Saturday, March 10, for the first of five shows on this first leg of the UK tour.

The last time they were here, they were just a little support group to Boyzone. Now they're the hottest ticket in town. They will return next month for another five gigs. Tour manager Anto is reminiscing about his early days on the road with Westlife and how Wembley was always the one that they aspired to playing as the headline act.

'I remember driving them around England in a little van doing the under-18 clubs where the show started at six o'clock in the evening.

Driving up and down the motorways of the UK I'd point out a rock 'n' roll truck and they'd say, "Who do you think that might be?" I'd say, "It's probably Lenny Kravitz or Bob Dylan going to Wembley." And they'd go, "Yeah, one day we'll do Wembley."

'Then we got to open for Boyzone at Wembley and they were going. "One day we'll be here and it'll be our show. It will be our stage and there will be other support bands looking at us in that light." Now it's all here for them. So their dream has come true.'

'Saturday the tenth, Sunday the eleventh, Monday the twelfth, Tuesday the thirteenth, Wednesday the fourteenth...Wembley! Can you believe it?' Nicky says as the Westlife tour bus wends its way to the venue from the very posh Conrad Hotel at Chelsea Harbour, where the boys have set up camp.

'I remember Ronan Keating saying, "Wembley is sacred. Savour every moment of it." '

Shane is looking out the window of the coach as Wembley Arena comes into view.

'Oh, lads, look up ahead, it's the fans,' he says. 'They'll start screaming in about 20 seconds.'

Right on cue the hundreds of young girls waiting patiently outside the venue on Saturday afternoon are howling their heads off as the bus passes by.

'Oh, lads,' Shane says. 'This is the day I've always wanted to see. This is the best day so far.'

Nicky flicks back the curtain on the coach. 'See all the fake merchandise for sale. Look!'

The guys strain their necks to catch an eyeful of the touts who are flogging Westlife souvenirs.

'There are more here than there were for Boyzone, look!' Nicky adds as he scans the army of Westlife followers who are going wild with excitement.

The boys are escorted inside the venue to the dressing rooms. Shane, Kian and Nicky have the very plush room where people like Janet Jackson have chilled out before their concerts. There are leather sofas, a state-of-the-art sound system and a fridge stocked with champagne, wine, spirits and mineral water.

It's small and luxurious and can't cater for all five stars, so Mark and Bryan are down the corridor in a very large, but basic dressingroom.

It's just the luck of the draw.

Shane and their manager, Louis, wander out into the empty venue to soak up the atmosphere. Leaning on a crowd control barrier, they chat like two farmers over a fence.

'I remember when we were here supporting Boyzone and we were in their dressingroom, I asked Louis, "When are we going to play here?" He said, "Two years." It seemed like such a long time to have to wait. But it has gone in a flash,' Shane says.

'Now I want you to do Croke Park (Ireland's national Gaelic sports stadium) and Madison Square Garden,' Louis tells him.

Shane is beaming, the broad smile cracking his face.

'All the greats have played here. I saw Britney Spears here,' he says. 'I haven't been to many live shows here, but I've watched all the Take That concerts from here. And I watched Boyzone's first gig here, the one they released on video.'

Turning to Louis, he asks, 'Do you remember that Boyzone video – the one where they're in white on the front of it, against a blue background?'

'That was a good show, wasn't it?' Louis says.

'It was actually a good show,' Shane agrees. 'Myself and Kian used to watch it the whole time back in Sligo. We used to say, "We'll be there someday." It's hard to believe today's the day.'

As he tucks into a chunk of roast beef with mash before the performance, Mark is also revelling in the magnitude of the moment.

'It's a little bit different to a normal gig. I'm going to be up on stage performing at Wembley to a packed audience and that is an absolutely thrilling feeling to have,' he says between mouthfuls.

Like the other lads, Mark had experienced a huge adrenaline rush earlier when the coach whizzed past the front of the arena and he spotted the Westlife sign proudly proclaiming their appearances.

'I'd seen it a few times in the past for Boyzone, the Spice Girls, Britney and Whitney Houston. But when I looked up and saw that it was Westlife tonight – and all the other nights as well – I had really messed-up feelings. We'd driven in a few times before, but it was always for someone else; we were never the main attraction, the reason why people were coming here. This time we have drawn the crowds ourselves and it's more special.'

His mind wanders back to the first time he became aware that Wembley existed. Unlike most young guys, the introduction wasn't through the soccer connection with the famous stadium.

'The first thing I remember about here was when I went to see Michael Jackson in Dublin back in 1987 or '88 and he was going to Wembley the next day. I was only a kid and it was a big mystery to me as to how he got from Dublin to Wembley. Now I'm here myself. It's just very surreal.'

In fact, when he arrived for his evening meal, Mark had panicked. He didn't have a pass and was freaking out for fear that he wouldn't get served.

'Shit, what am I going to do?' he asked.

Then it slowly dawned on him that it's a Westlife gig. He's one of the stars of the show. The caterers are Westlife's own staff. And he's the boss.

'I still keep thinking I shouldn't be here,' he says. 'When we were rehearsing it didn't sink in. It's only when I look at our stage in the venue that I realise just how big everything has gone for us.'

It's a long way from Westlife's humble beginnings as IOU, when they played to a couple of hundred people back in their native Sligo.

'Y'know,' Mark reflects, 'this might sound weird, but both things for me have been a big, big thrill. Back when we were doing 200 people the thrill was right up there at the top for me, on a scale of one to ten. And this is also right up at the top. This is a thrill in an obvious way because we are performing in front of loads of people in a really prestigious arena. But it was even more fun in the early Sligo days because it was all about the enjoyment of the performance. There was no commercial aspect to it. It was all about the enjoyment of the performance and getting people to come into a theatre to enjoy themselves. The kick for me is performing and it doesn't matter where it is. This might sound stupid, but I sometimes prefer to do a small gig, just a little club full of people, instead of a big arena.'

Over in another corner of the catering room, Bryan's dad, Brendan, and mum, Mairead, are enjoying a pre-show meal.

'As a kid I used to dream of playing soccer at Wembley Stadium,' Brendan reveals. 'It never happened for me, but a least I'll get to see my son play the arena. That's good enough.'

Wembley Arena tonight is a blaze of colour and screaming fans. As the crowd files out at the end, still buzzing with the excitement of the show and its grand finale, the boys are on their coach for the return trip to their hotel.

Kian is admitting that he didn't feel a buzz up on stage tonight. It's not that there was anything wrong with the show, but he didn't get an adrenaline rush.

'It just didn't happen for me,' he says. 'But that can happen sometimes for no particular reason.'

Louis is telling them that he loved the show. 'Lads, you're a hundred times better than I've seen so far. But there's still room for improvement.'

'Oh, always the bitter word,' Shane laughs.

'I'm serious,' Louis frowns.

Tonight, however, the boys are going to celebrate. Playing Wembley is good enough reason, as if they need one. Back at the hotel, they shower and head for Home House where Shane holds court, doing hilarious impressions of Louis, various record company personnel – all of whom are sitting right there in front of him and cracking up with laughter. Now he's mimicking Ronan Keating and Stephen Gately, sounding uncannily like the ex-Boyzone pair. He is definitely 'Mr Entertainer'.

Some of the Westlifers have slipped away to a club called Propaganda and it's not until the early hours of the morning that everyone starts making their way back to the hotel.

It had been a glorious day for Nicky, one of those that you cling on to for dear life, trying desperately not to let it slip away. The type of day that you'd love to bottle, to be opened whenever you're feeling down and need a morale boost. Ever since he'd landed his place in Westlife it had been Nicky's dream to perform at Wembley Arena. Today that moment had come and it felt damn good. In fact, it had been such a buzz he didn't feel the need to drink in the club tonight as he celebrated with his girlfriend, Georgina.

As he reflects on his life during the taxi journey from the club to Westlife's hotel in the early hours of the morning, Nicky reckons it doesn't get much better than this. The early aspirations of soccer stardom may have turned to dust, but fate has dealt him another lucky hand or two. Glancing down at the beautiful girlfriend resting her head on his shoulder, Nicky smiles. He has it all. A career in one of the top three biggest boy bands in the world and personal happiness with the sweetheart from his school days.

As Nicky looks up his heart jumps with fright as there's a car shooting out from a side road into the path of his taxi. With lightning speed he grabs Georgina and pulls her into his body. The taxi driver swerves wildly to avoid a collision with the other vehicle and smashes into a wall. Nicky's whole body is propelled forward and his head wallops off the front seat.

There's a sickening sound of metal being crushed and scraped as the car grinds to a halt.

'Georgina! Georgina! Are you OK?' Nicky asks in a state of panic.

'Yee-hh,' she says, her voice croaking with emotion.

As luck would have it, there's already a police car parked on the opposite side of the road, with the lights flashing. Nicky and Georgina get out of the car, shaking from the shock of the nightmare that has just unfolded, their legs barely able to support them.

The taxi carrying Louis Walsh comes upon a police patrol car by the side of the street. Louis notices that there's been an accident. Two cars have been in a smash. In the dim light he notices a familiar figure.

'That's Nicky!' Louis exclaims, sitting bolt up-right in his seat. 'He must have been in that crash. Stop the car. Quick! Quick!'

He jumps out and runs towards Nicky, now spotting Georgina by his side.

She's crying from the sudden shock of the accident.

'Are you alright? Is anybody hurt?' Louis asks in a panic.

Nicky nods. 'I've had a bang on my head, but we're OK. The police said we can leave.'

'Here, there's room in my taxi. C'mon, let's get out of here,' Louis says, helping the shaken couple to his car.

Georgina, still trembling and in tears, had been terrified at the scene of the accident when the police informed the couple that they were also dealing with a report that there were two men running amok in the vicinity with swords.

'I just wanted to get away from there as quickly as possible,' she tells Louis.

When the taxi arrives at the Conrad, Nicky quickly ushers Georgina past a group of Westlife fans who've been hanging around outside hoping to catch a glimpse of their idols. The couple don't notice the girls as they race to the comfort and safety of their hotel room.

'Nicky's been in a crash,' Louis is telling everyone as the rest of the Westlife revellers arrive from various clubs.

Sunday afternoon there's a group of German girls sitting in the foyer of the Conrad hotel. They're devoted Westlife fans who've made a pilgrimage to the UK to see their idols perform at Wembley. And they've booked into this ultra-plush and very expensive hotel, where the illustrious neighbours in the fab apartments across the little harbour include legendary actor Michael Caine and pop icon David Bowie.

As the female gathering builds up around the lifts to the rooms where Westlife are enjoying a late sleep, a member of staff hovers around looking a little concerned.

'Are you residents?' he asks.

'Yes,' they reply.

'Can I see your room keys?'

Among the foreigners are a group of English fans who have slipped in.

'I'm sorry, but it's residents only in this area,' they're told.

The girls leave without protest and join the little army of Westlife fans who are gathering outside. Westlife are due to return to Wembley at one o'clock this afternoon for their second performance. They also have a busy schedule today. It includes a select performance for 70 lucky fans in the afternoon at Wembley Arena, followed by TV and magazine interviews with several European media types. It's an action-packed evening before the show. Bryan and Kerry are the first to appear down from their hotel room, accompanied by a pretty little blonde girl.

'This is Nicola, a friend of ours,' Bryan says. 'Isn't she gorgeous!

'We've just ordered a taxi to take us to McDonald's.'

As the cab rolls down the King's Road he asks the driver to stop at a cash machine. He's got no money. Stars, they never carry cash!

Inside McDonald's Bryan and Kerry's appearance causes just a ripple of excitement. As they join the queue, the young girls in front are clearly flustered.

'It's Bryan from Westlife,' one whispers.

But there's no fuss.

As Bryan orders the food, a staff member asks him for his autograph. But there are no fans besieging him. Outside we hail a taxi back to the hotel and Bryan comments on the low-key attention he received in McDonald's, compared to the fan-mania in places like Newcastle.

'London is different,' he says. 'People are more laid back. They just look at you and say, "There's Bryan." It's no big deal in London because probably five minutes before we went in some other famous type walked in. It's kind of like that in London.'

Back at the Conrad we board the Westlife tour bus, but there is still no sign of the other guys and Anto is desperately trying to round them up.

While they're waiting, Bryan points to a swish Aston Martin car parked on the forecourt of the hotel and reveals that he has a wager on with a record company executive for that very same sleek motor.

'I bet him my BMW for his Aston Martin that Uptown Girl will be bigger in Europe than in the UK,' he says. 'The Aston Martin is worth £140,000.'

Kerry throws her eyes to heaven.

'Bryan, you are not driving an Aston Martin. It's far too fast for you. You drive too fast.'

'I like fast guys,' little Nicola pipes up.

Kerry and Bryan look at each other and burst out laughing.

'That's my girl, Nicola,' he says.

It's two o'clock as the tour bus departs from the hotel with all of Westlife on board. They're running an hour late. Backstage at Wembley during the sound check, it's obvious that Bryan dotes on the girl who has touched his heart. Despite the cheeky image that is portrayed through his interviews, he is clearly a big softie with a heart of gold, particularly where children are concerned.

While Nicola saunters off to the dressing room with Kerry, he reveals how they met after their minder Paul found a letter from her parents among the Westlife fan mail.

'It was a very sad story, like so many that we receive,' Bryan sighs.

'Nicola was born with her heart on the wrong side and, as a result, she has a lot of health problems. It is so hard on her mum and dad as they're also coping with the fact that Nicola's brother is a paraplegic. When Paul gave the letter to us it touched all our hearts. I was nearly in tears reading it.

'Her parents said how much it would mean to Nicola if she could meet Westlife and we all immediately wanted to do it. Paul contacted Nicola's mother and she couldn't believe it because we get so many letters like this and it's not possible to look after all of them.

'So we arranged for Nicola to meet us when we were appearing on CD:UK around Christmas time. It was quite difficult for the family to make the trip because Nicola's brother needs 24-hour care. It's so hard on the parents.

'When I first met Nicola I was really moved because I couldn't understand how somebody so perfect and beautiful could have such a defect. It's just so unfair. She is the warmest, most beautiful child you could ever meet. She made me feel warm when I met her.

'I think Nicola has made a difference to my life. She has made me realise how beautiful people can be. She has such a problem and she has been so sick, but yet she's a little angel.'

Nicky isn't feeling well. On top of the car crash last night, he's just smacked into a door backstage at Wembley shortly after arriving and bashed the same side of his head that was banged up in the car last night. He's feeling all panicky and nervous. Worse still, he's falling asleep. Someone suggests that he should go to hospital for a precautionary check. Falling asleep after you bang your head is cause for concern. There is always the danger of slipping into a coma.

Nicky is taken to hospital and will miss this afternoon's performance, all the media interviews and the 'meet-and-greet' sessions with fans.

There is also a question mark over his fitness for the second Wembley show tonight. When Westlife do their sound check at three o'clock, Bryan takes Nicola up on stage with him. He catches her hand, puts his arm around her and they waltz to the songs. The Westlifer minds her like a hen hovering around chicks. Nicola is beaming with delight. He makes her giggle when he changes the words of I Have A Dream to 'I have a dog!'

This afternoon is an endurance test for the four boys as they are dragged from room to room backstage at Wembley for a whole series of interviews and meet-and-greet sessions. At 3.30 p.m. just after the sound check, there is a German TV interview in one of the rooms along the corridor.

'I used to speak German in school,' Bryan tells them, as he impresses everyone with a couple of phrases.

There is also a small group of fans to meet – competition winners on London's Heart FM radio station – before they do their live performance on stage.

'I'm sorry to have to tell you that Nicky can't be here. He's feeling poorly. Hopefully, he'll be in the show later tonight,' the presenter tells the fans. The four Westlifers perform a set of six songs and afterwards they do a video recording of their congratulations to manager Louis Walsh for the Irish Music Awards in Dublin a couple of weeks later – he's won a Lifetime Achievement Award, but it'll be a closely guarded secret until the big night.

At 5.20 p.m. they meet a large group of competition winners and do another round of interviews. With so much happening there are no spare moments for snacks and just about enough time to take a pee.

'This shouldn't be happening,' Mark says, throwing a little tantrum when he realises there is no break.

'We got here late, so there's no time,' Anto tells him firmly.

The boys gather in a large room and sit at a table while fans file by for autographs and photographs. Mark gets a hug from some Austrian fans.

'I didn't think when I woke up this morning that I would be kissing Austrian girls today,' he says, suddenly cheering up again and turning on the charm.

Bryan is telling a female journalist from Germany that 'Nicky always forgets his lyrics, but Mark is even worse.' Then the conversation turns to Uptown Girl and Claudia Schiffer. 'I used to have a crush on her,' Mark admits. 'She's the perfect girl for the video because she has a posh image. It's a relief to be able to release a fast song. It shows that we're not boring.'

'So what are the best and worst parts of being in Westlife?' the German interviewer asks him.

'The worst is being away from our families, not having a place to settle and living out of a suitcase,' Mark reveals. 'And the best is when we're on stage.'

By the evening, Nicky is back in the venue.

'They've given me the all clear to go on stage,' he says. 'They didn't do a scan, but they checked my reflexes and stuff and everything seems to be working OK.'

Nicky now realises that he should have had a medical check immediately after the accident. 'The doctor asked me, "What speed did you crash at?" I said it was about 40 or 50 miles an hour. He said, "You should have come to hospital last night. If you crash at 20 miles an hour we put you in a collar as a precaution." I guess I'm very lucky.

'I was also lucky that I hadn't been drinking last night, so my reflexes were pretty sharp. I was sitting behind the driver and my immediate reaction was to grab Georgina because she was sitting in the middle. I hate to think what would have happened if I hadn't held on to her.'

Georgina is singing the praises of Louis.

'I was never so happy to see anyone in my life last night. Louis came out of the darkness like an angel. He was brilliant. I was really freaked out, particularly when the police said they were dealing with guys who had swords.'

Nicky reveals that he immediately telephoned his mother, while Georgina phoned her mum and her dad. Neither the cab driver nor the UK police were aware of just who had been in the smash. But with the daughter of the Irish Prime Minister and a member of Westlife involved, it is inevitably going to hit the headlines.

'As soon as I got back to the hotel I rang my Ma to tell her what had happened, even though it was the early hours of the morning. But I was afraid that she would hear it through the media and think it was an awful lot worse that it was. Mam is a terrible worrier and it's something I've inherited from her.'

Before the show, Shane's brother, Peter, who is a doctor, gives Nicky another examination to ease his worries.

'He says I'm slightly concussed,' Nicky says. 'There's nothing that can be done for it. All I really need to do is rest and take it easy. But there's no chance of that. Instead, I'll be going out on stage in front of 12,000 fans.'

Showtime comes around and there's a minor panic when a spark from the opening pyrotechnics sets off a fire in one of the monitors. In the true tradition of showbiz, the boys don't miss a beat as minder Paul, who is on duty at the front of the stage, quickly grabs the monitor and stamps out the flame.

By the third song it's obvious that Nicky is struggling through the performance. The other four compensate with an extra effort and the audience is going wild, so they obviously haven't noticed that Nicky is just a little out of sorts tonight.

Cuddly toys are being thrown on stage by adoring fans and the Westlife quickly kick them off to the wings where members of the crew scoop them up.

The fans don't realise that the lovable little bears and dolls can cause chaos on the set if they get caught up in the workings of the moving towers.

You can almost see the tabloid headline: WESTLIFE'S SHOW SABOTAGED BY TEDDY BEARS!

For their song, My Love, Westlife invite out 'a friend of ours.' It's their little pal, Nicola.

'This is Nicola; she's Westlife's best friend,' Bryan tells the audience. 'She's going to take my place.'

The little girl's eyes are twinkling with delight as she gets to live out every youngster's dream.

After the show, Nicola is returned to her proud parents, but becomes tearful as she says goodbye to the boys after one of the best days of her life.

Back on the coach, Bryan is still raving about the 'angel' who has touched his heart.

'Nicola is really special and the fact that I'm going to have my own baby makes me really aware of how I would feel if my child had an illness or a medical condition. My child isn't even born yet and already I feel such love for my baby. I look at Kerry and I love her to bits and now I love her stomach as well. I am really protective when I'm picking her up and hugging her.

'I just love babies and growing up I've always been a big fan of kids. It might not be a lad thing to say, but it's just something about me; I love children and not in the Gary Glitter freaky way. Children are such precious things. I love what I am doing, but the most important thing in my life is Kerry and our baby.'

The Westlife coach reaches the Conrad just as Kian's dad Kevin, mum Patricia, little sister Marielle and kid brother Colm are arriving. They're over to see the show and to spend some time with Kian. Tonight everyone is staying in.

'It's the first time in five weeks that we haven't gone out,' Bryan says. 'With Nicky not feeling well everyone has decided not to go out.'

Bryan disappears to the bedroom, but then returns to the hotel bar for a nightcap. We sit and chat and Bryan reveals that he's a cheap date.

'I'm not a big drinker. I'm wasted after a couple of beers.'

Some of the German media are among the residents and he chats with them like old mates. Songwriter Herbie Crichlow, whose unique hit-making talent has been utilised by a whole plethora of acts, including Five and the Backstreet Boys – he wrote their smash hits Show Me The Meaning Of Being Lonely and Quit Playing Games With My Heart – also arrives at the resident's bar.

'This guy is a genius,' Bryan says, as he hugs Herbie.

Bryan, who is now full of the joys of beer, drags Herbie over to a piano that's been sitting forlornly in a corner.

'I've written a song with Bryan Adams and I'd like you to hear it,' Bryan says, struggling to bash out the melody of a tune called This Is It.

Herbie is genuinely interested and encouraging. 'I'm hoping it will be on our next album,' Bryan tells him.

Eventually, it's time for bed.

'Kerry will think I got lost,' he says, before disappearing up in the elevator at 2.30 a.m. in the morning. He has to be up at seven o'clock to provide his beloved with tea and toast.

The next morning Nickymakes the headlines: WESTLIFE NICKY AND GEORGINA IN SHOCK AFTER TERROR CAR SMASH!

'Just as well I told me Ma,' the Westlifer says as he reads how 'a sober night out may have saved his life and that of his girlfriend.'

Sligo town at three o'clock on a Monday morning is a sleepy, eerily quiet place. A cold March breeze sweeps through the streets, sending scraps of discarded paper swirling around the roadway. The majority of the inhabitants are tucked up in their snug terraced houses around the centre of the provincial metropolis.

But the street lamps cast shadows from a few stragglers who're wending their way home after a night on the town. Kian Egan, dressed in jeans, bomber jacket and baseball cap, is one of them. The Westlifer is in an upbeat mood. His life at this moment is as near to perfect as he could wish. He's had a rare weekend at home, hanging out with his family and catching up on all the gossip with old mates. And later tonight he'll savour the thrill of Westlife's first Dublin show at The Point, which has played host to everyone from U2 to the Spice Girls.

Flanked by two friends, he's telling them how it has been one of the best evenings of fun he's had in ages. As the trio wanders towards Abrakebabra, a local kebab takeaway shop, Kian is suddenly struck by the false appetite that follows a night of boozing and suggests an early morning snack. The takeaway is closed when they reach it. Two guys hanging around the doorway engage Kian in conversation. He knows them from school and they're around his own age. The banter between Kian and the locals is light-hearted small talk.

'How's it goin?'

'What are ya up to?'

But as Kian turns to leave, one of them suddenly swings a plastic bag containing two cans of beer and strikes him across the head. Then all hell breaks loose as blows rain down on Kian and his mate. The Westlife star can't believe what's happening. But he has the presence of mind not to retaliate. Instead, Kian walks away from the danger zone, battered and bruised. Staff at the kebab shop alert the police to the incident and they arrive on the scene. Although Kian is shocked and badly shaken from his ordeal, he doesn't appear to be seriously injured. Nevertheless, the Irish garda insist on taking him to the hospital for an examination, which confirms that he has minor cuts and bruises. When Kian eventually arrives home he slips into bed without waking his parents to tell them about the fracas. Better to leave it till the morning.

Bad news travels like wildfire. No sooner had Sligo town come to life that Monday morning than the word was around town. 'Young Kian Egan was beaten up in a row down town this morning.' It was only a matter of time before the media would get hold of the story. The timing made it a perfect news event for the press, with Westlife launching the Irish leg of their Coast To Coast tour in Dublin that same night.

For Kian, it couldn't have happened at a worse time. Of all the shows on the tour, the Dublin ones were extra special. Now, this morning, a black cloud hangs over him, threatening to spoil his party. When he wakes up the evidence of his early morning run-in with young thugs is plain to see. His nose is cut and badly swollen. And he has two black eyes. Kian is also faced with the painful task of breaking the news to his mother.

It's every parent's worry that a son or daughter will return safely from a night on the town. When Kian's mum, Patricia, sees the state of her son's face she gets upset. How could something so awful happen in their home town?

But she realises that, despite the visible cuts and bruising, Kian has been lucky to escape serious injury. Nevertheless, she senses his torment that one of the potentially best nights of his life – Westlife's Dublin show – has been ruined by the incident.

When the news reaches Shane at his home in Sligo, he immediately jumps out of bed and rushes around to see his friend and fellow Westlifer. Shane's heart is pounding on the eight-minute journey in his black Jeep as he tries to make sense of what he's just been told. Westlife have been around the world and have visited cities where the crime rate is among the highest on the planet, yet nothing like this has ever happened. It's almost unbelievable that such violence should occur in their home town where they've never doubted their safety.

Kian is halfheartedly packing for the trip to Dublin when Shane arrives. He's shocked by his pal's dishevelled appearance and the cuts and bruising on his face. Shane gives Kian a comforting hug and sympathises with him. Kian is almost close to tears and in a state of depression as he recounts the details of the attack to his Westlife pal.

'I feel so sorry for him,' Shane says. 'He's in bits because of the show tonight. It has really spoilt it for him. I didn't think this would ever happen in Sligo.'

Louis Walsh's immediate reaction is one of fury when he hears that Kian has been out on the town in the early hours, putting himself at risk.

'Kian, I don't believe what I've just heard. What were you thinking of? You're a star. You can't be doing those kind of things nowadays. There is always someone waiting to have a go.'

Kian is having none of it.

'Don't start on me, Louis. I'm not in the mood. You have no reason to have a go at me. It wasn't my fault.'

Louis calms down.

'Kian, the good thing is, you haven't been badly hurt. I'm just thinking of your welfare. There are certain things you can't do nowadays. You're too high profile.'

'It was my home town, Louis. I thought I was safe,' Kian protests.

'Well, you've learned a good lesson and it could have been an awful lot worse,' Louis points out. 'But don't let those guys get you down. They're just losers. You're the one who's making something of your life. Just put this behind you and it'll be a great show tonight. We'll all be there and we'll have a laugh.'

Ronan Keating is green with envy when he sees Westlife's massive production and extensive wardrobe for the first time on opening night in Dublin.

As he wanders around backstage in his new trademark denim jacket, hand-in-hand with his gorgeous ex-model wife Yvonne, Ro's eyes are popping out of his head. He's comparing it to Boyzone's first concert in The Point at Christmas 1994.

By comparison to Westlife's multi-million pound stage production, with its spectacular lighting and massive moving towers, Ronan is telling fellow guest pop star Dane Bowers how Boyzone had a black stage, poor lighting and just their own performance to rely on. Pointing to Westlife's space suits, Ro added: 'Boyzone didn't even have costumes. We went out and borrowed firemen's jackets and hats from the local fire station.'

It seems someone has hit the fast-forward button as Ronan can't believe how quickly the time has gone. It feels like it was only yesterday that Westlife were the new, young greenhorns with everything to prove, supporting Boyzone on tour and looking up to him for advice and guidance.

'This is a strange moment for me,' Ronan says. 'I'm standing backstage with these boys who all of a sudden are WESTLIFE with EIGHT Number One singles and selling out 11 nights at The Point. Just two years ago I was standing backstage with them when they were supporting Boyzone on the road and I was their co-manager. They were still building their fan base and learning their stagecraft. That's why I love this business because it's totally unpredictable. It can change people's lives overnight. Look at Westlife, they have it all now and fair play to them, they work hard for it.'

Nicky is bouncing around the dressing room with excitement. This is one of the landmark moments in his life. Performing his first full stage show at The Point.

'The other shows have been great, but to bring it all home to Dublin is the icing on the cake,' he says. 'The Point has so many memories for me. I used to come to all the pop shows here, acts like Boyzone, The Cranberries and East 17, and I'd go home on a high, thinking, jeez I'd love to up there doing that. Now it's actually happening. I'm playing literally on my own doorstep because my home is just 15 to 20 minutes from here.'

Dane Bowers, who now seems to be a permanent fixture in the Westlife camp, is chatting in a corner with Bryan. He loves the party vibe in Dublin and when he discovered that the boys were planning to paint the town red after the show, he hopped on the first plane over today.

Pauline McLynn – 'Mrs Doyle' in the *Father Ted* TV series – pops her head in to say hello. And she jokingly offers them a cup of tea.

'Ah go on. Ye will! Ye will! Ye will! YE WILL!'

Two tall, clean-cut boy band types stroll over to Bryan, throw their arms around him and give him a matey hug.

'Thanks for putting us on the bill, Bryan. It was fantastic out there, a brilliant buzz. I never thought I'd ever perform at The Point,' one of them gushes.

Bryan laughs.

'Don't mention it. Look at the times we had together! I still think those were the best days.'

As they walk away towards the arena to take their place among the audience for the Westlife performance, Bryan reveals that the guys, Darragh Dean and Tim Madigan, are members of the support group, Cartel.

'Cartel is my old band,' he reveals. 'Darragh, Tim and myself formed it together here in Dublin and I was in it right up to the time that I was picked for Westlife. In fact, before Westlife, I contacted Louis, who was then managing Boyzone, and asked him to check us out. I didn't know at the time that he was putting Westlife together, but he told me all about this new boy band he was starting and he said I should come along for the auditions.

'When I was chosen for Westlife it was the end of my time with Cartel, but when I look back on the group they were the best days of my life. We didn't have any big record company behind us and we weren't on the daily treadmill of promotion and interviews and everything else that goes with a career in the major league. It was us doing it for ourselves and that gave us a lot of personal satisfaction. In Westlife everything is done for you.

'Things were happening for us on the Dublin scene right up to the time I got into Westlife. I really thought Cartel was going places as a group.

'Somehow fans even got hold of my mobile phone number and were constantly ringing me. It was a real buzz.

'I first met Darragh and Tim at a karaoke party and we really hit it off. Somehow the talk came around to forming a group. It was one of those nights where we were full of enthusiasm because we'd been up singing for hours and it developed from there.

'It wasn't just some kind of fancy notion, we were deadly serious about the group. I used to rehearse with Darragh and Tim every day for two hours in an old church. Our voices gelled really well together and then we started doing gigs and we'd impress everyone by singing *a capella* where our voices were the instruments. People were going, "Wow! Those guys have voices, they can really sing," and suddenly we started building up a huge fan base. There was a massive buzz around the town about us.

'We took Cartel as far as we could. But to move to the next level we needed Louis Walsh. He had made it happen big time for Boyzone and now everyone wanted him to manage their band. In the end, I took his advice and went to the auditions for Westlife. It was the end of my time with Cartel, but Darragh and Tim understood. They would have jumped at the opportunity if it had happened for them and we're still the best of mates.'

The media interest in Westlife's first night at The Point is unprecedented.

There's a scrum of photographers jostling to get a close up of Kian's smashed face. In the city's newsrooms space has been allocated on the front pages of all the local dailies for the shot that everyone wants to see.

There have been wild rumours that he's badly scarred. It's been said that he's even had stitches to one deep gash. For blood-thirsty newshounds, this is a great 'angle' as Westlife open their show in town. Forget the music.

To hell with the performance. This is the 'real' story of the night.

Backstage, meanwhile, a Westlife make-up artist is totally engrossed in the task of concealing the evidence of Kian's run-in with gurriers. Layer after layer of make-up is being applied to his eyes and around his nose to mask the cuts and bruises.

By stage time only a cut on his nose is still visible.

Westlife are more nervous than normal before tonight's show. Of all the venues, including Wembley, that they've played so far, this is the most important one in their eyes. It's the seal of approval in their native Ireland for their stage production and performance that will mean the most to them. There are also family and friends out in the audience and it would be so embarrassing if there are any individual or collective cock-ups.

They also want to impress RONAN.

There is bitter disappointment etched in the faces of the photographers as they realise that the prospect of a sensational picture has bitten the dust.

All lenses are focused on Kian as his tower turns and he becomes visible to the audience. But images of a badly scarred face are instantly wiped away as the snappers peer through their superlenses.

The show goes off like a bomb, with the wild Dublin audience creating a spine-tingling atmosphere. On stage, the five boys just can't stop smiling as they soak up the applause and adulation of the home crowd. This is what makes it all worth while. Even Kian appears to have wiped out the memory of the horrible experience he'd suffered in the early hours of the morning.

It certainly hasn't affected his performance tonight.

'I was nervous. I think all of us were nervous out there tonight,' Kian says afterwards. 'A lot of my relations were among the audience and when you know your family and friends are out there you tend to give it that tiny bit extra because you want to impress them so much.

'We also wanted to show Ronan that we could do it. He was

great to us in the early stages of our career. He gave us a lot of sound advice and created an awareness of who Westlife were back then. Now we're on a whole different level and we wanted to prove to him and everyone else that we have what it takes to be where we are today.'

Westlife cut the umbilical chord from Ronan since the demands of his solo career meant that he wasn't spending any time working with them.

'We discussed it with Ronan and agreed to go our separate ways. The good thing is, there was no big row with him over the business side of it. We've parted as friends and he'll always be a good mate to Westlife. Ronan is a gentleman in the way he does things.'

There's a big party afterwards and Ronan and Dane join the boys to celebrate their successful homecoming. As the booze flows, Shane Filan slips into his regular party piece, mimicking Ronan and Stephen Gately. Ronan rolls around his seat with laughter and tears flow down his cheeks.

'He is so ME it's scary,' Ro splutters as he struggles to catch his breath.

Late into the night Ronan and Shane are huddled together like bosom buddies, talking in foreign tongues. It's amazing how drunk people always seem to understand each other.

It's the day after the concert and Kian has an appointment with a Dublin dentist. As a result of the assault in Sligo, one of his fillings has come loose, requiring routine work. But as Kian leaves the dental surgery, he's confronted by a photographer from a local tabloid newspaper.

With no make-up hiding his prominent black eyes, the Westlife star pleads with the snapper not to take his picture. But the snapsman is intent on shooting his prey.

Kian is angry.

'How did you know I was here? Please leave me alone,' he demands. He doesn't want his injuries splashed across the newspapers.

The next day the front page of the *Irish Sun* has a massive image of a morose-looking Kian with large dark rings around his eyes. The singer is upset.

It's not just the fact that his black eyes are displayed for the whole country to see. But the Westlifer has an angry expression on his face, and he fears it makes him look like a thug in the eyes of the public.

A few days after the attack, Kian is philosophical about it. Although it had occurred on the morning of an important performance, he feels it could have been worse.

'If we'd been shooting a video that day, or doing a photo shoot for our album sleeve it would have caused a lot more problems for everyone,' he points out.

In the aftermath of the assault, Kian has decided not to press charges against the two culprits.

'It's not worth the hassle,' he says. 'The thing is, I could have knocked lumps out of those two guys, but they're not worth it. Maybe they think that they have one up on me now, but at the end of the day I have the last laugh. I'm the one who's lucky to have a successful career; I'm travelling the world, meeting interesting people, having fun and getting paid for it. They're back home in Sligo doing not very much except sitting on the side of the street drinking cans of beer every night. I'm sure they would love to trade places.'

If there is a downside to fame and pop success on the world stage, it's the constant, full-on attention it creates. Fame can't be switched off when Westlife are on their holidays or visiting their homes. It follows them everywhere, as Kian's dramatic encounter outside a kebab shop in Sligo proves. If the singer hadn't been a successful Westlife star, he probably wouldn't have been singled out for a mindless beating that night. The incident makes Kian realise that he can no longer go back to a regular life in his home town. There will be always danger lurking in the shadows, particularly where there's alcohol being consumed.

The Westlife pin-up reveals he has now been forced to hire a personal minder when he socialises on the local club scene.

'I don't go out by myself any more in Sligo,' he says sadly. 'It's annoying because I've always gone out by myself in my home town. I didn't see any reason not to. The thought of any kind of danger never crossed my mind for a second. But now I see how things can quickly turn nasty. So I've hired a local guy to keep an eye on me. Nobody will mess with him because he's got a "name", not in a bad sense, but people know that he's not to be messed with. I don't use him when I'm going out to dinner with my family, but he'll be there in the background when I'm in a local nightclub. Things can happen in a club. Other guys might want to make a name for themselves. So I'm not taking any chances from now on.'

Westlife's new lifestyle in Dublin is as near to normal as they've experienced in three years. There is no daily grind of rehearsals or interviews. No mountains of clothes to be retrieved from bedroom floors, or suitcases to be packed and unpacked. No early morning calls from Anto and mad dashes to airports to catch flights.

With a record breaking eleven shows at The Point – they beat the nine sell-out performances notched up by their predecessors Boyzone – the boys have free days at home. It's an opportunity for them to chill out, but they're still racing around like lunatics.

'The thing is, we find it impossible to calm down,' Nicky explains. 'It's the same whenever I get home for a break. I don't slow down like I should do and I never sit in. I might sit for an hour, but then I'll be on the phone to my mates organising a game of golf. That game of golf might lead to a meal and on to a club. Or I will go out for a day with Georgina's dad or her mam or my Mam and Dad, bring them out for dinner. Everything is centred around making up for lost time.

'My Mam is always giving out to me for not resting up. Sometimes I come home and I've got a headache or a cold or I'm dying with 'flu and she's insisting that I go to bed and I'm saying, I promised Georgina I'd go out or I promised my mate

I'd call over. Mam says, "One of these days you're going to fall down." And she's right. Every couple of months I'll have a really bad couple of days where I'm in bed suffering from the 'flu.

'The strange thing is, I can lead a crazy jet-set life for months, with late nights, early mornings and no proper food or exercise and I'll be fine.

'But as soon as I stop my body suddenly gives up. That happened to me before Christmas. I had a couple of days off and I woke up in my hotel room dying.

'I was so bad I couldn't lift my head off the pillow. I phoned Anto with my mobile and said, 'Anto I'm really sick and need a doctor. But you're going to have to get a key to my room from the hotel because I can't get out of bed.' It turned out that I had a severe case of tonsillitis. I was put on 15 types of tablets. We were due to go to Stockholm to do promotion and then on to Asia and the Far East but I had to stay behind. Georgina came over and stayed with me until I was well enough to go home.'

Nicky and Georgina have found their dream home off a country road just outside the picturesque village of leafy Malahide by the sea on the north side of Dublin. Today the Westlife star drives up to it in a very flash Mazda MX5 sports car, which he uses as his mode of transport during the series of concerts at The Point.

Set on an acre of prime land, the four-bedroomed mansion oozes character and is beautifully cocooned by trees and greenery. A long driveway sweeps the visitor up to the forecourt, where two giant oak trees stand on guard at the front of the house. Inside, there are spacious living rooms and the massive garden is like a football stadium. It's a world away from the modest three-bed terraced house where Nicky grew up in the working class community of Baldoyle, a sprawling suburban area also located on the north side of the city.

'I always thought I could never live in a big house in the country, that I would be afraid there at night time,' Nicky reveals as he peruses plans for the development of the grounds. 'I still don't know if it's going to be our home for the rest of our lives. Remember, I grew up in just a normal terraced house in Baldoyle, although it's a beautiful house in a very friendly housing estate, with neighbours on each side.

'But this house seems perfect now because it's very hard to find, there's a drive up to it and it's very private. Georgina and myself can go in, close the gates behind us and we have complete privacy. My family home in Dublin is totally accessible and I have fans calling there all the time. They come all the way from places like Switzerland, Sweden, Asia and Japan and they video the place. You open the door and there's a video in your face. It's not what I need when I go home for a break. So this is just perfect.'

This desirable property has been snapped up by Nicky for £750,000. In a city where the average three-bed house now costs £200,000, it is not considered terribly extravagant for a Westlife pop star.

'I know everyone thinks we're absolutely minted beyond belief, but we're not. So the price was right at the time.'

As he wanders around the vast expanse of the garden, the city slicker shakes his head and smiles.

'I'm not used to this! Loads of land. But I'm going to make the most of it. There's going to be a five-a-side football pitch in that section to the left. Over there by the trees I'm going to have a tennis court. We plan to have all the area around the house landscaped and the garden will also have a fountain feature to set it off, with lights all around.'

The excited young couple are now making daily forays into the city stores in search of beds, comfy seats and all the other bits and bobs that make up a love nest.

Their romance first blossomed at the local school in Baldoyle when they were both in third year at Plunkett College in the Whitehall area of Dublin, with the pair exchanging coy glances across the room during tuition.

He remembers going home that evening and announcing to his mum, Yvonne,

'I've just seen the girl that I'm going to marry. She's in my class at school.'

'That's great, son,' Yvonne replied without a thought as she prepared the evening meal.

Nicky, however, couldn't pluck up the courage to ask Georgina out on a date, although he never stopped talking with his pals about the tall, slim, raven-haired beauty whose eyes like deep ponds had left him mesmerised. Nicky asked one of his friends to act as an intermediary, as the guy shared the same bus home with Georgina.

The result was devastating for Nicky. The word came back that she wasn't interested. Georgina later clarified this version of events by revealing that she hadn't actually made any comment when asked because she thought the friend was winding her up. Two years later, Nicky and Georgina still hadn't got together. And he was still hankering after her like a lovesick puppy. Then another of his mates, Colm Costello, decided to act as Cupid. He approached Georgina and told her that, 'Nicky fancies you and he wants to ask you out.'

Nicky was steaming with rage when his pal told him about his initiative.

'You did whaaat? I could kill you!' he ranted.

Eventually he cooled down and asked, 'What did she say?'

'She said yes,' his pal replied.

'She said Ye-ye-yes? She said YES! Jeezus I love ya!'

The friend's matchmaking was a spectacular success as the young couple soon became inseparable.

Nicky still shudders at the memory of his first meeting with Georgina's dad, who was then the Irish Minister for Finance, Bertie Aherne – now Ireland's Taoiseach (Prime Minister). As an ace soccer goalie on the Irish soccer scene, Nicky had squared up to many an intimidating opponent in his day. But none of them was as daunting as his first face-to-face encounter with the Minister for Finance over Sunday lunch at the city's Skylon Hotel just a short hop from Dublin Airport.

'I was a nervous wreck,' Nicky recalls. 'Mam was teaching me table manners before I went out. She kept telling me to work from the outside in with the cutlery. I was so nervous, I just watched Bertie and did whatever he did.

When he dunked his bread roll in his soup I thought, "Yeah, cool, if that's OK by him," and I followed his lead. I remember that I didn't have a lot to say. I just replied "yes" and "no" to whatever he said. And I'm sure that first time was just as awkward for him as it was for me. But he did everything he could to break the ice. He insisted that I call him Bertie, as most people do in Ireland because he has that down-to-earth kind of personality. And he's big into sport, so that took up a lot of the conversation.'

Nicky and Georgina had nine months of a regular life and courtship before they had to face the first of many tests to their commitment when he was selected to try out for Leeds United soccer club. It was an experience that has steeled them against the regular and lengthy separations that life in Westlife has imposed on them.

'Myself and Georgina seem to have been away from each other all our lives, apart from the time we were in school. When I went to Leeds I only got to see her every two months. When I got dropped from Leeds, I was home for about a year and that was a great time. Then I got into Westlife and it's been a relationship by phone most of the time because I'm away so much. We sort of grew into the regime of being separated and that helped an awful lot, but it's still hard to deal with.'

In fact, at one stage, Nicky had toyed with the idea of joining the Irish Garda (police) and it was Georgina who encouraged him to audition for a place in Westlife, then known as IOU.

'At the time I was doing karaoke shows and Georgina suggested I should audition for IOU. I knew that Louis Walsh was involved, so that clinched it. I didn't want to waste my time with bands and managers who didn't know what they were doing.'

Ask Nicky what he finds so attractive about Georgina and he simply responds, 'She's just beautiful. She's so placid and caring. I didn't know that before I went out with her because it was looks that first attracted me to her. But she's just a gorgeous person.'

Their love faced its toughest challenge during the first summer that Nicky was in Westlife and Georgina went off to work in America with pals. 'I think that was the closest we came to breaking up,' he admits. 'We were on the phone to each other four or five times a day, but when we got back together after the two to three months it felt like we'd grown apart; Georgina also looked different, her hair had grown a couple of inches, but we soon got back to our old selves.

'Through all the enforced separations it's never got to the stage where either of us has wanted to say, "Ah, look, this is silly." We are just too close now for anything to break us up.'

As a desirable pop star, Nicky has all kinds of beautiful girls hovering around him, vying for his attention in the vain hope that they may woo him.

But the Westlifer is so secure in his relattionship with Georgina that he appears to be oblivious to the temptations that are in his midst.

'To be honest I see Georgina as my rock and I don't know how

I would have coped with this life if she wasn't there for me. The one-night stands with other girls isn't an issue because those girls are there for a Westlife star and not for a person. It's not what I want, it's not the road I'd go down. Georgina knows that, she knows me so well. There is so much trust involved on both sides.'

As Nicky strolls through the bare rooms of his newly-acquired palatial residence, the country squire in the making shows that he's still a lad at heart as he points to the spot where he intends to install a pool table for evenings in with his male gang of friends. Away from the world of pop, the Westlife star has remained loyal to the bunch of buddies he used to hang out with before he hit the big time with Westlife. There's Paul, a Robbie Williams lookalike with a wacky sense of humour; 'Skinner', who cuts a double for Paul Gascoigne and has a zany approach to life and 'Cos', a tall, striking, self-assured bloke. Together they help Nicky to maintain a sense of reality and keep him grounded. Occasionally, they also drag their famous mate away from Georgina for a boys' day out. Invariably it involves fiercely competitive sporting activities.

'Because I'm away with Westlife so much, I spend nearly all my time with Georgina when I'm home and we also go out with our friends. But I also have my time with the lads. On a day like that, Georgina has come to learn that she won't be seeing me, which she hated at first. But now she actually organises a day with the girls to give me a lads' day out. Georgina is great like that, she gives me space. That's healthy too because if I was living at home with her under ordinary circumstances we wouldn't be with each other morning, noon and night every day of the week. I would have a day where I'd go out with friends because everybody does that. That's the way normal life is.

'I love the time I have with my mates. We are so competitive and there's always some competition going on when I'm home. We have a FIFA day on the Playstation and we all gather in a room in one of our houses. We pick our team and then the competition is fierce. We call it the 'champion for the belt.' It could go on from 12 noon till four o'clock the next morning. Girlfriends will ring and we'll say, "Gee, listen, I'm in the middle of the game and I'm two-nil down and I'm very annoyed. Can I call you back in ten minutes?" It is THAT serious.

'There are days when we go down to the snooker hall or we go golfing and every game is fought as if our lives depend on it. I love those days. It's just typical lads kind of stuff and Westlife is never mentioned, so that's total relaxation for me. Sometimes if we finish around six in the evening we'd ring the girls and organise to go to the pub or a club. That's when Westlife might come back into play. If you turn up at a club door in Dublin as a group of ten people, you won't get in together. So I'd ring our security Paul Higgins and ask him to organise for us to get into Lillies, which is one of the city's best known clubs and Paul has contacts there. That's where it's an advantage being in Westlife.'

Bryan and Kerry also have their 'fairytale' home to furnish and decorate, and it's a labour of love for the besotted couple. Their seven-bedroomed mansion surrounded by woodlands and tucked away in an exclusive cluster of nine family homesteads amid the hills of County Wicklow, 30 minutes from Dublin's city centre, is breathtaking.

'Every time I drive up to it I just can't believe I'm living in a house this big,' Bryan says as he swings his swanky BMW on to the driveway and takes in the impressive size of the residence that screams star status.

Like a child unwrapping his Christmas presents, Bryan adds excitedly, 'It's my dream home. It's beautiful. I love it.'

He is, after all, only 20 years old.

Although a modern dwelling, it oozes character. Bryan wanders into the kitchen; it seems to go on forever. Three rooms of an average three-bed semi could comfortably fit in here. The remnants of toast, a jar of marmalade and used cups sit on the table from that morning's breakfast.

There's a large dining room that could comfortably seat a soccer team and their partners for dinner, leading off the kitchen. The fact that it has yet to be furnished adds to the impression of enormous size. A door off the dining area takes the guests into another empty room. Bryan has the smile of a cheeky kid as he struts to the centre of it.

'This is going to be a lads' room,' he announces. 'It's going to be a games room with a pool table and over there and I'm going to have my music section. It will have a piano and my guitars and that's where all my discs and awards will be displayed.'

A sprawling conservatory with exotic plants sweeps around the side of the house. It's the perfect chill-out room with spectacular views of the surrounding woodland and the rolling garden that is home to a large variety of trees, shrubs and flowers. It's a world away from Bryan's frenetic lifestyle on pop's merry-go-round. A sea of calm after the storm.

Bryan and Kerry have been happily plotting and planning the interior decor, sifting through interior homes magazines for ideas on furniture and fittings. Now they're finally getting the chance to browse through Dublin city furniture stores as they set about the task of kitting out their own little palace.

Boys being boys, the first item on Bryan's list is a pool table for his games room! After that, Kerry can pick and choose whatever she likes. But even with a big budget, it isn't easy to decide on which items of furniture are suitable, or what blends in with the colour scheme and what will fit in a particular space. It's an exercise that demands huge concentration and lots of time, but the famous young couple are also coping with endless requests for autographs from shop assistants and customers. They are a young couple so obviously in love as they hold hands, stroke each other's arms and, in this starry-eyed state that comes with the first flush of romance, don't even quarrel over colour schemes!

Backstage at The Point during one of the Dublin shows, Georgina is escorting a familiar Irish public figure, dressed in casual but smart jacket and pants with matching blue shirt and tie and accompanied by two burly gentlemen in sober suits, along a narrow hallway. It has a series of doors with A-4 sheets of paper taped to them. The signs read, Dancers Room, Musicians

Room, Production Room...Westlife Dressing Room.

The Irish Prime Minister (Taoiseach) Bertie Aherne, a tall, well-built, man with receding grey hair, chubby boyish face and cheeky smile, glances all around these unfamiliar surroundings.

Nicky is by the door of the boys' dressing room, waiting to meet the leader of the country, whom he now casually addresses as 'Bertie.' He may be one of the world's big political figures and the most powerful man in Ireland, but tonight he's Georgina's dad and he's come to see her boyfriend's band play a local venue.

As Nicky takes Bertie inside the dressing room to meet the other members of Westlife before their performance, the atmosphere is warm and relaxed.

'How'ya, lads!'

'How'ya, Bertie!', they respond in unison.

They've all met before. The Taoiseach was among the glitterati who attended Westlife's very first showcase at Dublin's trendy Red Box venue in March, 1999.

'They're really great. I think they're going to put Ireland on the map, as much as Boyzone have done before them,' he said way back then.

Tonight, Bertie appears genuinely excited at the prospect of sitting back and enjoying a night of sheer escapism from the affairs of the nation and the problems of Northern Ireland.

'Georgina has been telling me so much about the show. In fact, she talks non-stop about it,' Bertie laughs. 'I'm told I'm going to be very impressed and I don't doubt it.'

Then he chats in a corner with Westlife's manager Louis Walsh, telling him what a great job he's doing for the music industry.

'I'd better watch it, you'll be after my job next,' Bertie laughs.

'They're not the Number Ones I want,' Louis giggles.

Georgina leads her dad, who is accompanied by two Special Branch detectives from the Garda, out into the arena where the cacophony of sound is a deafening mixture of whistles and screams. But, from the opening scene of Westlife's dramatic entrance, the three VIPs seem totally captivated. As they become acclimatised to the hysteria of the thunderous sound of the adoring fans, they just can't take their eyes off the stage. It's clear that they're enjoying every moment.

Just before the final song, Flying Without Wings, the threesome leave their seats and begin walking towards the exit. But, as the opening bars of Flying Without Wings sound around the auditorium, Bertie stops in his tracks.

'Wait! Wait!' he says loudly to his minders. 'I gotta see this. I gotta see this!'

He'd obviously remembered Georgina's advice, 'Don't leave before the last song. There's a big surprise.'

Bertie takes several steps back, accompanied by his 'shadows', and watches from an aisle as Westlife soar over the heads of the audience. Watching his expression, it's obviously a an impressive experience. Just before the final moments, Bertie does his disappearing trick and has left the building before Westlife return to earth.

Nicky and Georgina are driving home when she receives a call on her mobile.

'That was a fantastic show. They've really come a long way in two years,'

Bertie tells his daughter.

'I told you Dad!'

Then he's on the phone to Nicky.

'Well done! Georgina was right, it's a brilliant concert.'

The three Sligo boys, who are staying in the same exclusive hotel they made their home-from-home during rehearsals for the show in January, are enjoying days out golfing, trips to the cinema, shopping and hanging out with their families and friends who have travelled down from the north west of the island to visit them.

Kian is an idol to millions of girls around the world, has the career of his dreams in pop, a very healthy bank account and gets to perform every night at Ireland's top concert venue, but during these 11 shows in Dublin he admits that his biggest pleasure is being able to drive his car.

'I've learned that at the end of the it's the simple things in life that give the most enjoyment,' he admits.

As Kian slips behind the wheel of his sleek BMW, he explains, 'You have to remember that I'm only 20 years of age (he'll turn 21 on April 29) and most guys of 20 don't get to own a BMW. I do, but in my case I hardly ever get to drive it. So this week is a real treat for me. I drive down to The Point every evening for the show and when I come off stage I run straight to the car. The key will be in the ignition, security will have it started and ready to go. We shoot off at speed to avoid all the traffic leaving the concert and it's a great buzz as it's a high speed getaway.

'The cops don't stop us because they know what we're doing.'

Down at the venue tonight before the show, Kian is tucking into fish and chips and anxiously awaiting a call from his sister who's on the way from Sligo to see the show. The concerts, he admits, are extra special when there are family members or close friends in the audience. 'It's a real buzz,' he says.

Kian smiles with pleasure as he recalls his father's delight when he'd first seen the show at Wembley.

'I wanted to shock my parents with the impact of the show, so I didn't show them the set backstage before the performance on the night they were there. And they were astonished. My father is a quiet man and he'd normally go, "Well done, son! I'm proud of you." But afterwards he was reliving the whole show and picking out little highlights he remembered. He was like, 'And then there was this bit! And that bit!'

'My father had never been in London before, so that's why I brought them to Wembley. So for my father to be in London for the first time and see his son playing Wembley, I can imagine it must have been quite a strange feeling. In 40 years time, if my kid does what I'm doing, I would be just as happy to sit in the audience in Wembley for the first time as well.

' I'm sure I would have a shiver down my spine, going, "That's my young fella up there".

'One of the biggest kicks I get from Westlife is being able to do things like take my Mam and Dad shopping in London. Not that my Dad thanked me for it – like most men, he hates shopping. But I took them along to Harrods and my Mam got a dress, shoes and a handbag for my sister's wedding in the summer.'

Being the resident band at The Point has created a family atmosphere backstage in the catering and chill-out area, which has a pool table, Playstation and a TV section with lots of couches.

Although the up-tempo 90-minute show is physically demanding, Kian reckons that the current show is less stressful than doing promotion.

'The hour-and-a-half on stage is gruelling and you've got to be mentally and physically fit, but the regime is not as hard as promotion. When we're doing promotions, we fly from one country to another, get up at nine in the morning and finish at 12 at night, then get up at seven the next morning and finish at eleven that night. With this show, we're getting out of bed at two in the afternoon. We come in and do two or three hours promotion. Then we do the show and meet up with everybody afterwards to have a few drinks and talk about the performance. It's much more relaxing.'

As he watches Bryan shooting pool with blonde dancer Lene, he admits that Westlife will be sorry when the curtain comes down on the final show and they have to move on. 'There's a great vibe backstage here. There are so many friendly people around. Just look around, people are watching football on the TV, there's a pool game going on, we're eating the best of food and everybody is happy. There are no bad vibes and no arguments. It's a happy environment.'

His mobile rings and it's Kian's sister who has arrived at the venue. She's having difficulty finding the route to backstage.

'Hang on, I'll come and get you,' Kian tells her.

Anto arrives on the scene at that moment.

'Kian, the meet-and-greet is happening now.'

There are 100 excited fans corralled in a backstage room eagerly anticipating the arrival of their idols in the flesh.

'Anto, I can't do this now. I've got to find my sister.'

'Kian, it's happening right this minute. The other guys have gone ahead,' Anto says firmly.

Kian is fuming. 'Look this is not fair, my sister is out there trying to get in.'

'Give me her mobile number and I'll go find her,' Paul offers.

Kian passes on the number, but he's so upset as he enters a room full of young Westlife fans that he can't force a smile. For 20 minutes a morose Kian is trapped as fans file past, each stopping briefly for his autograph and an occasional photograph.

Sometimes fame can be a pain in the butt.

Bryan slips off his pants, pulls on his white soccer shorts and an Adidas top. As he laces up his football boots, Kerry reaches down and takes a novel from a pocket in the BMW, rolls back the front seat and flicks open the pages.

'This is good. You can see the match from here,' Bryan says.

'Yeah, Bryan. But I'll probably just have a relaxing read,' she says.

'Whaa-at! You're not going to watch me do my David Beckham stuff!' he teases.

'Bryan, you just go and do your lad's thing,' she laughs.

He tenderly strokes her blonde tresses. 'Are you sure you don't mind hanging around here?'

'I'll be fine, Bryan,' she says.

It's a day off for Westlife in Ireland, so Bryan has a rare chance to turn out with his team, Aer Lingus, in a city league.

The location for this evening's encounter is a sports ground in the concrete jungle of Tallaght, a sprawling working-class residential belt on the west side of Dublin.

As the game progresses, a gang of youths on the sideline spots Bryan out on the field of play.

'Go on, ye bleedin' faggot,' one roars at the Westlife star.

Suddenly he's the target for a torrent of abuse. Bryan is oblivious to their insulting jibes. Then the gang, aged from seven to 17, notice the BMW. Now it becomes a target. The gang slowly converge on the parked vehicle near the pitch, and as Kerry looks up from her book she's instantly alarmed and then frightened by the leering youths who have surrounded the car. They are now hurling abuse at the terrified young woman, who clearly fears for her safety. Bryan spots the commotion and races over to Kerry. She is in tears. He's furious and announces to officials that he's pulling out of the game to take her away from the hostile scene.

Various members of the opposing team from the Tallaght area come to Bryan and apologise over the incident. They announce that they are now abandoning the match as a result of the shocking behaviour of the fans.

'OK, lads, I appreciate that it's nothing to do with you guys,' Brian acknowledges, with a pained expression.

As Bryan drives away the gang of youths hurls stones at his car.

'They're just a bunch of no-hopers,' Bryan fumes.

It had been horrendous intimidation of a young woman and in the aftermath of the incident Kerry is distraught. A few days later Bryan lets it be known that his badly shaken fiancée no longer feels safe in Ireland and wants to return to the UK.

'I've had a really tough job to convince her to stay,' he reveals. 'It may be only one low-life gang of guys, but they have blackened her image of Ireland. She'll always have that vision of what Irish people are like because of what they did and that's sad because there are so many good people in Ireland.

'A handful of gurriers have ruined it for her and I blame the parents of those kids for having them out there terrorising a pregnant woman. It's a disgrace.'

It's not the first time that the Westlife star has personally experienced animosity from young Irish guys who begrudge him the success he has enjoyed on the world stage.

And it's not just Bryan who suffers verbal assaults.

'We all get it in the neck when we're out and about here at home, particularly in Dublin,' he reveals. 'The sad thing is, it only happens in Ireland. Everywhere else we go in the world people applaud what we do. And we've certainly never experienced anything like that in England. It's not that we're looking to be treated any differently to everyone else, but we certainly don't deserve the abuse and the taunts we get at home.

'A lot of the young Irish male population seem to have a grudge against us. Whenever I'm out in my car I get dirty looks from guys and they give me "the finger." I get "Queer!" and "Faggot!" roared at me. It's very sad, really. I remember Boyzone and, later, Ronan Keating saying that they used to get that all the time, and probably still do. I found it hard to believe at first, but now I've experienced it at first hand. And look what happened to Kian!

'There's a famous quote from Bono about the Irish attitude to success, compared to how the Americans view it. Bono says a Yank will look at the guy with the big house on the hill and say, "I want to be that guy." In Ireland, they say, "I want to GET that guy." And, sadly, it seems to be so true.

'You would think that they'd be delighted to see fellow Irish guys flying the flag. We're holding records in England and taking over the UK charts and people at home are slagging us off for it. It just doesn't make sense.

'We've helped put Ireland on the map in places like Asia. They all now know out there who we are and where the country is. It's just a shame that those guys at home don't see that we're doing the country proud.'

CHAPTER 4

Bus life and Europe hopping

Westlife are in a foul mood. Tempers are so frayed among the group that a huge row threatens explode any second.

The time bomb has been created by one of those bizarre days where a week's work has been packed in to 24 hours. Worse still, a series of cock-ups has sent the boys' morale plunging into a dark pit. They are shattered and very, very hungry.

It all began in Birmingham after the last show of the UK and Irish tour. Westlife had been dragged out of their beds after just a few hours sleep to catch a 6 a.m. flight to Cologne in Germany for a special appearance on Viva TV.

Germany is the second biggest market in the world and is hugely important to Westlife, who are now making a major impact in that territory.

Getting the opportunity to perform six songs on a Viva special, with interviews in between, is a major boost, so they're totally up for it.

'If you really break Germany, you can add on an extra three

million sales to each album,' Kian, the astute businessman of the group, points out.

Westlife arrive in Cologne at ten in the morning and finish their TV appearance at five in the afternoon, grabbing a quick McDonald's meal in between.

Then they set off on an hour's drive to Düsseldorf for a flight to Copenhagen in Denmark. There's a two-hour wait before their flight, so the boys decide to while away the time by tucking into some tasty hot food, as they're like a pack of hungry wolves after the day's work.

Then comes their first major disappointment of the day.

Anto breaks the bad news. 'There are no hot dishes to be had anywhere in the terminal right now.'

'Ah, Anto, tell me you're joking,' Nicky cries.

All five are now looking at him with pleading eyes.

'Sorry lads, I'm deadly serious. There's no hot food.'

Bryan's jaw drops. 'Anto, I gotta eat.'

'There's nothing I can do about it. There is no food. Let's go up to the business lounge and see if there's something there.'

Anto leads the way and five dejected Westlifers shuffle along behind him unenthusiastically.

The executive lounge is almost deserted, with the exception of two businessmen in dark suits, sitting side by side on a black leather couch and poring over the pages of a report.

As the boys scan the refreshments area, their hearts sink. Biscuits and peanuts are the only fare on view.

'I guess it's peanuts and coke,' Kian sighs as he drops his hand luggage and saunters over to the counter.

They eventually board the plane with great expectations. The in-flight food on air travel may not be their favourite, but tonight it will be as welcome as a gourmet meal.

When the service trolley eventually arrives and they frantically whip away the covers of their trays, their jaws drop open and the lads glare at Anto in silence.

'Don't blame me, lads. I didn't order it,' he says indignantly.

The boys shuffle the food around with their fingers before placing the cover back on the tray.

Cold reindeer sandwiches are as welcome at this moment as breaking wind in a spacesuit.

'Ah, lads, this can't be happening,' Bryan says, shoving his food away.

'I can't eat this either,' Nicky adds.

The reindeer is returned to the trolley untouched.

For the rest of the journey Westlife fantasise about big juicy beefburgers and chicken snack boxes in Copenhagen.

When they arrive, it looks like their luck is in. Bryan spots a Burger King restaurant on the way to the transfer lounge. There's another hot food shop further down the line.

'Yee-yesss!' he shouts, punching the air with his fist in a fit of delight, as his legs gather speed.

His elation and the high spirits of the rest of the Westlife troupe is short lived. Like a mirage in the desert, the boys discover that all the little food shops closed 20 minutes earlier.

There's a cloud of doom and gloom hanging over the party as

they struggle, without a word, towards the boarding gate for the last leg of the trip to Oslo.

But as tour manager Anto checks the departures monitor he gets a sinking feeling.

Oslo isn't registered on it. Instead, there's a flight to a place called Stavanger.

'What's going on, Anto?' Kian asks.

'Dunno!'

A clearly worried Anto goes off to check out the situation and when he returns the look on his face says it all.

We're in trouble.

'There's been some kind of cock-up and we have to take this flight to Stavanger,' Anto announces.

'Where the friggin' hell is Stavanger when it's at home?' Kian asks tetchily.

'It's about two hours west of Oslo.'

'Whaatt! There's another two hours on to the journey when we get there. I don't believe you,' Bryan wails.

'Yep!' Anto says curtly. He's in no mood for arguments.

The flight to Stavanger takes one hour. The boys keep their spirits up by clinging on the hope that there will be a McDonald's open when they arrive.

It's midnight in Stavanger and the prospect of finding a late-night fast food store in this strange place doesn't look good. After a quick tour around the metropolis their fears are realised. It's like trying to find a needle in a haystack in a foreign city at this hour of the morning. They decide to continue the road journey to Oslo and pray that there'll be a roadside café en route.

It's the early hours of the morning, snow is falling, it's freezing cold, everyone is tired and hungry. At this moment, the Westlife dream has turned into a nightmare.

'Sometimes I hate this life,' Bryan sighs as he tries to find a comfortable position to rest his head. He's hoping to fall asleep and wake up in a restaurant.

Eventually a service station that serves fast food is discovered. Trevor, the driver, rolls the bus into a parking bay and there's a mad scramble down the steps.

Bryan is leading the way.

'Oh, lads, food!' he roars, 'Yee-yess!'

Shane, Kian, Nicky and Mark are in hot pursuit.

'What do you want, lads?' Anto asks as he scans the choices that are displayed in pictures on a wall behind the service counter.

'The chunkiest burger in the house,' Bryan responds.

'Burgers all round then, lads?'

'Yeah!'

Ten minutes later Westlife attack the order when it arrives.

'These are absolutely disgusting,' Kian splutters as he chews a mouthful of the greasy, wafer-thin offerings.

But it's not a time to be choosy when you've just struggled through a famine.

'God, I wish I hadn't eaten that,' Mark says, rubbing his stomach. 'It feels like a big mass of gunk down there.'

Back on the coach the Westlifer are moaning and groaning.

'I'm feeling slightly sick,' Kian says, then he drops off to sleep.

After Birmingham, Cologne, Düsseldorf, Copenhagen and Stavanger – all within 24 hours – the Westlife bus finally arrives in Oslo at 2.30 in the morning

By this stay, the boys feel like they've done the five-date European tour even before it begins.

The prosperous city of Oslo on a sunny Saturday afternoon is a lively metropolis, with young lovers strolling up and down the Karl Johans Gate, the main pedestrian thoroughfare, which stretches for a mile and a half and has an endless variety of café bars and eateries

Oslo is one of the smaller capitals of Europe, with a population of 480,000, and they all seem to have converged on this buzzing street today.

It's thronged with colourful people from all walks of life. There's a chic middle-aged couple, wearing designer casual gear and adorned with expensive jewellery, sauntering into Café Bacchus, an obviously popular coffee house situated on the square beside the city cathedral.

There's a female punk, sporting a Mohican hairstyle in a dazzling display of orange, blue and white, wearing Doc Martens with a skirt bedecked with chains and topped off with a little leather jacket. She's locked arm-in-arm to a six-foot-four tall shaven-headed bloke with four rings dangling from a left nostril and tattoos on his neck, giving the impression that his whole body is covered in artwork.

Tourists are wandering around the corner and into the National Gallery to view such gems as the nation's best-known painting, Edvard Munch's *The Scream*.

Meanwhile, Westlife are spending this brisk, sunny day behind closed doors being interrogated by the local media about their lives and ostensibly amazing times as the glitterati of pop.

In the evening, after they've talked the talk, they're itching to walk the walk. This is a major decision – what to do and where to go. It's a rare night off for the boys, so their security, Paul and Fran, are faced with the mission of sussing out a hot spot where the boys can party without being mauled by over-zealous fans.

Someone has a contact in a local restaurant, so they decide to dine there before sampling Oslo's nightlife.

Later, as they leave their hotel, the pop quintet are pursued by hordes of stunning blonde female fans. This is every guy's dream, but the reality is a little scary. Out on the street the girls are grabbing at the Westlifers as Paul and Fran try to fend them off. Once they're safely indoors again, Paul breathes a sigh of relief.

'The problem with packs of girls is that the situation can spiral out of control and someone could get hurt. You can't take your eyes off the lads for a split second because that's all it takes for a disaster to happen. We always have to remember that there are crazy people in the world and it just takes one to cause a nightmare. Look at the number of celebrities that have been killed.'

Over dinner, Kian admits that achieving 'fame' hasn't dramatically enhanced him as a person. It's not something that's tangible. It doesn't bring a feeling of being superhuman or more wise or even happiness.

'Fame isn't something that makes your life fantastic and wonderful when you get it. It's not a feeling. It's just a word for all the attention around you. If nobody paid attention to me, I wouldn't be famous. Sometimes all that attention can be a pain in the backside and there's probably one day in every month where I think, "I wish to God I wasn't doing this." But half-an-hour later I'd be fine. It's gets me down sometimes, but I wouldn't like to be back in Dunnes Stores (the Irish supermarket chain) packing shelves or in college working my ass off.'

When they get to the club later in the night it's even more manic. Although a VIP section has been cordoned off for the five singers, their dancers and members of the crew, the Norwegian girls are hell-bent on scoring with a Westlife star. Their harassed security duo spend the night pulling scantily-clad females out of the area and escorting them away from the boys.

The Westlife heart-throbs could have the pick of the beautiful blonde girls who're smothering them with attention tonight. Gary Barlow admitted after Take That broke up that he had succumbed to the temptations of fans and enjoyed a string of brief encounters with nubile young ladies in his hotel room during the heyday of the supergroup. But the twilight zone of groupies and manic fans is a self-imposed no-go area for the guys in Westlife.

There are no Westlife rules, written or unwritten, about picking up girls for one-night stands as they weave their way from country to country. It's the boys themselves who are acutely aware that it's fraught with danger.

Lessons had been learned at the start of their career when Kian was the victim of a 'kiss and tell' story in a UK tabloid. An English barmaid he'd met before the group notched up their first Number One hit with Swear It Again and were propelled to stardom, recounted lurid details of her night of passion with Kian. It was a horrendous shock for the Westlifer. He was particularly upset that it caused embarrassment to his family back home in Ireland.

'I cried my eyes out over that story,' Kian admits.

That incident was a wake-up call for Kian. It made him realise that he's no longer seen by some people as a person, but as a name to be exploited. The boys have long since realised that the majority of the girls are buying in to a fantasy. They are attracted to the slick, well-groomed Westlife images that are portrayed through TV shows, videos and the glossy pages of teen magazines. They are chasing a star rather than an ordinary human being. It's all part of the fun, but it makes it difficult for them to find that 'special' person to share their lives. They still have a go, but approach with caution.

'Every country we go to we could be with local fans if we wanted. Any time we go to a club, there are girls who are there for the taking. They make that quite obvious. I think we're in the best job in the world to meet girls, to be honest. But taking a total stranger like that back to your hotel room is too messy and too dangerous. It could turn horribly wrong,' Shane says.

'I'm very choosy when it comes to girls. Very picky. I don't like to take advantage of the fact that fame can land me a girl. I'd rather be with somebody I'd meet in a club who mightn't know who Westlife are, or if they do know, at least they're not full-on fans. Ninety-nine per cent of our fans are fine, but there are some out there who are just too extreme and in the psycho area. There is no knowing what they would do. You do learn to read people, though. I can spot very early in a conversation if the girl wants to be with me for myself or for the fame. If the conversation is all about Westlife, then I know it's a fame thing.

'It's one thing enjoying all the attention from girls – and we do because we're normal fellas and what young guy wouldn't get a thrill from gorgeous girls calling his name and shouting, "I love you!" – but at the end of the day I'm searching for a girl who is into Shane Filan and not Shane Westlife.'

But as a normal 21-year old with burning desires, Shane confesses that he doesn't live like a monk.

'Over the last couple of years I've met a few girls and I've been with them, whether it's for a couple of months or a few weeks. Nothing that was too serious. It's not easy to start a relationship when we're on the move all the time. Bryan is the exception, but he found Kerry and it was brilliant because she was in the business and understands what it's like. Nicky is very fortunate that his relationship had been firmly established before his life became a crazy one with Westlife. Myself, Mark and Kian are in the same boat. But things can change over night.'

Despite the trauma of being betrayed by a girl, Kian insists he still enjoys the thrill of the interaction with the opposite sex and is adamant that he'll embrace a relationship if it happens.

'I'm just human like everyone else; I have the same needs, the same desires and the same drive. Just because I'm in Westlife doesn't mean I have to turn down every opportunity that comes my way. I'm always wary and I make sure that I stop, think and use my judgment before getting involved. But when I'm in a club surrounded by beautiful Page Three girls or models or dancers, I'm definitely looking at the possibility of something happening. After all, I am a hot-blooded male.

'If it feels right then I'll go for it and I have been involved with girls, but so far those encounters haven't developed into serious relationships. If I'm in Spain and I meet a girl I really like and if I'm with that girl for two days, all of a sudden I have to move on and it's impossible to establish something lasting. It's the same trying to find a girl back home in Ireland. Who wants to get involved with somebody like me when I'm going to be gone for months on end?

'I know it does look like a brilliant life from the outside and for the most part it is. Not many people in life get the opportunities I'm getting at this age. I have nothing to whinge about in terms of my actual career. It's only if someone asks me about my personal life that I have to be honest and admit that it can be lonely.

'I look at Nicky and Bryan and they are ringing their girlfriends all the time when we're away. I don't have that. Instead, I'm on the phone to my mother and my friends back home. I know that one day it will work out; in the meantime I'll motor on and when I find a real love I'll find it.'

Kian doesn't rule out the possibility of finding true love with a fan. But he does make a distinction between the hordes of young girls who hang around hotels and those who are simply fans of their music.

'There are often good-looking girls our own age who check into the same hotels and whether or not the single guys in the group date them is a personal choice. There are certainly no rules saying we can't go with them. We can use our own judgement and if it feels right, then why not. And it depends on what you call a fan. A fan is a person who likes music. The fans outside hotels are not there for you, they're there for Westlife. When A1 arrive in town, the same fans will be outside their hotel. It's better to meet fans outside of that circle.'

MTV Europe is playing their video for Lay My Love On You, which features scenes of the boys playing soccer, wearing the strips of an Irish club called Bray Wanderers from County Wicklow. 'We filmed that in Asia,' Nicky reveals. 'The reason we're wearing the Bray Wanderers kit is because the Dublin's boys wouldn't wear the Sligo jersey and the Sligo boys wouldn't wear a Dublin jersey. So we settled for Bray, County Wicklow.'

◁ Kian, in after-show recovery

▽ Practising Backstreet Boys moves in Kuala Lumpur

△ Bryan, Nicky and Kian have a knock around in Kuala Lumpur

△ Westlife answer questions in Kuala Lumpur

△ Fans in Manila

△ Kian

Shane

△ Nicky

Bryan

△ The Heavenly Band

Westlife's personal security Fran Cosgrave is the butt of jokes today after his embarrassing incident while checking into the hotel. Like most of the guys he uses a pseudonym to avoid being hassled in his room by fans. Yesterday the name was Bond, James Bond.

Fran had gone to the bank to get some cash while everyone else checked in.

Upon his return, Fran went up to the receptionist and asked to check in.

'The name is Bond.'

'Have you got a reservation, Mr Bond?'

'Yes.'

'What's your first name Mr Bond?'

'James.'

'We don't seem to have a reservation,' the reception says, raising her eyebrows.

'Look, I'm James Bond and I'm definitely staying here tonight!'

'We don't have you here, Mr Bond,' the ruffled receptionist insists. 'Perhaps you are in our other hotel.'

The normally unflappable Fran is now in a flap as he marches off to their sister hotel.

'I want to book in, please. The name is Bond,' he announces agitatedly upon arrival.

'We don't seem to have a Mr Bond here. Can I have your first name, sir?'

'James.'

'Hold on a minute, sir.'

The receptionist calls over a male supervisor.

'Sorry, your name again?'

'Bond. James Bond.'

'Ahem, yes, we don't seem to have you here, Sir.'

'This is ridiculous,' Fran flips. 'I'm here with a group of people. Have you got a Mr Cruise? (Anto's pseudonym).'

'Yes we do, sir. All his party has checked in, apart from Mr Cosgrave.'

'Em, that's me.'

'I see, sir. You're not Mr James Bond then?'

'Eh, no.'

The Vallhall in Oslo is a brand-new indoor sports arena and on this Sunday evening it will host only its second-ever pop concert. Norway's boy band of yesteryear, A-Ha, featuring Morten Harket – the man with the finely honed and chiselled features who is still a heart-throb to thousands of besotted women around the globe – had performed in concert at the venue just a few nights earlier. This evening, thousands of girls are descending on the very same hall to see five famous Irish lads in the flesh.

As they file through the security gates, the fans, many accompanied by boyfriends, are clearly in an excited state of anticipation as they giggle and babble in little groups.

Backstage, Westlife are tucking into roast chicken with all the trimmings. Anto sticks his head around the corner and announces, 'Lads, the support act wants to meet you. They're the group who won Popstars here.'

No Angels, Norway's answer to Hear'Say, are hovering in a hallway. There are three girls, a blonde with black streaks, a petite oriental with red-tinted hair and a tall, dark beauty. With them are the two towering guys who complete the band – one of them looks uncannily like a young Morten Harket.

'Hi, guys,' Shane greets them, still chewing on a chicken bone. He introduces Mark, Bryan, Nicky and Kian.

'So how has it been going for your group?' Kian asks.

One of the girls reveals that No Angels have topped the charts with a song called Tick Tock and it's been the biggest selling single ever in that territory.

'You look like Kym from Hear'Say,' Bryan tells the dark-haired girl of the group.

Then he adds with a cheeky smile: 'But you're better looking than Kym.'

The conversation turns to Westlife's next single and Shane reveals that it'll be When You're Looking Like That.

'We're going to South Africa and we'll be shooting the video there, so I'm really looking forward to that as it'll be our first time in that part of the world.'

'We've gotta go and get ready for the show, so best of luck guys,' Kian adds, as No Angels troop out towards the stage for their performance.

Along the corridor a member of the local security team is reading a Westlife interview in the Sunday newspaper, *VG*. In the article, Bryan admits that he'd been watching porn on TV in his hotel bedroom the previous night. It had been a disappointing evening, he reveals, because he'd wanted to go out, but he was 'knackered' after watching TV.

Then the interviewer asked him how long he's been away from Kerry.

'Obviously too long,' Bryan quips.

Back in the dressing room Shane removes his socks and his feet are covered in black fluff.

'This is not dirt,' he says, alarmed that people will jump to the wrong conclusion. 'I actually have a thing about clean feet. I wash mine about four times a day, roll up the trousers and do a real good job on them.'

There is a minor panic in the wardrobe department. Fiona has discovered that the zip is broken on Bryan's Uptown Girl outfit and there's no sewing machine at the venue. She's only got one option – sew it manually.

'Oh well, here goes,' Fiona sighs, threading her needle.

As she expertly sets to work, Fiona reveals that all the costumes are showing signs of wear and tear from frequent washing. Because the boys have lost so much weight since the start of the tour – the result of their high-energy nightly performances – many of the outfits no longer fit them properly.

'We've had to shrink-wash a lot of stuff,' she says.

As she inserts the final stitches on the boiler suit, Fiona tugs at the zip and it moves up and down.

'Let's hope it doesn't burst during the performance,' she adds, crossing her fingers.

As they change into their space suits, the boys do their vocal warm-ups. Then Shane slips into his managerial style pep talk.

'Remember, lads, this is the first European show,' he shouts over the din of vocal acrobatics as Mark and Bryan limber up.

'It's back to basics now, lads. Keep everything very tight. Let's have full concentration from everyone. We want to make a really good impression with our first show here.'

Bryan's mobile phone rings before he leaves the dressing room. It's Kerry. 'I'm just about to go on stage, honey. Call you right after the show,' he says.

Out in the arena the Westlife set is dwarfed by the massive interior with its high ceiling. It is also the first concert that doesn't have a seated audience.

As the excitement builds, the 11,000-strong army of fans are straining their necks, hoping to see the five famous figures making an appearance any second now.

The journey from the boys' dressing room to the stage is visible to the crowd on the left side, so the boys are escorted to the backstage area through a route that takes them outdoors. It's short walk to a back-door entrance, but the lads have to wade through mud in their space suits before they reach it.

'Where are you taking us, Anto?' Nicky asks slightly alarmed, as he plods through the muck. 'Are you sure this is the right way?'

'Have I ever led you astray yet?' Anto quips.

'Yes!'

There is a huge explosion of sound when Westlife make their

entrance – and that was just the crowd. The impression of mainland Europeans being more reserved than the UK and Irish audiences is soon demolished. Their whoops of delight can be heard at the Royal Palace 15 minutes away in the heart of this very clean and comfortable city.

Instantly recognising that they've caught the imagination of their Norwegian fans, Bryan feeds off the frenzy.

'We couldn't have picked a better European city to launch our European tour,' he tells the Oslo audience during the first interaction between songs.

They burst into spontaneous applause.

'Do you want to know why?' he asks.

They scream their heads off.

'Because you've got the best-looking girls in the world,' Bryan shouts. As the roars of delight subside, he then adds: 'And the blokes are OK too.'

This entertainer has the perfect timing of a seasoned comedian. And he prowls around the stage like it's his second home.

The show tonight in Oslo is a lot slicker than the UK and Irish concerts because Westlife aren't allowed to run over time. Now that the tour is on the move every day, it's going to be a nightly and daily race against the clock to dismantle the set and rig, load it up into the trucks, get it on the road and set it up in the next city for the following evening's concert. It normally takes 18 hours to build up the stage, now the rigging crew have to do it in ten. Westlife still perform the same number of songs, but there is less on stage banter between the boys.

'That was a good show tonight,' Kian says afterwards as the coach sails along the motorway on a nine-hour journey to Stockholm. 'I think the fact that the crowd was standing made it a little bit different. It created a really good atmosphere and the audience got totally involved. It felt good out there for me.'

Even Bryan's hastily repaired Uptown Girl suit stood the test of the exuberant performance.

Shane, who had earlier given his fellow Westlifers a pre-show team boost, is happy too. But he is reluctant to be cast in the role of group's commander in chief. Sipping a bottle of mineral water and towelling his head as he relaxes in the coach lounge, he says: 'I wouldn't say I'm the leader, but I always try to give a little pep talk before we go on stage, just to make sure that everyone is focused, which they usually are anyway. It makes me feel more comfortable going out on stage.'

In the mould of his pop idol Michael Jackson – he once took a chunk of grass home from a Dublin concert venue as a memento of Jacko's concert – Shane is the ultimate professional on stage. Every note and every move has to hit the bullseye every time. Anything less than 100 per cent perfection will upset him. It's a praiseworthy attitude. But in another sense it can be a curse, stealing some of the enjoyment of his time on stage if there are even minor shortcomings.

'I'm too much of a perfectionist, to be honest,' he admits. 'I always want things to be better than they can possibly be.'

As one-fifth of a group, it can be frustrating when others let standards slip during a performance. Sometimes words are exchanged after the show.

'If somebody is not pulling their weight on stage for some reason, we all get annoyed about it,' Shane reveals. 'I would definitely say, 'What were you at out there!' And, likewise, people would say it to me if they felt that I had done something wrong. We always give advice to each other and if somebody is not pulling their weight we give out to them.

'Everybody is the same in the band and everybody deserves the same treatment. If one member is messing up, the other four deserve more respect than that.

'Every night one of us messes up. If we mess up and we don't mean to, well, things happen. But if someone messes up and they don't care, that's a problem that has to be sorted out straight away.'

There are two coaches in convoy on the road tonight, with Westlife's band and dancers sharing the second one. The 11 articulated trucks with all the stage gear will follow behind once all the gear has been packed on board.

Westlife find coach travel less stressful than jet-setting. There is no frantic packing and unpacking. No mad dashes to airports with tons of luggage in tow. No boring routine procedures like checking in, hanging around for hours before the plane takes off and waiting for luggage at the other end.

'We fly all the time, so to get on a bus is a bit different and a lot more laid back,' Nicky says. 'It definitely keeps the morale up on tour and it's good for building the team spirit.'

Their spacious upper lounge, which can comfortably seat ten people on long, soft couches, is luxurious with all sorts of mod cons for entertainment.

The boys have several choices of amusement to wind down after the performance, including satellite TV, a video, DVD, mini-disc system and Playstation. And they've got a fridge stocked with booze and soft drinks.

There's an extensive video library at the back of the lounge, with action-packed movies like *Terminator 2* and *Die Hard.* Jutting out from the eclectic collection are a couple of videos by other pop acts. *Backstreet Boys Live* and *Take That Live In Berlin* are sitting right there on the top shelf.

'It was interesting to watch those to see what it was like for them. I suppose subconsciously we pick up little tips here and there. You're always learning anyway,' Nicky remarks.

Tonight they're going to sit back and view *The David Beckham Story.* 'The people who made that sent it to us to have a look at it. Maybe they'll do something with us down the line,' Shane reveals.

Their home-from-home on wheels also has a fitted kitchen, with a fully stocked fridge-freezer and a microwave. There are toilets, and a shower that has just enough room to manoeuvre – big Bryan has the most difficulty twisting and turning as he scrubs up after a performance. The upper level also has ten sleeping berths. Like creatures of habit, each Westlifer still occupies the same bunk from their first tour on the coach when they supported Boyzone.

Mark had been quick off the, er, mark way back then. He'd hopped on to the bus when it arrived for that trip and after a quick recce he'd bagged the longest bunk. Shane wanted one on the lower level because he doesn't like heights. Nicky suffers from claustrophobia, so he opted for the berth over Shane.

'There is less head space in the lower berths, whereas the ceiling is much higher on these top ones,' Nicky points out. 'I like it. You do have a certain amount of privacy. It closes off with a curtain and there's a little light inside for reading and you put your mobile phone beside you.'

For safety reasons, the boys sleep with their feet facing towards the driver to prevent head and neck injuries in the event of a crash.

But getting off to sleep in a confined space and on a vehicle that speeding down the motorway can be difficult.

'You hit your head or you bang your legs just as you're about to drop off and suddenly you're wide awake again,' Mark reveals.

Then there's the problem of noisy mates who're not in the mood for sleep when you want to bid goodbye to the day. 'Some nights some lad will have a few drinks and be acting up. It does become, "Oh God, I can't get to sleep." There was one night when Kian was up singing for hours out the sunroof. Everyone of us was going, 'Kian, will you shut up and go to sleep.' Sometimes it's like that old TV series, *The Waltons*, with all the family saying, "Good night Mary Ellen", "Good night John Boy"... "Good night Kian", "Good night Mark".'

There are times when being cooped up with a gang of guys becomes frustrating, due mainly to the lack of privacy. Coach life can be particularly difficult to live with when, like Nicky and Bryan, you're trying to maintain relationships over the phone.

'It's virtually impossible to have a private conversation when we're in transit,' Nicky moans. 'No matter where you are, there are people around. You just learn to live with it, but you can't really have intimate discussions. There's a lot of, "I can't really talk now. Tell you later." Georgina and Kerry understand, though. They've been on the coach. They know what it's like.'

In the autumn of 1999, Westlife were on their luxury sleeper coach rolling along the motorways of Europe with Ronan Keating on board. Ro was then their co-manager and Westlife were the support act to big guns Boyzone, who were doing a month of sold-out shows on the continent.

Shane, Kian, Bryan, Nicky and Mark were staring out the windows like wide-eyed kids on a school outing, afraid of missing something.

'Look! There's a windmill.'

'See that funny wooden house over there!'

'What is growing in that field?'

Ronan sat back, observed their reactions with a wry smile and reflected on his first foray into Europe with Boyzone. It had been one of the best times of his life. Everything was new and exciting to him. Stephen, Keith, Shane and Mikey were also just like the naive Westlife lads back then, enjoying the thrill of being in a pop band, touring in foreign territories and getting their first taste of the big time.

One side of him wanted to be in Westlife now, so that he could savour the first-time thrills all over again. But the clock can't be turned back.

Tonight, as Nicky recalls that time on the road with Ronan and Boyzone, it makes him take stock of just how far they've come in such a short period of time. It didn't seem so long ago that Ronan was his idol and his inspiration. He remembers how, long before Westlife was formed, he approached Ronan in a Dublin club, shook his hand and said, 'You're an absolute legend and a credit to the country,' then walked away. Ronan had gone after him and said, 'You're a nice guy, thanks a lot!' Now, Nicky was getting a chance to make his own name in pop and Ronan was a part of that dream. Fate works in mysterious ways.

'It was amazing to have Ronan Keating on OUR bus then. Here was one of the lead singers of one of the world's famous bands, a guy we looked up to, and he was sleeping in the bunk bed beside us. It was weird back then, but now it would be quite normal because we don't think twice about who's who in the business today.'

Ronan would arrive on the coach with a big rucksack full of CDs and introduce the Westlifers to all kinds of music as they travelled from city to city. He was adopting a really serious approach to his job as co-manager and mentor to these young guns, passing on his knowledge to the next generation of the boy band scene. Nicky has memories of Ro one night telling the boys the life story of the legendary Canadian-born folk singer-songwriter Joni Mitchell and playing some of her songs, including her best-known track, Big Yellow Taxi.

'Ronan was then our co-manager and he spent the time passing on what he'd learned. He told us about all the great times with Boyzone, the breaks they'd got and how they'd party like mad when things were going well. But he also showed us the other side of life in a pop band. He warned us that there were low points when the pressure would become unbearable and grind us down. He told us how he'd cried in his room in Asia in the early days because he was so far away from his family and from familiar surroundings. It got him down big time and it's something we were likely to face as well.

'He was like our big brother, "Look lads, this is what's going to happen and when it does you'll know that you're not losing the plot. It happened to Ronan Keating and many others in the business. It's a normal reaction to the stress and strain."

'We did listen to him as if he was some kind of big guru, even though he's only three years older than us. But Ronan had been there since the age of 16 and we knew that he was telling us hard facts. It was sound advice.'

Westlife are back where it all started on the very same coach that was their 'home' on the Boyzone European tour, but now, in spring 2001, they're a supergroup on the road.

'I can't believe how quickly it has happened for us,' Nicky says today. We've got to this level in two-and-a-half years, whereas it took Boyzone six years to do the same. That's not saying we're better. They carved out the road and we followed from there.'

It's nine o'clock on a Monday morning and the Swedish capital of Stockholm, built on 14 islands and known as The City That Floats On Water, has a blanket of dark cloud hovering overhead. Today it's living up to it's nickname, as the streets are being engulfed by torrential rain. However, it doesn't deter the little army of Westlife fans who are literally camping outside the upmarket Sheraton Hotel. There are several girls tucked into sleeping bags and they've obviously spent the night waiting for their idols. Their perseverance pays off when they finally get to see a bleary eyed Westlife in the flesh as the boys arrive.

While the group, dancers and musicians sleep on coaches here during the European leg of their tour, they book day rooms in city hotels to wash and relax before embarking on local promotion in the lead up to the evening's performance.

Bryan saunters down to a bedroom where the five musicians are chilling out. He's the only person among both coach loads who looks totally refreshed and it's obvious he's brimming with energy. He slides down a bedroom wall and sprawls across the floor. He's cracking jokes and chatting about everything under the sun. There is no stopping him, even though at this moment the weary musicians just want to get more sleep.

As the conversation turns to the Asian tour that will follow on from Europe, Bryan says with a laugh, 'Lads, it's going to be a weird experience for you guys. We couldn't believe the reaction the first time we went out there. The fans are crazy. You'll be able to go out and about, but we'll be stuck in the hotel or the venue most of the time because there would be total chaos if we hit any of the shopping malls. Wait till you see it when we get there. It's mental. You have no idea. Ronan Keating warned us about it before we went out the first time. But it wasn't until we actually experienced it ourselves that we understood what he was talking about.'

Then the Westlife star suddenly pipes up, 'Anyone fancy a McDonald's for breakfast?'

All eyes light up.

'Now that's a good idea,' drummer Niall says.

Suddenly there's a little posse sneaking out the back door of the hotel.

Stockholm is familiar territory to Bryan and the rest of Westlife, as they've recorded their albums here. In fact, the fans regard them as locals by this stage. He knows his way around city like a seasoned tourist guide. Wearing a puff jacket and with beige baseball cap pulled down over his eyes, the towering star looks like an American baseball player as he struts around the side streets in power-walking fashion, leaving the musicians trailing in his wake.

'C'mon lads, keep up,' he teases.

There's a big grin on his face as he pushes open the doors of McDonald's, with his little army in tow.

The staff do a double-take, look at each other and stare back at Bryan. There are sharp intakes of breath as they realise that one of the top young pop performers in the world is standing right there in front of their service counter. In all the time the Backstreet Boys were in town, recording their albums and hit singles at the very same studios where Westlife churn out the hits, they were never spotted in the big M.

'A Big Mac please!' Bryan orders.

Then he asks, 'What do you want, lads?'

As he waits for the order to be served up by an attendant, several other members of the staff cautiously approach him for an autograph.

'Sure, no problem,' Bryan says, signing scraps of paper that are offered to him.

Suddenly there's a scrum around him. Apart from the McDonald's workers, the early morning customers who have arrived and got the shock of their lives to see a Westlifer standing at the counter are now forming an orderly queue for his autograph. This is turning into a one-man Westlife signing session.

The musicians sit back with a smile on their faces and enjoy their food, while Bryan struggles to meet the demand of his public. There had been only a handful of people in the beginning, but news of the Westlifer's presence seems to have been publicised around the city, as people are arriving from all directions.

Bryan looks to the Niall and the boys, showing signs of alarm. This could get out of control. The band stand up to leave and it's Bryan's queue to make his escape. With half a burger in one hand and a bag of chips sticking out of the right hand pocket of his fleece, he takes off down the street at speed with the little posse of musicians trying to catch up.

'That was a bit of fun,' he laughs.

Back at the hotel, there has also been a massive influx of fans since the boys arrived. Staff at the Sheraton are now busy erecting crowd- control barriers to ensure that Westlife have a safe passage when they're leaving later in the afternoon.

Bryan avoids the mayhem by slipping in through the back entrance unnoticed.

Upstairs in stylist Ben's bedroom, Shane is having his hair tweaked and gelled until it stands upright with little wisps jutting out at every angle.

As Ben masterfully whips his crowning glory into shape, Shane is reminiscing about the first time Westlife visited Stockholm. It was one of the most exciting days of his life. Although he'd been on several flights to the UK, the one to Stockholm just before Christmas 1998 was the group's first major trip outside Ireland and Britain. It was this visit to record at the Cheiron 'hit factory' which, in addition to the Backstreet Boys, has also produced big chart smashes for mega-selling Britney Spears, 'N Sync and Five, that Shane realised he was now in the major pop star league. He was jetting off to Europe to record an album, for gawd sake. It didn't get much better than that.

'That was a big day in my life, to go to Europe,' he smiles at the memory of it. 'It was the same for the rest of the lads, we were all jumping around with excitement. Our first "foreign" trip as a band. It was really cool. We had just signed a big record deal and we knew something was going to happen. We didn't know what. We certainly didn't think at that stage that it would be as big as it is today.'

Nicky, who has been relaxing against propped up pillows on the bed, suddenly springs to life.

'Do you remember the first time we were all together on a plane, Shane?' he asks.

Shane nods.

Nicky swigs from a bottle of mineral water and flops back on the pillows.

'I remember it so well. We were going to London to record. Kian and Mark had never been on a plane before. They'd never been outside of Ireland. That was funny, watching their reactions. They wanted the window seats so that they could see Dublin from the sky taking off. 'Look there's Ballymun,' Kian was saying, pointing to the high-rise flats not far from the airport. And then when we landed in London they had their noses pressed against the glass, to see if they could spot Buckingham Palace or Wembley. The five of us were like a bunch of kids. Nobody knew us then. We didn't have security and there was no Anto to mind us or lead us. We'd arrive at the airport and there'd be a driver from the record company waiting patiently with our name on a placard. Nobody gave us a second glance back then. Then on the journey into the city, you'd hear Shane going, "Look at that Porsche!"'

Shane laughs.

There's no stopping Nicky once he's on a roll. The garrulous pop star may be in Stockholm today, but at this moment he's that young kid starting out in Westlife. He crosses his legs, rests his arms behind his head, bouncing his elbows off the headboard of the bed, and laughs out loud.

'Jeez Shane, do you remember the wrestling matches?' he asks.

Shane winces and throws his eyes towards the ceiling.

Nicky giggles. 'We used to stay in a small hotel in Fulham, right beside Chelsea Football Club grounds, and we'd all eventually gather together in one room. We'd start off chatting, but then the horse-play would start. We'd turn the beds up on their side, strip off to the waist and have huge wrestling fights. It would be the Dublin lads against the Sligo lads. Then there'd be Bryan against me and Shane against Bryan or Kian. Bryan was big and strong. Kian was muscular, but he was small. Mark was physically big and me and Shane were little terriers, we'd never give up. Because we had no clothes on top, we'd end up covered in scratches and bruises.'

Nicky turns to Shane again.

'Remember the time you got hurt?'

Ben is touching up Shane's facial features with some light make-up before they set off for media interviews down town. Shane glances in the mirror and nods at Nicky, who is bursting to tell his story.

'Bryan was wrestling Kian, then Shane jumped in and Mark

jumped in. We were all wrestling and then we all broke away. Then Bryan jumped on Shane causing him to twist his back. He screamed with the pain. "I can't believe you did that!" he was shouting at Bryan.

'That reminded me of the days when my school pals would come around and we'd be messin' and Mam would say, "Will you boys stop that, it'll all end in tears." It was a bit like that. Shane sulked for a while, but you couldn't fall out with Bryan. He's a big baby really and he'll have you laughing again in seconds.'

Westlife may not be a band who trash hotel bedrooms in the tradition of rock 'n' roll groups of yesteryear, but they came damn close to earning a bad-boys reputation during those first faltering steps on to the pop-go-round when their harmless fun left a London bedroom looking like a bomb had exploded.

As Nicky tells it, Shane and Bryan had been wrestling each other when they went straight through the door of a fitted wardrobe. There was a huge creaking sound, then the crackling of timber breaking. The two boys had gone crashing through the door, ending up inside with splinters of wood everywhere and metal clothes hangers jangling around their ears. As they pulled themselves clear, Nicky recalls their horror.

'Oh shite, what have we done?'

There was only one sensible thing to do. They did a runner the next morning without a word.

'We never did pay for the damage,' Nicky admits today, with just a hint of guilt.

Anto arrives in with the itinerary for the afternoon and evening.

'It's a busy one lads,' he says, clearly trying to whip them into an action mode. 'As soon as Ben is finished dolling you up, we've got to move fast. The cars are outside. You've got interviews from 4 p.m. with *Aftonbladet*, the biggest daily/evening newspaper; *Expressen*, the second biggest daily/evening; *Okej*, a monthly teen mag and *Frida*, a monthly girl teen mag. Then there's a live interview with Power Hit Radio, there's a meet-and-greet with fans and then we go to the venue where you'll do an on-line chat with fans before the show.'

Outside the Sheraton, the boys run the gauntlet of a hundred fans who are still staging a vigil in the pouring rain. On the short journey to Power FM radio station, where all the interviews are scheduled to take place, Anto shares a car with Kian and Nicky.

He's reminding them that Stockholm is where Westlife picked up their very first fans outside of Ireland when they were recording at Cheiron, a shabby looking one-storey, cabin-style building at the bottom of a block of flats near a motorway.

'The Backstreet Boys had been recording in the same studio the previous week. The girls thought it was the Backstreet guys who were still inside doing the business.

'They were hanging around the studio and as I walked past a window they knocked on it and called me out. I went outside and said, "Hello! Who are you looking for?" They went, "Is Nick Carter there?" I said, "Nick Carter is with the Backstreet Boys."

She said, "Yeah. Is he in there?" I said "No." Then they asked, "Is Howie there?", and they went through all the Backstreet names.

'I said, "There's a new band in there called Westlife," and they went, "Who are they?" So I pulled the guys out and said, "Some girls want to meet you."

'The boys were delighted, of course, it being their first time meeting gorgeous Swedish girls. They were called Mia, Charlie and Andrea.

'Charlie had just shaved off all her hair and her eyebrows, so she looked a bit strange, but she was a great kid. Andrea looked a bit like Madonna and Mia was a real stunner. After that first meeting, the girls began to follow us and they became the first Westlife fans outside of Ireland. Whenever we come to Stockholm to do any kind of shows we always make sure to give them complimentary tickets. They're coming to the show tonight.'

The afternoon interviews have gone well; by this stage there isn't a question the boys haven't encountered before. But some recent stories about the boys have filtered into this territory and they form the core of the questioning. Kian has been asked about the assault he suffered in Sligo on the morning of the Irish shows.

Nicky, meanwhile, has been constantly queried about his wedding plans, following remarks he made in a recent *Hello!* feature. 'Every journalist said to me, 'I hear you are getting married.' So I had to explain that I have no plans to marry at the moment. The question that was asked of me in *Hello!* was, 'Would you like to get married and have children?' And if you ask any one of us that question, we are all going to say 'Yes.' I told *Hello!* that Georgina and myself will eventually get married. But nobody picked up on that amazing word, 'eventually', so I've spent the whole afternoon going from interview to interview saying that hopefully I'll get married and have children...EVENTUALLY.'

The venue for tonight's show is The Globe, a magnificent tiered concert hall that holds an audience of 18,000. Westlife have sold it out. As the car carrying Kian and Nicky reaches The Globe, Nicky bends his head down and peers up into the sky, exclaiming, 'Look, Kian! See the roof! It's like a big igloo stuck on top of the building.'

Kian cranes his neck and huddles down in the back seat. 'Where is it?' he asks.

'There!' Nicky tells him.

Kian stretches forward into the front seat and looks up from the windscreen as the car reaches the backstage entrance.

'Ah, it's too late. You can't see it from here,' Nicky adds.

As all the cars arrive, Westlife are ushered inside for their sound check.

'I didn't think we'd get a sound check today,' Shane says. 'I thought the crew would still be working on the construction of the stage, but they've made great time and it's all ready for us.'

Afterwards, the boys are escorted to a room which is clinically clean and almost bare apart from five lap-tops sitting on a long bench, which has a cluster of chairs. All around the world, fans are waiting patiently to link up with Westlife for a web chat.

To the cynical who doubt that it is actually the stars themselves who are answering the questions, this confirms that, at least in Westlife's case, the fans are getting the real deal. Kian and Mark, in particular, are very fast and efficient on the computer keyboard as they frantically tap out their responses.

While the boys are having their pre-show meal backstage, the venue is already filling up.

Bryan slips out to the side and peeps through a door. All the tiers are filling up with young fans. There's a colourful sea of strobe lighting building up.

'Wow!' he says, 'It's some venue.'

It had seemed massive earlier during the sound check and now with the audience piling in, it looks like a giant ant hill as people are occupying every space, right up to the roof.

Bryan goes backstage and phones Kerry on his mobile. As the others eat in a section that is cordoned off from the trucks parked indoors and has been converted into a make-shift restaurant, Bryan natters away on the phone to his beloved, pacing up and down.

'Ah, you should see this venue, Kerry, it's got loads of tiers and it's gigantic...yeah, it is full, there's about 17,000 out there tonight.'

Showtime finally comes around the roar of the crowd nearly blows the 'igloo' off the roof.

As he struts around the stage with his microphone in hand, Bryan sparks off more wild cheers when he tells the crowd that Westlife are officially 'Swedish.'

'Do you want to know why?'

More ear-splitting cheering.

'Because 90 per cent of our songs are written by Swedish people. You have the best songwriters!'

Hands are in the air, clapping wildly.

'Coast To Coast was, of course, recorded right here in Stockholm.'

Tumultuous applause.

And, as the crowd is finally settling down, Kian adds: 'And we love Swedish women!'

Suddenly The Globe is going mental again. Westlife are setting their European audience on fire.

Instead of going straight back on to the coach after the up-beat performance, Westlife stay behind for an hour to meet some of the Cheiron songwriters who came to watch their songs being performed live during the group's first full stage show.

'You guys learned to dance,' one of them quips, as they troop into the dressing room and are offered bottles of beer.

They may be the hottest songwriting team in the world right now, earning multi-millions from the hits they've given Britney, the Backstreet Boys, 'N Sync and Westlife, but these guys could pass for a bunch of brickies on a building site. Their dress sense is casual and low key and their manner is quiet and understated.

Some have long hair, others tightly cropped. They're the ordinary man on the street. In every sense, they're the backroom boys of pop, shunning the limelight as faceless writers and producers, yet reaping the rich rewards.

They enjoy success without the fame. It's the way they like it.

As Anto eventually rounds up the Westlife boys for the coach trip to Copenhagen, Nicky and Bryan have gone missing.

Toilets are checked. The wardrobe department is scoured. Several little rooms along a corridor are scanned.

Eventually security supremo Paul Higgins tracks them down.

They're out in the venue, helping the road crew to load up stage gear on to the articulated trucks.

'The rest of yez are a lazy shower,' Nicky quips as he dusts down his clothes and trails off to the coach.

Trevor the coach driver, a clean-cut forty-something with a Gary Lineker smile, shakes his head with disgust as he surveys the debris strewn around the front and back lounges of his gigantic motor, after the boys hop off at the next stop in Copenhagen.

'Those guys are so messy,' he sighs.

He's ferried Boyzone, Bon Jovi's crew and Michael Jackson's entourage during his career as a chauffeur to the stars and Trev reveals that, without a shadow of doubt, Westlife are the worst litter louts of the lot.

'Look!,' he points to a half-eaten sandwich that has been cast aside on a seat by the window. Several fast-food containers and empty drinks cartons are piled up on the table and some have spilled on to the floor.

'I don't think they like to get the bin dirty,' the coach master mocks.

A hand-written sign prominently displayed by Trevor on the fridge door reads: 'I'm not your mother. Wash your own dishes.'

It's obviously invisible to the Westlifers.

'Yeah, they don't pay any attention to it,' Trev sighs. 'They look at it, laugh at it and throw the dirty dishes in the sink.'

There has been no major damage on the tour so far, although Kian hasn't won any star ratings by throwing up on the coach the morning after a big party night.

Despite their shortcomings, Trevor has a soft spot for the five lads. 'They're good boys otherwise,' he insists, without a hint of sarcasm.

Their driver and surrogate mother has long since discovered how to put a smile on their faces.

'My main mission, once we take off, is to find a fast-food outlet that serves up southern fried chicken. I have to find a route that passes a Kentucky or such like within half an hour of leaving. Get that and they're sorted.

'Everyone's happy.'

Trevor has the engine ticking over as the final strains of Flying Without Wings are echoing throughout the arena and then five figures in white come sprinting through the darkness and jump on board. Trevor leaves skid marks on the surface of the backstage compound as he powers up the Westlife bus and heads off into the night, jumping ahead of the concert traffic.

The boys are on a high. 'Ninety-five per cent of the shows are really good, so we're always in great form when we come off stage,' Kian reveals.

Westlife are enjoying their life on a coach around Europe. It gives them a proper sense of being on tour as a band.

Sitting in a corner of the coach lounge, testing his skill on the Playstation, Mark has the look of a pop star who is living his dream. He seems happier now than at any other stage in the life of the group. The days when he suffered severe home sickness are behind him. In just two years, he's cut the umbilical chord from the family home and has settled in to a life of non-stop travel.

As Mark muses over his new-found contentment, he acknowledges that the Westlife live tour is a huge part of it.

'I love touring. My personal love in life is performing. That's what I like to do the most. That's what I'm in the bloody thing for. When you're on tour, you're performing every night and I couldn't be more in my element. I look forward to getting on the bus, having a chat, playing with the Playstation, having a drink or whatever we get up to on the tour. When I ask how long the journey is going to be, I'm hoping it's going to be longer. I am going to be devastated when it's all over.'

The 'quiet one' in Westlife is displaying more attitude on this tour, having come through a pre-Christmas personal crisis over his life as a pop star. Mark had become disillusioned with the pop industry's emphasis on style, fashion and image, as well as the media's preoccupation with the personal lives of the stars. He felt the focus should be on the music and the songs.

As a person who clings on to real people and real life, the Westlife personality can barely tolerate the shallow individuals who populate the industry and its environs.

'So much of the industry is completely fake and so many of the people are so false,' he says. 'I joined a pop group to sing and I felt that so much of the time was taken up with talking about what we do, rather than actually doing it. I didn't want to know about hairstyles and clothes anymore.'

Mark never considered dropping out. Instead, he decided to stand up for himself. 'I was the type of guy who went along with things, so as not to rock the boat. But I decided that from that moment on I would learn to say no and take some personal control back into my life. I wasn't going to allow other people to put me under pressure.'

The turnaround in his life also came in January with the rehearsals and the opening of the tour. 'Once we started working on the live show everything made sense again. This is why I joined a group. Not to get a new hairstyle or a new outfit, but to sing. I couldn't be happier.'

Although Mark has a reputation of being the loner of the group, an elusive character who slips away into his own world when he's not on duty with Westlife, he has totally embraced the big touring 'family' that also includes the musicians and crew. It takes him back to his childhood in Sligo and his participation in the local musicals, like *West Side Story* and *Grease*, that nurtured his love of the stage and of performing in public.

'This tour has reminded me so much of those days in Sligo,' Mark reveals. 'A big room of people get together and rehearse for whatever musical and everyone is aiming for the same end result – a massive show that is going to be the talk of the town. It's been the same with this Coast To Coast tour because it's not just us five lads touring around.

'It's a big gang and I love that feeling.'

It's the early hours of the morning on the coach in Germany after a long, hard day. Westlife are tired and edgy. There had been an early morning call, a full-on schedule that left no down-time for proper breaks or a decent meal and everyone had wanted a piece of them. They'd smiled through all the stress and strain in public, now it's time to let off steam behind closed doors in the sanctuary of their own coach and among their own little group. They're winding down over a few bottles of beer. Someone suggests watching the video tape of a TV appearance they'd done for the promotion of Uptown Girl in Germany. It seems like a good idea. Bryan sets it up and they all sit back to view their performance.

As he watches, Nicky becomes agitated. The boys are singing live and he's furious that his microphone isn't turned up properly, so his voice isn't coming through. He blames Anto, who says that it wasn't his responsibility. Nicky insists that Anto should have checked it. 'This is TV in Germany in front of ten million people,' he shouts across at the tour manager. As the argument continues, it gets more heated. In the midst of it, Nicky fires a bottle of mineral water at Anto, but it misses, hits Ben and the water spills all over him.

'Oh shit!' Nicky gasps.

It brings the argument to an abrupt end.

Full of remorse, Nicky goes over to Ben and gives him a hug.'

'Sorry pal.'

Nicky and Anto don't speak for the rest of the night.

Anto explains later that in the early days he used to do all the sound mixing for Westlife. 'I'd go into the TV studio and say, "He sings this line, he sings this line" and I'd oversee the mixing of the sound. But now I don't do that because I have a lot more to do. But Nicky obviously thought that it was me who was in the sound booth that day and it was me who didn't turn up his mic.'

The next morning Nicky breaks the ice and apologises to Anto.

'I was really out of order last night. I'm not usually like that, but I got really annoyed because my mic wasn't up. I realise now that you weren't in the sound booth because Ben actually told me where you were, that you were upstairs checking your e-mails in an office.'

Anto is magnanimous. 'OK, shit happens. Let's carry on and get on with it.'

Nicky later insists that the incident is completely out of character for him.

'I am the least likely out of all the guys to lose his temper quickly. We actually counted one day all the incidents that we've had where people really had a go at each other, not physically, but head to head as in screaming at each other or Anto or Paul or Fran. And I was the one who had the least rows. It was like Bryan and Anto, Shane and Anto, Bryan and Shane and so on. Mark was even above me. I was chuffed, although my incident with Anto was probably the worst out of them all. But the worst temper of all is Kian's. Jaysus, Kian would cut you in half if he wakes up in the morning and gets out the wrong side of the bed. And as quiet as Mark is, if he loses his temper he would go through you for a short cut.'

Nicky then recalls how a prank Anto pulled on Kian blew up into a major public row in an airport.

'We were on an early flight after a late night and we were all knackered. Kian had just forked out £5,000 for a lovely Rolex watch two days earlier. Everyone of us fell asleep as soon as the plane took off, except for Anto. And while Kian slept, he slipped the Rolex off his wrist. None of us knew a thing about it. We arrived at London Heathrow, got off the plane and as we were half-way down the terminal, Kian suddenly started shouting, "Me watch! Me watch is gone!" He was in a real panic, a bloody five grand watch, no wonder.

'I grabbed him and said, 'Where was the last time you remember having it?' He remembered taking it off in the hotel before we left and didn't recall putting it back on. He was nearly crying and wanted to go back and check the plane.

We kept asking him questions, trying to jog his memory, but he was in a state and all he could say was, "I don't know! I don't know!"

'At this stage, Anto held up his arm and was tapping his wrist going, "Look at the time! Look at the time! We have to go." At first none of us took any notice. Anto was shoving the watch in our faces, "Look at the time. What time is it?"

Suddenly Kian copped his Rolex on Anto's wrist and you could see the anger just rising up in his face. Anto ran and Kian took after him. Kian was kicking him around the airport. It was serious kicking, he wasn't messing. We were trying to calm him down. "Kian, don't be kicking him!" It was turning into a big scene and attracting a lot of attention. There were all these people from England getting off an aeroplane and seeing a member of Westlife kicking the shite out of some fella. God knows what they thought of us. Eventually, Kian calmed down, but he warned Anto, "Don't you ever do that to me again." Personally I would have been just so relieved to get me watch back that fighting with Anto would have been the last thing on my mind.'

There are only five shows on this short hop across the continent as Westlife give their European fans the Coast To Coast live experience.

'We're actually losing money on this part of the tour. We would need to do a lot more concerts to cover the costs of transport and staging,' Nicky reveals. 'But we wanted to show

European fans what we can do. Once the word spreads about this show – and the reviews are great – it'll be much bigger the next time around.'

It's time to pack again.

'God, how I hate this bit,' Nicky sighs.

'Living out of a suitcase is just a complete nightmare. You have to constantly keep track of clothes that are clean and clothes that have to go to a laundry somewhere along the line. Even deciding on what to bring with you on trip is a nightmare, particularly if we're going to be visiting all kinds of climates on the same tour.

'It could be the depths of winter in one place and heat waves in another. Last year we were in Italy doing promotion, then we had to fly on the Los Angeles to shoot a video and fly back to Sweden to record. We went from wearing vests to thermal underwear and overcoats.'

Anto arrives back from foyer of Westlife's hotel in Germany, struggling under a mountain of cards, cuddly toys and other assorted gifts that have been handed in by fans.

'Ah, lads, this is getting ridiculous,' he sighs, dropping the enormous haul on to a kingsize bed in Bryan's room.

Westlife could fill an articulated truck with all the teddy bears, dolls, books, clothing and jewellery they've received from girls on this trip.

'I'll arrange for them to be passed on to a local charity,' Paul Higgins suggests helpfully.

'Good idea.'

Bryan is sitting in a corner of the room reading a letter he's picked out of the collection.

'We normally donate cuddly toys and other suitable items to charity or children's hospitals and homes,' Anto reveals.

'Some of the personal gifts the boys get are absolutely incredible and weeks of painstaking work goes into the making of them. They get a lot of amazing artwork, paintings and drawings of their images. There are crocheted and knitted jumpers with their faces on them.

'One of the nicest items I've seen came from a Japanese fan, who was obviously an expert in origami, the art of folding paper. It was a glass bottle about two foot long and six inches high and it contained about 5,000 love hearts. There was a message for one of the boys in each individual love heart. It must have taken a year to do.'

Bryan looks up from the letter he's reading and prompts Anto. 'Remember the goldfish!'

Anto laughs. 'That was one of the strangest gifts that was given to the boys by a fan, while we were in Toronto. Bryan being Bryan he wanted to take it home. I said, "No way, Bryan. I have enough trouble looking after the five of you without having to take care of a fish as well."

But Bryan was adamant and he turned up in the airport with it. We were going to be flying from Toronto to New York and then on to Dublin. I couldn't believe he still wanted to take the fish with him. Then I got a brain wave. I convinced Bryan that the fish would explode due to the pressure on the plane. He fell for it...hook, line and sinker.

'So if the Canadian fan is reading this, a custom's officer in Toronto is now the proud owner of a Westlife goldfish!'

CHAPTER 5

Fan mania in the Far East and a birthday surprise

Man-mountain Paul Higgins is fleeing through Jakarta's main airport like a jet, dragging Nicky along with him for dear life. There's a strange, wailing sound echoing throughout the interior of the building, which is as hot as a baker's oven.

Like a swarm of bees, hundreds of manic young Indonesian girls are swooping down on the two frantic men who're running like scared animals, trying desperately to reach a safe haven inside the departure gates.

Suddenly another wall of fans appear in front of Paul and Nicky.

'Jaysus, where did they come from?' Nicky pants.

Somewhere along the journey, the team of local security guarding Westlife has gone missing and now it's just Paul and Nicky on their own, being engulfed by their frenzied followers.

It's like a terrifying scene from the Alfred Hitchcock horror movie *The Birds*, as they're swamped by the mob.

'Keep going! Keep going!,' Paul is urging his Westlife charge. He sweeps his arm in front of him in a bid to move one of the fans out of their path; but the local teenage girl is so slightly built that Paul's gentle push lifts her off her feet and suddenly she's airborne, flying three to four feet off the ground.

'Oh shit!' Nicky gasps, as he rushes forward with two arms outstretched to break her fall. Like a major sporting moment in re-play, the girl seems to descend in slow motion. Nicky demonstrates the skill that almost earned him a place as a Leeds United goalkeeper when he catches the nymph in his outstretched arms, stopping her from bouncing off the ground.

Still moving, he slips her gently from his grasp.

There's no time for sorrys or thank yous at this moment as Paul steers Nicky to a gate. It's the wrong one and because of the chaos exploding behind the two guys, there's no persuading the police to allow them through.

'This can't be happening,' Nicky pants.

The pair are back in the middle of the mayhem, with their sweat-soaked clothes clinging to their bodies as they race to another gate. Finally, they gain access, and Nicky collapses in a heap on the floor. Paul is bent double, hands resting on his knees as he recovers his breath. He's got to do this all over again with the other boys.

They, meanwhile, are circling the airport in a bus, as the fans had pounced on it and violently rocked it from side to side, almost bursting in the windows, when they first parked outside the International Departures.

As Paul prepares to go into the war zone again, two policemen arrive in to the lounge to discuss how to deal with the hysteria.

Paul informs them that the rest of his group are on a bus somewhere in the vicinity of the airport, waiting for the signal to stop and unload the human cargo. The police, fearful of the pandemonium developing into a riot, get security clearance for the Westlife bus to drive straight on to the runway and up to the waiting plane. Anto, who is holding all the passports, tickets and visas, checks them through.

Finally, everyone makes it on board in one piece and Paul, shattered and dishevelled, falls back into his seat on the aircraft and announces, 'I'm wrecked! Look at me, I've just lost a stone in weight.'

Welcome to South-East Asia.

The fan-mania in this part of the world is so intense that it actually makes Westlife question just how far they're willing to push the fame game. They discuss among themselves what it must be like for Madonna, Michael Jackson and Tom Cruise, having to constantly cope with this extreme attention whenever they venture out into public places.

'I could never live like this full-time,' Kian admits. 'If it was like this back home in Ireland or in the UK it would be a total nightmare. God love Michael Jackson, we only taste it when we come over here. He's had this since he was about seven. You can see why he's a freak, totally understand it. He has never experienced or seen real life because he can't go out and do normal things. It would be impossible and unsafe for him, like it is for us over here.'

Westlife had been prepared for the onslaught of fans on this trip to Indonesia. They had been steeling themselves for the battle, like fully-primed soldiers going into action. While it is still a shock to the system, today's experience is nothing compared to the terror they felt the first time they visited Jakarta, Indonesia's capital city.

'We were like lambs to the slaughter because we didn't know that anyone knew us over here,' Kian reveals. 'We arrived, got our trolleys and waited by the conveyor belt to collect our bags. The next thing we know, there are 300 girls marching in on top of us. They walked from the arrivals right in to the baggage claim, which is something you wouldn't be allowed to do back home.

'All of a sudden they're dragging us out. We had no security with us and were totally unprepared for the situation. We were scared shitless as we beat our way out into the main arrivals area. But it was worse out there. It was like walking into a football stadium, there were thousands and thousands of girls and they all ran at us.

'Mark was by my side and the two of us put our heads down and prayed as we pushed our way through the screaming girls. I remember looking up and seeing a bus, hoping it was ours, and pushing like hell to get to it. The trolleys were gone, the bags were all over the place, but all I cared about at that moment was getting on that bus.

'We made it, with the fans clamouring on board as well and Anto kicking them off. Then we took off, leaving the bags behind. I'll never forget the sensation of my heart pounding against my chest. It was so, so scary.

'After that, each of us had two security guys full-time for the rest of the visit. They rarely get bands here and when they do, they go bananas.'

This time around is no different. Westlife are a phenomenon in this region, where their Coast To Coast album is expected to hit official sales of one-and-a-half million. In fact, they're the biggest selling act in Indonesia of all time – even bigger than Shane's childhood idol Michael Jackson.

At least 3,000 fans have invaded the airport as the boys arrive in from the previous day's concert in Bangkok. But a more bizarre sight is the couple of hundred airport staff who've surrounded the Westlife plane as they're disembarking. It's like the turnout for a head of state. And they all want photographs and autographs.

Westlife are then literally spirited out through a side route by airport officials to avoid the chaos, leaving the rest of the crew to face the disappointed throng.

Suddenly the star emphasis shifts to Westlife's musicians as they're pestered to sign autographs and pose for photographs.

'I'm not a star,' drummer Niall is protesting, as a group of girls implore him to scribble his name on their sheets of paper.

'You look like them,' one of the girls responds.

On the journey to the hotel, the cars pass a family who are bombing along through a cloud of dust on a rickety old motorbike. The man is steering the bike by the side of the road in searing heat and smog, while the woman cradles a baby between them.

Kian points out the family scene that is a reality check for Westlife about the quality of their own lives, despite the stress that goes with their bizarre job.

'Apart from the whole crazy fan aspect, the main memory I took away from here the first time was the poverty. I'd never seen anything like it in my life.

'Of course there are people living in terrible conditions back in Ireland and there are homeless on the streets, but it seemed like a whole nation over here was just barely surviving. I've been told that the majority of people earn five dollars a month.'

It's a shocking statistic that has stirred Westlife's social conscience.

'We were actually talking about doing a free concert in Indonesia, but it's probably a crazy idea because it would be so difficult to control. How would they cope with 600,000 people turning up when running a normal show is a nightmare in terms of security?' Nicky says.

But Westlife have refused to play the corporate game in this part of the world by supporting the campaign of multi-nationals to stamp out the illegal trade in counterfeit goods like CDs. 'Piracy is huge over here and you can see why, people can't afford the official stuff,' Kian says. 'We've been told that for every one of our albums sold, four bootlegs are bought on the black market, which means we don't get a penny from them. A million people can afford to buy our official album and the other four million get a bootleg. But that's not wrong to us because it means that people who can't afford it will get to enjoy it.

'We've been asked to support the "Say No To Piracy" campaign in this territory, but we've refused. Bryan wrote, 'Thanks for all your support – Piracy, Your Decision.' You can't expect poor people to buy your album in a shop at full price, when they can get a pirate version on the street for three pounds. They're struggling to put clothes on their back and food in their mouth, never mind bloody playing concerts to 20,000 people a night, making millions of pounds and driving nice cars.'

Westlife's Jakarta hotel is already under siege, with fans crawling all over the front of the building and taking up residence in the lobby. Nondescript cars are used to ferry the boys into an underground carpark and from there the bemused quintet and various members of their entourage are led through the hotel kitchen and along a series of passage ways to a staff lift.

Once Westlife reach the floor that has been totally reserved for them, it becomes their 'prison wing', with a team of ten local security guys guarding them around the clock. They are literally trapped here, as their appearance in any of the public areas of

'The police and security were literally boxing the heads off each other. That's just life in this part of the world. It's a little bit different to home.'

'Yeah, just a bit,' Nicky laughs.

The first Westlife show here in Jakarta has been a major triumph, sending the audience home smiling. But with fan frenzy at a peak in the city, the morning flight to Malaysia is going to be nightmare.

Anto, Paul and Fran consult the local promoter about the security arrangements. A series of phone calls follow and he comes back with a solution.

'The army is being drafted in to get us out of the airport,' Anto informs the boys.

'Cool!'

Westlife are buzzing from the show, but they're confined to their hotel...AGAIN!

'Anyone for cards?' Nicky suggests.

The following day, Friday, May 25, I'm in Kuala Lumpur ahead of the group and just in time to hear the DJ on a local breakfast radio show telling residents of the Malaysian capital that, 'Westlife will be arriving at Kuala Lumpur airport at 1.20 this afternoon. The popular boy band will be here at 1.20.'

There's now no chance of the Westlife entourage quietly slipping into the city.

The palatial five-star Sunway Lagoon hotel, where the boys are staying on this visit, is already crawling with fans at 9 a.m.

Security inside the awe-inspiring building has cordoned off a section of the foyer where the quiet and polite young girls, equipped with cameras and autograph books, are corralled, so as not to disrupt the normal business of the day. With their 'quiet and polite' demeanour likely to blow up into total hysteria if Westlife come through the massive doors, the flimsy security tape seems totally inadequate.

But, unknown to the fans, other plans are in place to ensure the boys gain access with the minimum of fuss.

By the afternoon, the scene is heating up at Kuala Lumpur's spanking new, glass-fronted, space-age airport where hundreds of fans have gathered to greet their idols when they touch down. A massive team of local security in yellow waistcoats is on stand-by to guide the guys safely to their cars.

There's a deafening scream from the hordes of girls, who now look like they're having a spasm attack as they frantically jump up and down when they spot Bryan coming through arrivals. Just behind him are Mark, Kian, Shane and Nicky with Paul, Fran and Anto. Camera flashes are going off and a human wall suddenly surges forward.

The Westlife party is being tossed around in the mêlée, like ships in a storm. Bryan has his baseball cap whipped off, Nicky's hair is being tugged and he hangs on to minder Fran's belt as they make a drive towards the exit. Kian can't see where he's going as he's caught up in the craziness, so he's hanging on to Paul's belt and being tugged along at speed. Shane is in serious danger of losing his shades, not to mention lumps of flesh, as he ploughs through the heaving mass. The yellow-jacketed crew are sweating in the intense heat as they struggle to get the boys into their vehicles. Then they're off.

'That wasn't too bad,' Nicky remarks in all seriousness, while he runs his fingers through his hair as the car roars out of the airport.

Kian, who looks totally shattered, is talking about his bizarre experience earlier that morning in Jakarta when two hotel staff confronted him in his bed, hounding him for his autograph.

'Anto knocked on my door at eight o'clock to pick up my bags. I got up, opened the door and went back to bed, still half asleep. As Anto walked in, two staff walked in behind him and when he left he didn't pay any attention to them. Suddenly they're at my bedside, a 50-year-old man and a 30-year-old man, going, "Excuse me, sir, sign!, sign!" I said, "I'm trying to sleep. I'll sign when I get up." They were insisting, 'Sign now! Sign now!' So I got up our of my bed and I said, "Get out of my room! What the fuck is this? Give me a life! I'm in bed trying to sleep."

'There I was in my boxer shorts literally shoving them out the door. I don't mind signing autographs for people, but not when I'm being hassled in my bed first thing in the morning when I'm knackered and trying to sleep.'

At the Sunway Lagoon Hotel, about 20 minutes from the commercial centre of Kuala Lumpur, there is disappointment for the fans who've been anxiously awaiting the boys arrival since early morning, jumping up and rushing towards the doors whenever any group of Westerners arrived in cars. There are communal sighs as they spot the yellow jackets running across the forecourt of the building. They quickly move en masse to the front doors, but realise almost immediately that their efforts are in vain. The Westlife cars are already in the underground carpark and the boys are making their way past the kitchens and up the rear elevator to their suites.

'I've never seen the lobby of a hotel in these parts,' Nicky observes as he arrives on the executive floor of the hotel. 'But I can tell you what all the kitchens look like!'

Mark is in a panic. He has a huge collection of CDs with him on the trip and the container bag has gone missing amid the confusion at the airport.

'Can you check it out and see if it's among the rest of the luggage somewhere. There's £700's worth of CDs in it,' he tells Anto, as he paces around by the lift, waiting to receive the key card to his room.

Twenty minutes later all the luggage arrives up to the floor. There's a big blue case sitting in the middle of various sized suitcases and hold-alls.

'That's it!' Mark sighs. 'I thought it was in the boot of the car I was travelling in.'

'Nah, it got dumped in with all the other stuff on the band's bus,' Anto informs him.

Mark shakes his head and smiles. The loss of his CD collection would have been devastating. The eclectic mix of music from old-school soul to standards from musicals and latter-day R&B

and pop help the Westlifer to survive life in a hotel room on tour. While the other members of the group will often congregate in one room to pass the time between work commitments, it's rare to find Mark among the gang.

It's not that he's anti-social; he just seems to get lost in his own world. Being located in a room next to Mark gives an insight into his lifestyle. He sings for hours alone behind closed doors.

'Oh I never stop singing,' Mark later admits. 'I've brought a stereo with me on this tour and I always sing along to the music. It's just me exploring my voice, singing along with all these different artists. There is so much music out there to listen to. I'm always taking it in and being influenced by it. It's what I live for, it's what I really love. I'll watch TV as well, or phone family and friends and send e-mails. There are times when I love going out to a club, but I like staying in more than going out.'

Bryan calls his pals in to show off his suite, which has rooms the size of small concert halls.

'Look at this!' he says, swinging his arm around the enormous expanse of the front lounge. 'You could have a great party here.'

Westlife have less than an hour to unpack, freshen up and get some styling touches from Ben. Then the rest of the afternoon is a hectic schedule of promotion. There are several TV interviews, including one with the local MTV. And a large group of print media is waiting patiently in a meeting room on another floor for a Westlife press conference.

As Nicky hangs around for Ben to finish tweaking Shane's hair, he's musing over soccer ace David Beckham's new Mohican hairstyle, which is pictured in a newspaper that has come in from the UK. 'I can't believe he's done that!' Nicky says with a frown.

Bryan is sifting through a copy of *Smash Hits*. 'Jessica Simpson is back on the scene, lads,' he announces with a nod in the direction of Shane and Kian. 'She's split up with her fella.'

Shane holds up a stunning photo of Britney Spears in *Top Of The Pops* magazine. She's sporting figure-hugging pants with a belly top. 'Be honest, lads,' Shane says, pointing to the pic. 'Is there anyone here in this room who wouldn't shag Britney?'

Silence.

'Everyone wants to shag Britney,' he laughs.

'She is seriously gorgeous, though,' Kian chips in, as if it needed to be stated.

The interviews that afternoon are no less raucous. At the press conference someone asks who has the longest body part in Westlife?

'Oh that'd be Bryan,' Nicky quips. 'He's sometimes mistaken for a man with three legs!'

Later, Mya from pop TV show *Wavelength* wants to know what's been happening in Westlife 'since I last saw you?'

'Bryan's going to be a daddy,' Nicky informs her.

'I'm having a little bábó (baby),' Bryan says, then adds with a cheeky smile, 'Yeah, I hit the target.'

'Will you have more children?' Mya asks.

'He was lucky enough to score once. He'd never do it twice,' Nicky mocks.

By late evening, with all the promotion wrapped up, the boys are ravenous and a massive order goes out for Kentucky Fried Chicken, which is now their favourite food on the tour in these foreign parts.

Everyone veers towards Nicky's suite as they wait for the nosh to arrive. Some sit around a dining table, others flop back into couches, and soon the conversation develops into a friendly argument about the merits of living in Sligo and Dublin.

Shane is adamant that his home town of Sligo has everything he needs in life.

'It's only got one taxi,' Bryan mocks.

'It doesn't have McDonald's,' Nicky claims.

'It does, too,' Shane responds.

'But there's so much more to do in Dublin,' Nicky point out.

'I don't care, I have everything I want in Sligo, it's a really cool place to live. When I go home there, I'm treated like a normal person. I'm just "young Filan" to the locals. The people in Sligo are not star-struck and I like that. It's nice to go home and have that kind of normality. I'm no better or no more important there than anyone else in the town. That's why I want to live in Sligo and not in Dublin, because I think you get more attention in Dublin.'

Shane talks about the new family home he's having constructed for his parents in the countryside, a mile-and-a-half outside Sligo town.

'They were always going to build it, now I can do it for them, which is kind of cool,' he says. 'They're now at an age where they can retire. It'll be a big house with lots of rooms for family get-togethers.'

At present, the Filans live over their modest town-centre café, The Carlton, where Westlife fans regularly drop in hoping to catch a glimpse of their idol Shane. 'Our family was the first to sell burgers and chips in Sligo,' he says proudly.

Then Shane reveals another ambition. The pop star wants to take over The Carlton and become one of the leading business lights of his home town.

'I plan to buy it off my family and, obviously, they'll still be involved in the running of it when I'm away. But it's something I plan to put my money into as an investment and maybe in a few years time I'll turn it into a bar or a fancy restaurant or a nightclub. Then I'll be able to say, "I own that!"'

Tonight the boys can chill out – although they can't go out – here in Kuala Lumpur. They've got a free night. Down in the bar their musicians are knocking back beers while a local group entertains hotel guests doing cover versions of hits of the day. In fact, the Malaysian singer does a mean Robbie Williams on Angels.

It's just past midnight when Mark, Kian, Bryan and Nicky join the group, having learned that the coast is clear as all the fans have vacated the lobby. By this stage the hotel band has also packed up and left. But there's a piano on the stage and the boys are in the mood for a sing-song.

Suddenly there's a big party vibe as Mark, Kian and Bryan gather around the piano. They spend the next couple of hours singing tunes, covering a cross-section of gems from The Beatles to the Rolling Stones, while band member Tim Maple tickles the ivories.

It's getting on for 3 a.m. by the time everyone decides to call it a night, or rather a morning. Despite being exhausted when he'd arrived in Kuala Lumpur yesterday afternoon, Kian seems to have been recharged and he's beaming as he heads off to bed.

At noon later that day the sun is shining in this paradise resort with its swaying palms, luxurious green spaces and rich expanses of shimmering grass, developed on what was once a desolate tin-mining area. The nearby water park, which boasts the world's largest surfing wave pool, is alive to the sound of happy families having fun.

Two familiar figures in dark shades and colourful shorts are lounging by the pool, topping up their tans and sipping cool drinks. It's band members Richie Taylor and Niall Power.

This is a luxury that is out of bounds for the Westlife stars, who are forced, for security reasons, to remain on their hotel floor until it's time to go to the concert venue later in the evening. Neither is there time for them to go exploring Malaysia, taking in the islands of Penang and Langkawi. Both have fine sandy beaches and warm seas, while the latter famous for its snorkelling and diving.

It's 4 p.m. as Anto wanders around the hotel corridors, knocking on bedroom doors and announcing, 'The cars are leaving for the venue in ten minutes.'

Kian's door opens and he wanders out into the corridor, wearing a T-shirt and shorts. He looks half-dazed, like he's just come out of a coma.

'I can't believe I've slept right through till now. I only woke up when Anto came banging on my door,' he says with surprise, staring down at the inviting pool below, where the last of the sun worshippers are still soaking up the final rays.

The lack of proper sleep in the previous days had finally caught up with him, Kian admits, as he waits for the rest of the troops to gather for their trek through kitchens and out to their cars.

'I was shattered yesterday. I couldn't move. So I really needed that sleep. We never get enough, to be honest.

'You go to bed and two hours later you're called for a flight. Then you fall asleep on the plane, but it still leaves you tired and dehydrated. It's horrible. You catch a couple of hours here and a couple of hours there, but it's no good. You have to get several hours of undisturbed sleep before your mind is totally rested.

'Any doctor will tell you that.

'OK, last night I could have gone to bed early because we didn't have anything on, but it was also enjoyable to do what we did as a gang of friends.

'It was enjoyable to go down to the bar, have a laugh and a singing session around the piano.

'I only had one beer, but it turned out to be a great night. To not do that occasionally takes the fun out of touring.

'When I look back at yesterday, I don't think about the press conference or the interviews we did early on, I think about the craic we had last night.

'You do need to have those nights to survive a tour like this. The fact that we are constantly moving and haven't been home for so long makes it hard to cope with. I have been finding it a real struggle some days. It's a long way from home. Nothing is familiar to us here. Apart from all the other people on the tour, we don't get to see our families and friends.

'I've been trying to get through to Irish mobiles for the last two days to link up with people, but I'm not having any success. But there's no point in complaining. I'll just have to get on with it.'

Nicky's jaw drops as the Westlife cars arrive at the venue for the afternoon sound check. He jumps out and sprints into the centre of the gigantic arena, spinning around to take in the huge expanse of the place.

'Ah no! If I'd realised we were playing here I'd have organised a football match for the afternoon,' he wails.

This is a state-of-the-art, 100,000 seater soccer stadium. It could be Wembley Stadium.

Nicky roars to the other Westlifers who are trailing behind. 'Lads! Can we get a ball somewhere? We gotta get a game going!'

A member of the crew, who've been busy setting up the stage and equipment, kicks a ball into the centre of the field.

Nicky's eyes light up with delight.

'Lads! C'mon, let's have a kick around,' he roars.

Bryan, Shane and Kian respond immediately and race on to

the pitch. Mark clearly isn't a sports fanatic as he disappears backstage.

'I'm back where it all started,' Nicky shouts as he takes up position in goal.

The temperature is in the nineties and humidity around 80 per cent as the four Westlife lads strut their stuff at speed à la Beckham and Keane, watched by a team of bemused local security guys.

'Let's have a penalty shoot-out,' Nicky adds as tour manager Anto pleads with them to do their sound check.

'I'm looking after a bunch of kids here,' Anto sighs.

The tour manager has another worry. He's just discovered that the barriers at the front of the stage are not adequately secured and are likely to collapse under a minimum of pressure.

'I'm warned the promoter that unless it's sorted there'll be no show tonight,' he reveals.

The layout for tonight's Westlife show has been designed to cater for 20,000 fans. The stage, which looks like the head of a pin as it's dwarfed by the giant arena, sits out on an area of the field, with rows of white plastic chairs in front of it. The rest of the audience will be accommodated in the stand. Behind the stage, several small white marquees have been erected as dressing rooms for the band and musicians.

In the half-hour build up to the show, Westlife slip into their white suits and psyche themselves up for the performance by singing Backstreet Boys' songs.

Anto's assistant Maria sticks her head through the flap of the tent and advises the boys to rub on the mosquito repellent. 'You'll be eaten alive on stage if you don't,' she warns. From inside the tent, the boys can hear Anto's voice blasting around the arena.

'What's going on?' Shane asks.

Security chief Paul Higgins sticks his head in and announces that there's a problem. Fans have spilled out of the stand and invaded the area in front of the stage. This is a seated show for safety reasons, but they're standing and surging forward.

With the A1 tragedy in Jakarta hanging over the tour, Anto is refusing to start the show until everyone is seated.

'Westlife can't begin the performance until everyone is sitting down. Please return to your seats,' Anto pleads.

Out in the crowd, Paul and Fran are desperately trying to spur the local security into action. But chaos reigns. The army of men in yellow jackets can't seem to grasp what is required in this situation.

Like knights in shining armour, Paul and Fran make regular plunges into the pack of fans, scooping up two girls each at a time and carrying them under their arms to the safety of open ground before guiding them towards the seats in the stand.

Back in the tent, Westlife are still amusing themselves with their Backstreet Boys performance, aping the dance moves of the American boy band.

Stunning Miss Malaysia World, who is tonight's Uptown Girl, is also waiting patiently in the wings.

Forty minutes after the concert is due to begin, Anto is finally happy that order has been restored and it's now safe for the performance to begin.

'Westlife thank you for your co-operation,' he tells the audience.

Minutes later, as Westlife burst on stage like lions cut loose from a cage, it's instantly obvious that the delay hasn't diminished either the excitement or the enthusiasm of the crowd. They're screaming with delight at every swagger, every wave and every wink of an eye.

Even the mosquitoes appear to be enjoying it.

After the opening songs, the boys are clearly struggling to cope with the heat of the night. The temperature is in the nineties. Anto runs on to the stage with bottles of ice-cold water to revive them. They're towelling the heavy beads of sweat from their faces. Changing costumes is a nightmare. The sweat-soaked clothing is embedded in their skin and the inner layers are almost impossible to remove. Worse still, they're now changing into jackets and jeans.

'Oh man, I'm going to die out there,' Nicky pants, as he peels off his top and bottoms and slips into his jeans, T-shirt and leather jacket.

'We should have made this one the stools tour,' Kian jokes.

Mark can't believe his eyes when he cops a banner being held aloft by a group of Malaysian girls near the front of the stage. It's in the Irish language and reads: 'Lá breithe faoi shonas Mark!' (Happy birthday, Mark!). He's set to turn 21 on Monday.

Apart from a minor panic when a small group of fans slip through the security cordon and is found wandering around backstage, the show goes without a hitch.

'The feckin' heat on that stage, man, was unbelievable!' Kian pants as his car leaves the venue at speed, led by police outriders. He shakes his head and the perspiration rains down on the back seat.

'Starting songs with big leather jackets and woolly trousers practically was a killer in that furnace. And for Uptown Girl we had boiler suits, with jeans and T-shirts underneath...I nearly died out there.'

Kian is surprised that the audience sat down for the entire show. 'They normally don't sit down. They normally squash each other up against the front barrier and you have 50 security pulling two people out every second. But Anto warned us going on stage, 'If I say to you, 'Stop the show!', you have to stop.' He felt watching the audience before we went on stage that he was going to have to do that. But they were well behaved in the end.'

Kian, Nicky and Shane seem oblivious to the six police outriders who are swiftly clearing a path for the Westlife car as it speeds back to the hotel.

The last time around, a helicopter had to fly in to airlift Westlife from a public appearance in Malaysia.

'It's not like home. The fans don't leave when an event is finished here. They hang around and in that situation it was the only way out,' Kian reveals.

Shane is recalling the thrill he experienced the first time the group had a police escort when Westlife was formed.

'We were doing the 2FM *Beat On The Street* (Irish radio roadshow) in Dublin. I remember thinking, this is so cool having the garda stop the traffic for us. Now we just accept it as part of the job.

'We have to get a police escort most places we go nowadays. I never think, "This is unbelievable. I'm so famous." It's just something that has to be done for safety reasons.

'You don't know what can happen in foreign territories. They want to make sure that you are safe when you're here and that you'll come back again.'

Back at the hotel there's a dinner in honour of Westlife, organised by the sponsors of the tour. But the boys have a 5-a.m. alarm call for a flight to Singapore where there's a concert tomorrow night, so they've decided against partying.

Despite the pressure and stress of coping with the problems at tonight's concert, Anto has to ensure that everyone has their bags packed and all the hotel bills have been paid, so that there are no delays in the morning.

Shane and Kian are hanging out in Nicky's room and Anto is imploring them to organise their packing for the morning flight to Singapore.

'If you pack the bags now, I'll take them and you won't have to worry about them in the morning. Otherwise, I'll be knocking on your door at 4.30 a.m.'

He's getting no reaction. Anto shakes his head with frustration and wanders off.

Bryan has left the door of his suite on the latch and Anto drops in to check that he's packing.

'Bryan, have you got your bags packed?'

'Anto, get out of my room I'm on the phone,' he shouts from the bedroom.

'The crap I have to put up with at times,' Anto says with a frown. 'Trying to get them to pack their clothes into their bags to be collected can take two-and-a-half hours. Bryan is definitely the worst because he walks into a room, drops his suitcase and that's where he works from. Anyone coming in or out of the room has to step over this clothes explosion. You can imagine somebody putting a bomb in his bag and the explosion sending clothes all over the place. That's what it looks like.

'There was one incident in a hotel in London when Kerry was staying with Bryan. She dropped her bag right inside the door next to Bryan's. You couldn't see the carpet of the hotel room because it was covered in clothes.

'The housekeeper came to me and said, "We can't clean the room because we're not supposed to move personal affects, we are supposed to work around personal affects."

She refused to do the room because it was in such a heap.

'When it comes to packing, Shane is the best. Nicky is very good. Mark will ask me, 'When do you want the bags?' If I said I wanted them outside his door at 2 minutes, 45 seconds past midnight, he will have his bags out at 2 minutes, 45 seconds. He is very precise, Mark. Very precise. Kian can go either way. Sometimes he's on the ball, sometimes he's not on it. If he is full of sleep he can't function at all. Then we have a row. But we're usually OK after a while.'

At this stage, tour fatigue is beginning to reveal cracks in various sectors of the Westlife camp. There have been a series of blow-ups among individuals. People are tired from early mornings and late nights, drained from air travel and stressed out from the daily grind of staging a live show.

Anto admits that in his personal role as tour manager he has to soak up a lot of hassle to make sure that everything runs smoothly.

'I try not to flap, or get annoyed or get stressed out about things, but sometimes it's impossible not to react. Paul and myself had a serious argument on the tour. I disagreed with the way he handled an incident at an airport. But as head of security he thought it was the right decision. We were both tired and both dealing with 200 fans trying to maul the boys and it ended in a seriously heated row between the pair of us. We didn't speak for a week. I actually cried when I realised that I'd lost the respect and friendship we'd had. But then we made up and gave each other a hug. It's not worth losing a three-year friendship over a stupid, silly argument.'

When the Westlife boys let off steam it's normally Anto, Paul and Fran who feel the force of it on tour. 'We're the first in the firing line, the first to take the impact of their anger when they're upset over something because we're the one who runs their lives. We're the ones who pull them out of bed in the middle of the night to catch a plane, when all they want to do is sleep. They shout at me. They tell me what I am and what I'm not.

'I have to take it on the chin. It's not my job to be abused, but it's my job to get them out of bed. If it means them giving me a bit of a hard time then that's what the job is.

'But their anger doesn't last very long. They quickly realise, "Hold on, I'm being an asshole, this guy is only trying to get me out of bed so that I make it to the plane on time to do the next concert." '

Anto returns to his own room, completes his own packing and zips up the suitcases. Then he checks that he has everyone's passports and tickets before heading off on his rounds again to give the boys a final baggage call.

'Sometimes I love the job and love what I do. Sometimes I absolutely hate it because they're being a bit awkward and arsey. One individual might be grumpy on a particular day and it makes life harder for everybody else. It rolls on to the next person, then he gets grumpy and it turns into a horrible day.

'Sometimes they can be quite demanding and very rude, probably because they think they can get away with it, and I suppose they do in a way. But generally they're well behaved and good fun. With Bryan, it's better to caress him instead of fight him. Within two or three minutes he's fine. He will call out and say, 'Fair play to you!'

Most days are trouble-free and out of seven days, two will be fantastic. I suppose that's the same with most people's lives.'

Manilla airport is under siege.

The news of Westlife's arrival in the capital of the Philippines has leaked out and hundreds of fans have invaded the shabby building. Security chief Paul Higgins looks worried as he returns after checking out the situation. Excited young girls are like an army of ants covering arrivals area.

'There's no way we're going to be able to get through there in one piece,' he warns.

Paul consults the local airport security and arrangements are made to slip the boys through another exit, thus avoiding immigration.

There are some fans in pursuit as Westlife race to their cars, with the local boys in yellow waistcoats on hand to help out.

Two members of the local paparazzi are in a fury over being denied pictures of the boys by Paul, who is frantically trying to get the group out of the danger zone.

Suddenly the photographers turn on the Westlife security man.

'You are in our country now!' they shout at him.

'I don't care whose country it is, I have a job to do,' Paul pants, as his head swivels around the area to make sure that Kian, Shane, Mark, Nicky and Bryan are all on board.

'OK, we're outta here!' Paul roars.

But as he turns to get into the car, the irate photographers are kicking and punching him from behind. Paul is boiling with anger as he slams the door of the car, but otherwise he's unhurt.

After a successful concert in Singapore, one of the wealthiest countries in South-East Asia and so clean and environmentally conscious that they fine you for dropping chewing gum on the street, Manila is a shocking contrast.

Bare-footed Filipino children are shuffling along filthy thoroughfares. The roads are choked up from bumper-to-bumper traffic and some people are using masks to protect themselves against the fumes, dust and grime. It's 90 degrees in the shade and 20 locals are crammed into the famous Filipino 'jeepney' taxis that have room for a dozen and are painted every colour of the rainbow, as well as being decked out in tassels, badges and horns. They seem have everything except air-conditioning. Along the streets there are huts that families call 'home' and rows of run-down buildings.

These are the stark images of Manila's economy and the lifestyle of the majority of its ten million inhabitants that Westlife capture as they're whisked to their hotel from the airport. It's the only slice of Filipino life they'll get to see on the trip. The Manila Galleria Suites hotel is coming into view and it's surrounded by fans. Westlife are going back to 'prison' on the floor of a 30-storey hotel, with a team of Filipino security guys set to guard them around the clock.

Their route to their rooms are all too familiar as well – it's past the kitchens and up the back elevators.

Shortly after they arrive, the lift from the lobby starts making regular stops at their floor. Girls are riding the elevator and stopping off at the Westlife suites hoping to catch a glimpse of one of their idols, or slip past security to their rooms. Someone jokes that Uptown Girl has now been replaced by 'up-and-down girls.' But the ever present and vigilant local security team ensure that the young Filipinas don't leave the lift.

Two hours of the afternoon are spent in interviews with local TV networks, including MTV, then Westlife are free until the show tomorrow night. But they've nowhere to go and they're becoming frustrated with the regime.

'Shane just told me that he wants to go home,' Anto reveals. 'I asked why and he said, 'I'm sick of this crack. I can't go out of the hotel. All we can eat is hotel food. If we go somewhere to a restaurant we have to go with ten or 15 security people. It's a movement of six or seven vehicles. I just want a normal life.'

But Anto isn't overly concerned by Shane's outburst. He's heard it all before on these foreign trips. 'Right now he's feeling a little fed up with it all and he just wants to go home to Sligo and ride his horses. But he'll come through it.

'They're caught up in the bubble out here, completely isolated from real life and sometimes they can lose touch with reality. With all the travelling and the different time zones it can freak them out.

'Nicky rang me in the middle of the night the other night and went, "Anto, where am I? Where am I?" I said, "You're in Bangkok." And he was like, "OK. What time is it?" It was four o'clock in the morning. He said, "Oh, sorry, Anto, I was just a bit freaked out. I didn't know where I was".

'He just needed reassurance that he was still on planet earth. That happened to him before when we were on a foreign tour and he actually rang Georgina back in Ireland to ask where he was. I think we were in Warsaw in Poland at the time.

'You lose track of the days and the weeks. They run into each other. I phoned my partner, Elizabeth, back home recently. It was 8.30 in the morning Irish time and I said, "You're late for work." She said, "I'm not going to work today." It was Saturday. The only date you know is the date you're going home and how far away it is.

'All of us on the tour put our private lives on hold to do this kind of work. We have chosen to be travellers of the world and our partners accept that this is how we make our living. But it's not easy for anyone to cope with.'

Shane has cooled down and is putting this crazy lifestyle into perspective. 'Four years ago I was back in Ireland, doing marketing and accountancy in a college in Limerick. I was looking out the window and dreaming of being in a band. It was the time that the Backstreet Boys had Backstreet's Back on release and Boyzone were in the charts with Isn't It A Wonder. I wanted to be THEM. I wanted to be doing what I'm doing now. I didn't want to be an accountant, I wanted to sing.

'I didn't imagine that four years later I'd be in Manila, complaining about being trapped in a hotel by hundreds of fans, having sold 12 million albums in two years. It's not that I'm ungrateful. I enjoy coming over here and doing concerts. It's staying on the hotel floor that I don't like. I want to be able to see places, but I can't.'

Shane's annoyance had been sparked off by the fact that Paul and Fran had returned from an expedition to the massive shopping mall attached to the hotel and had been raving about the variety and the bargain prices.

'They were talking about the Diesel shop and the big jewellery shop and I wanted to go down and have a look to see if there was anything nice,' Shane reveals. 'But they said I couldn't possibly go down because there were hundreds of fans. That's kind of annoying when you can't have a bit of a life over here. We just come in, do a gig and fly out.'

The Westlifer says that, being confined to his room, he can now understand why some of the big rock 'n' roll bands of the past had a reputation for wrecking hotel rooms and throwing TV sets out the window.

'I haven't reached that stage yet,' Shane laughs. 'But I can see why those bands freaked out and did that, particularly as those rock bands used to go on tours that lasted 12 to 18 months. We've done four months now and it's one of the biggest tours for a pop band and it is hard. One of the things that upsets me when I'm over here is that I can't sleep properly. I'm the best sleeper in the world normally, but when I go to different time zones I don't sleep and I'm tired all the time.

'One of the hardest parts is being away from your family and friends, and I'm so far away from Sligo. If I'm not in Sligo I'm not as happy as when I'm in Sligo. I'm so far away here and it's a different culture and different food. It's coming towards the end of the tour and we're all getting edgy at this stage. We just want to see our families and stuff.'

Bryan has just been on the phone to Kerry and is feeling the strain of being torn apart from her for so long, particularly as her pregnancy is rapidly progressing and he's missing out on some very special moments.

'I've missed Kerry's four to six months stage where she really gets bigger,' he sighs. 'Every time I ring her she's going (adopts English accent) "Bryan, I'm getting fat." And I go. "You're not getting fat, Kerry. You're having a baby!" She's at the point where women really start showing and I'm not there to see all those stages. When I went away she just had a little bump. I won't recognise her when I go home.

'Probably because it's our first child I wanted to be a part of every single second of it. I'm on the phone to Kerry 24 hours a day, but it's not the same. When Kerry tells me that she can feel the baby kicking, I want to be there to feel it. I want to be able to look back and say, "Yeah, I remember that time and I remember that bit." The thing is, I won't. I'll have missed out on so much.'

The only consolation is that Kerry is enjoying a good pregnancy after an initial fright in the first three months when the devastated couple thought they were going to lose the baby. Bryan shudders at the memory of that incident and reveals how

Nicky, Shane, Kian and Mark rallied round to support him through the nightmare.

'I was in London when I got the news that Kerry had started bleeding and was rushed to hospital with a suspected threatened miscarriage. It was the worst moment of my life.

'The boys knew was I was going through and they were with me through it all. I'll never forget that night how supportive they were. They were like a proper family that night and that really brought them close to my heart.

'It was such a relief when I finally got the word that it wasn't a miscarriage and that Kerry was going to be fine. Looking back on it now, I think this pregnancy has made us all grow up a little bit.'

Bryan doesn't know how he's going to cope when the baby comes along and he has to go off on foreign tours. It's not something he wants to think about right now. He'll cross that bridge when he comes to it.

Through all the tough times and the separations from loved ones, Bryan admits he has never considered leaving Westlife.

'No, never,' he says emphatically.

'There's absolutely no way I'd do that, particularly now that I'm starting a family and have a partner. I want to make sure that we are all going to be financially comfortable. I want Westlife to go on for a long, long time.'

Down in his suite, Nicky is relaxing on his kingsize bed, furiously tapping a remote control as he flicks through the channels. There are 27 channels, but nothing worth watching. He stops at a news report which reveals that more than 20 tourists have been kidnapped from one of the 7,000 diverse islands here in the Philippines.

He shakes his head from side to side. Turning off the telly, he says, 'This is a mad part of the world.'

Nicky is clearly edgy. He paces around the large suite in his stockinged feet. He stops by the window, hands clasped behind his back, and stares out at the view. It's an uninspiring sprawl of rooftops and there's smoggy haze over the city.

Nicky sighs. He too wants to go shopping to pass the time. But the Westlife star knows it's an impossible dream.

'Paul and Fran told me the that there's a great Diesel store in the shopping mall downstairs. They got loads of T-shirts. I said, "I have to go check it out, Paul." He said, "You're not going near downstairs. There are fans all over the place. You'd be slaughtered." So I'm stuck here.'

He goes back to surfing the telly channels. Twenty seven channels...and nothing on!

'Oh, well, at least there's the party later on,' Nicky adds, his eyes suddenly brightening up again.

It's 9 p.m. and Anto is tapping on the door of Mark's suite.

'Mark!'

'Yeah!' he calls out.

'I need you to come and sign some work permits.'

Mark opens the door. Inside, his room is tidy with just a few clues that someone has been living here. There are two massive piles of CDs neatly stacked on the floor near a stereo player. Seven or eight of the albums are loosely spread across the top of the bed cover. A lap-top is open and sitting on a glass table near a massive window which looks out on to the shimmering lights of the city. A half-empty bottle of mineral water is beside it, the top having rolled on to the carpet.

'Can you come now, Mark?' Anto asks.

'Do I have to go right this minute?'

'I'd like to get it out of the way, Mark.'

'OK, let me close down the documents on the lap-top and put it away.'

A couple of minutes later, Mark, still dressed in the grey T-shirt, navy sweatshirt, blue tracksuit bottoms and flip-flops he'd been wearing during his down-time in the hotel, follows Anto to the lift. Anto is making small talk and Mark doesn't notice him pressing the button for the penthouse suite.

It's a short stroll to the door of the penthouse. Mark has been here earlier in the day for the TV interviews, but every hotel corridor looks the same. As the tour manager pushes open the door of the suite, the interior is in darkness.

Suddenly there's a roar of 'SURPRISE!' The lights go up. Mark looks dazed. His mind has shut down and he's frozen on the spot.

'HAPPY BIRTHDAY!' the Westlife entourage roar in unison.

The penny drops and a shocked smile breaks across his face.

Shane, Kian, Bryan and Nicky lead the queue to give him a hug. Mark is still shaking his head with bewilderment.

Finally, he says, 'I need a drink.'

Wardrobe mistress Fiona, production assistant Maria, Filipino record company supremo Di and BMG's international promotions executive Heather Metcalfe are congratulating themselves in a corner of the room. They had been the leaders of a perfectly orchestrated conspiracy to give Mark a night to remember. All their plotting and planning had now worked a treat. It was clear from the silly expression on his face that the Westlife birthday boy had been totally unaware of the behind-the-scenes preparations for his party. He's standing there in his tracksuit bottoms, with his mouth swinging open as he tries to make sense of what's happening. Poor sod. But it's a moment that everyone was determined to celebrate on this trip.

After all, a twenty-first birthday is a landmark in everyone's life and should be greeted with great fanfare.

In his wildest dreams, Mark could never have imagined that on the day he turned 21 the occasion would be celebrated with a full-on party in the PHILIPPINES of all places.

Sipping his vodka and soda, Mark's eyes wander around the suite which is festooned with balloons and ribbons hanging from the ceiling. There's a proper bar with a crew of hotel staff busy dispensing drinks to the small contingent of revellers. Standing on ceremony adjacent to the booze counter are three chefs in their white regalia and hats, hovering over a large array of exotic dishes displayed in hot silver trays. There's a piano in another corner and a karaoke machine sitting on the floor.

Fiona, Heather and Maria have installed all the essential ingredients for a good knees-up. Now it's up to everyone present to create the party vibe.

Bryan, who tonight is the group's Sporty Spice in his white Adidas jacket, navy bottoms and trainers, topped off with a beige baseball cap, has obviously been nominated as Master of Ceremonies. He picks up a mic and calls for order. Then he summons Mark out to the centre of the floor.

'He'll kill everyone for doing this because he doesn't like surprises,' Bryan announces.

Handing him a small wrapped gift on behalf of the lads in Westlife, he says in a Cockney accent, 'Mark, you're a top geezer. It couldn't happen to a nicer bloke. Happy birthday from all of us.'

Then he adds, 'The drinks are on Mark!'

At this stage, a member of the hotel staff is lighting the candles on the specially prepared cake, which bears the inscription, 'Happy Birthday Marky!'

The boys gather round as Mark steps up to blow them out, then everyone joins in the singing of 'Happy birthday, dear Mark...'

But the party's only starting.

With Bryan in control of the karaoke, no-one is going to escape doing a turn in the spotlight. And Bryan selects the songs.

The professionals kick off the evening's singing entertainment. First up it's the Westlife boys struggling with classic tracks from yesteryear, which Bryan decides might be a good laugh to test them on. He knows Kian is a rocker at heart, so he gives him the Christmas carol, Away In A Manger, sparking off a burst of laughter around the room. Shane, Nicky and Mark have a go, as does Bryan.

Then the backing musicians keep the show swinging. Stage fright has gripped other members of the crew and they lurk in the shadows for fear of being hauled up to perform.

Two hours later and with people full of the joys of whatever they've been imbibing, there's a mad scramble for the mic as everyone thinks they're a pop star.

Nicky is sitting on the ledge of a window, chatting with Mark about his early days on the karaoke circuit in Dublin. 'Mark, this takes me back. It really does. Me and me Da doing the pubs and parties with our karaoke show. "Father and Son" we called ourselves. I didn't realise it at the time, but I was learning how to perform in public and it was building my confidence.'

In the middle of the hooley there's a break for 'Judge McMahon's Court.' The 'kangaroo court' has been introduced to the Westlife world tour, so that misdemeanours and differences that have surfaced during a particular day can be aired and sorted in front of the 'Judge'. This shadowy figure, sporting a white hotel towel over his head, has a day job as the jovial technical wizard behind Westlife's spectacular lighting effects.

Tonight he adopts a more stern persona for the official proceedings where a member of the crew, who shall be referred to as Mr X, is up on a charge of leaving the hotel that morning without clearing his bill.

At this point Nicky escorts in the 'prisoner', who is handcuffed and has his head covered with a red table mat.

As Bryan calls the court to order, the 'Judge' bellows, 'You are hereby charged with leaving your hotel without paying your incidentals, thereby expecting Westlife to do so.'

The defendant, wearing a garish shirt and denim jeans, is on his knees and remains silent.

'How do you plead?' the Judge demands.

There's still silence from the defendant.

'I was your lawyer until I discovered that I had to pay your bill,' Nicky adds.

The Judge is growing frustrated.

'How do you plead to being a little bollicks?' he demands to gales of laughter from the onlookers.

'Silence in the court!' the Judge snaps.

'Guilty,' the defendant meekly admits.

'Alright, we'll let you off this time.'

There's a round of applause as the defendant slinks away.

Then it's back to the music and Nicky displays his skill on the piano, impressing the party set with his interpretation of The Beatles song, Let It Be. Suddenly guitars are appearing and the Westlife band take over for a live show.

Mark is singing. People are being handcuffed to tables and chairs. Someone is capturing the celebrations on video. This is going to be a night that Mark will remember for the rest of his life. If he doesn't, at least he'll have a video to jog his memory.

It's 2 a.m. as the party begins to wind down. Someone discovers that there's a karaoke bar still in full swing on one of the lower levels of the hotel. It's safe to go down as there are no fans around at this stage. As Mark, Kian and Shane arrive, the DJ lines up Westlife songs and the dozen lucky Filipinas who have been on a night out with their boyfriends, go wild with excitement, bursting into applause and screams, as the boys duly oblige on the vocals.

Mark can't stop smiling.

It's the perfect end to a top night in his life.

The next morning security chief Paul gets a call from the birthday boy.

'Have you any idea who has the key to the handcuffs?' Mark enquires.

'No, why?' Paul responds.

'I've just woken up in my bed with handcuffs on!'

'I won't ask,' Paul laughs.

'Honestly, I have no idea how they got there,' Mark insists.

'OK, I believe you. Thousands wouldn't. I'll go find the key,' Paul giggles.

In the Westlife dressing room after the sound check the following afternoon, Mark admits he was mortified when he realised that he'd been set up for a party the previous night.

'My first thought was, 'Look at the cut of me!', because I was wearing track suit bottoms. I swear to God I didn't expect it at all. Because everything is so chaotic as we're on the move all the time to different countries, I didn't expect something so organised. I had thought that maybe we'd go to the bar for a few drinks, but nothing more.

'When Anto came knocking on my door I was just finishing going through all the e-mails from home. Instead of clogging up the phone lines, all my relations sent me e-mails to wish me a happy birthday. So I had been trawling through those.

'I didn't think anything of having to go and sign work permits as it's normal for Anto to knock on my door and ask me to do that. Most of the countries we go to we have to get work permits because we're actually working there and doing something that is creating an income.

'Even when I was going into the room and the lights were off I thought nothing of it. I'm used to weird things going on in Asia. When the light came on and I saw the balloons and everybody going, "Surprise!", I was still kind of half not copping on to what was happening. When I realised what was going on I was just in shock. I went silent. I didn't know whether I was supposed to make a speech or mingle or what. I ended up saying, "I need a drink."

'I think, basically, they picked the right thing to do for me. I don't think I would have liked a big, mad, glitzy, glamorous twenty-first bash you normally see. That's exactly what I wanted to do. There were a lot of personal touches to it. Fiona did the interior decor. She knows that green is my favourite colour, so all the balloons were green. She also knows that I like plain hamburgers, so the caterers had those for me.

'I think the karaoke came from me saying to the crew one day that we should have a bit of a get together so night and get a sing-song going. I love those kind of nights as they're something I used to enjoy in my early years when I was doing musicals in Sligo. It was unfortunate that my family and friends couldn't be there, but I was still amongst friends with the lads and the musicians and crew.

'And it was lovely to be the cause of everybody getting together.'

There are a couple of hours to kill before the show, but Westlife are confined to the indoor arena. Kian is in the dressing room making juice with an extractor, using a variety of exotic fruits that have been supplied for refreshments.

Nicky doesn't like the look of the food on the menu tonight.

'I guess it KFC (Kentucky Fried Chicken) again, guys. Can we get an order in?' he says.

Paul checks it out and returns with the news that, 'There's a McDonald's. Who wants McDonald's?'

'I'm only eating to survive on this trip,' Nicky says. 'I love Asian food back home. I love Chinese, and obviously this is the real deal over here. But you hear so many stories of the water not being purified and I worry about the hygiene and that puts me off eating the local grub. That's why I eat so much McDonald's and KFC. But obviously it's not that bad because all the people here are still alive.

'It's not a healthy lifestyle. I get spots. You put on weight. You lose weight. It's actually not as bad on this tour as when we're doing promotion, travelling from city to city doing interviews. We're not a group who get up in time to eat breakfast. So it's up and straight into an interview. You might get up at 11, go straight to the TV studios, get made up and then do the interview. That might take three hours.

'Then it's straight to the airport and by this stage you're starving and cranky and rowing with Anto. We'd say, "Anto are we going to eat?" And he'd say, "Yeah, yeah, when we get to the airport." When you get to the airport there's no guarantee that you're going to get food. There might be a thousand fans at the airport and we're whizzed through. Anto is under pressure because he has to check us in, so feeding us is the last thing on his mind. By the time you get to your next destination it could be one o'clock in the morning and you still haven't had a proper meal. You are crying out for a Mars bar at this stage. We've had many days like that and it's one of the downsides.'

Today in Manila Nicky admits that he has one major fantasy. In fact, it's been the same fantasy that has occupied his thoughts for the last few weeks.

'I just can't wait to get home and visit my Nana; her Sunday dinners are amazing. My favourite is turkey with stuffing, cabbage, mushy peas and roast potatoes. And it's the way she cooks them. If I got the exact same food somewhere else it wouldn't taste the same. Nana has that special touch and her own secret ingredients.

'Then there's my Mam's fry-ups. They're unbelievable. You look at the plate and it's a work of art with puddings and sausages, rashers, eggs and other little trimmings. I have such a craving for all of that at the moment. It's like the cravings women get when they're pregnant. That's me at the moment.

'It's funny how nothing compares to the food your mother made or Nana made. Like, we can eat out in the best restaurants in the world, but give me Sunday lunch at Nana's or my Mam's fry-up or her home-made sandwiches and there's no contest.

'When we were doing the Dublin shows, I was driving home along the Clontarf Road one of the nights and I was really hungry. As I was passing some of the "chippers" I thought about stopping and getting a burger and chips. I was still in my white stage clothes, because I'd dashed from the stage to the car. But I decided that I didn't want greasy food anyway. When I arrived home there was a fantastic surprise waiting for me. Mam had made my favourite sandwiches, which have egg, lettuce, onion, tomato and mayonnaise. I devoured them.

'The next night as the show was winding down and we were flying over the heads of the audience in The Point, all I was thinking about was my Mam's sandwiches. I was waving down at the audience, but my mind was on the sandwiches. I think I probably made an even faster dash to the car that night and the journey home seemed to take forever as I looked forward to relaxing with another plate of those delicious sandwiches. I walked in and Mam was sitting watching the telly. "Where are the sandwiches, Mam?" I asked with a smile. They weren't on the table covered in tinfoil as I'd expected.

"Sandwiches?"

'I knew by the look on her face that I was in for a big disappointment. "I just thought you might have made them again," I said, trying not to sound too distraught, even though I was devastated. I might have just performed in front of 9,000 fans, but the sandwiches were going to be the highlight of my night. "If I'd realised, I would have prepared them for you, Nicky," Mam said.

'I'd obviously laid on the guilt trip, though, because half-an-hour later the sandwiches arrived when I came down to the sitting room after a shower. I've often asked for them at eleven o'clock on the night before I go away with Westlife and she'd say, "No way." But she always give in.'

Bryan and Paul are having an argument over who has piled on the most weight during the tour.

The Westlifer initiated the argument by taunting the security chief.

'If you get any bigger, Paul, we'll have to get an extra seat on the plane for you.'

'With those wings you could fly the plane,' Paul retorts, tugging Bryan's waistline.

'It's all that deep fried chicken you guys eat,' Fran says.

'What's all this "you guys" thing. You eat them as well,' Kian pipes up.

'Yeah, well, I work out.'

Former fitness instructor Fran flexes his muscles.

'The damage you're doing on the inside is a lot worse than the physical damage. Your cholesterol level must be sky high.'

Nicky looks concerned.

'Right, I'm not putting my body through this anymore. Even if I have to eat vegetables three times a week, rather than burgers and chips every day, sometimes twice and three times a day. OK, lads, are we all agreed. A health kick from now on?'

'What about the McDonald's?' Bryan asks.

'OK, after the McDonald's,' Nicky concedes.

'Yeah, right!' Kian quips. 'I've heard it all before.'

After scoffing the McDonald's, Westlife sit around, rubbing their tummies and chatting about one of their favourite topics...CARS.

With money in the bank and boys loving their toys, several of the Westlifers have their hearts set on new motors.

It's an hour before stage time in Manila and Nicky is on the phone to a contact in Dublin getting the price on his dream machine, a Ferrari 355.

Kian rings his mum in Sligo and asks her for the phone number of Porsche dealer in Dublin. She'll call him back.

'I'm not sure whether I should get a price on a Porsche because I know I'll buy it,' he turns and says to Shane. 'I already have one car (a BMW). It would be stupid having two.'

The contact in Dublin comes back to Nicky with a price on the Ferrari. He won't have change out of £99,000.

'I don't think I could justify the money,' he sighs.

With a baby on the way, Bryan is now in the market place for a Range Rover. 'They're really safe machines,' he points out.

Paul, the security chief, has a friend in Dublin who's selling one that's practically new and in mint condition. He gives him a call and Bryan chats on the line.

'Yeah, I think I'm going to buy that,' he says to Paul at the end of the conversation.

Mark sits in a corner peeling oranges and looking on bemused by all the fuss over motors. He's the only member of Westlife who doesn't have a set of snazzy wheels to match the image of a millionaire pop star. Neither is he contemplating building a mansion or investing in property. Outside of the demands of life in the super league of pop with Westlife, Mark is hell-bent on keeping things simple.

'Number one, I don't have that much interest in buying a house or even a car,' he says.

'I don't see the point in buying them just because I have the money. I'll buy a house when I fall in love with the idea. It's just not important to me right now. I want to have a normal kind of lifestyle. I think the reason why the average person is the average person is because that's the best way to go through life. I don't want to lose the fact that I'm a 21- year old. Not every 21-year old has a house, a car and can afford to go on holiday to a nice place without thinking about it too much. I don't want to have an abnormal lifestyle because if you have an abnormal lifestyle in this world you are looked upon as abnormal and I prefer to fit in and not make too much fuss over anything. I probably sound like an awful miser.'

It's not that Mark hasn't had pleasure from the massive amounts of money he's earned through the success of Westlife. In fact, one of his biggest thrills was seeing the look on his Dad's face when he surprised him with a present of a Jeep.

Oliver Feehily, who sells and installs conservatories for a living, had made the long trek from Sligo to collect Mark from Dublin airport after a promotional trip abroad with Westlife.

'I arranged with my mum that they'd drive up to Dublin on the pretext of collecting me from the airport,' Mark reveals.

'On the way home I asked him to do a detour into Lucan (on the outskirts of Dublin), saying I had to collect something from a mate on the way. I was directing him down different roads and because he wasn't familiar with the area it was a lot of hassle for him, so he was actually getting a bit annoyed. I led him into the garage and told him I'd be back in a minute.

'A few seconds later I drove around the corner in this shiny black Jeep. Just like me at the surprise birthday, it took him a few seconds to realise what was going on.

'He was thrilled and that gave me a lot of satisfaction, to be able to do that for my Dad. It was quite practical for him as he uses it for his job. It's half-way between a van and a car, so he can use it to bring his equipment in the back and he's also a salesman, so it looks good for that job as well.'

As he slips into his white suit for the show, Nicky is still preoccupied with his dilemma over the Ferrari.

'I really don't think I can justify it,' he sighs.

This leg of the journey had started in Israel and taken Westlife on to South Africa, South-East Asia, Japan and back to Europe.

There were moments when the shock of the local culture or the devastation caused by internal wars jolted them out of their own privileged world.

Sitting on the balcony of his hotel in Tel Aviv, staring out at the opposite block of apartments, Mark observes how it looks like a building that's in the process of construction. There are still gaping holes to be filled in.

But on closer inspection he realises that this is a residential structure that has suffered the horror and ravages of war. The exterior has been ripped open by missiles and now he can see the sad remnants of what was once a family home.

A table with eating utensils strewn across it sits in the centre of one of the rooms. He imagines how little children once happily scoffed their food there as they noisily chatted and argued like normal youngsters, with the happy scene watched over by loving parents.

He fears to dwell on the terrible fate that has befallen the people who once called that room their home. Were they killed when the shells ripped through the walls?

It's at this poignant moment that Mark realises he's in a war-torn region.

There were, of course, the jeeps with armed personnel carrying massive weapons, the terrifying M16s and sawn-off shotguns, who escorted them from the airport and to the venue here and in Beirut.

Then there are the massive team of security, 15 guys all pistols and constantly hovering around Westlife whenever they leave their hotel rooms. There is the bomb squad who check their vehicles and do sweeps at the venues whenever they're on the move. And, although he hasn't heard any shelling, bombing or blasts of gunfire, he knows that there are incidents at this very moment somewhere close by.

Yet, bizarrely, in the midst of such conflict and devastation, normal life is going on all around. Westlife are playing a concert here before 20,000 local fans. The three-hour show will also feature performances from Five and Atomic Kitten and they've arranged to go partying afterwards.

Although slightly apprehensive, Mark wasn't scared or overly concerned about his personal safety as the Westlife tour headed into this region.

'We've been here before doing promotion and I was probably a bit more scared on that visit because I didn't know what to expect. But, other than the security, it was no different to any other foreign promotion. This time around we knew that there was a war going on. My first thoughts were, will there be bombs flying everywhere and machine guns going off? But I didn't really expect to be caught up in anything like that at the concerts. There is a part of me that doesn't care about the fact that there's a war on. I'm not thinking, "I can't wait to get out of here because I might be shot at or bombed." I don't know whether that's the brave side of me or it's the fact that I think nothing is going to happen to me here.'

Mark had also sheltered his parents from the worry of his visit to the war zones by deliberately playing down his tour of this region. 'I didn't make them aware that I was going into an area of war. I didn't say anything to my Mum about the fact that there is a lot of trouble here. That's simply because I knew deep inside that there was no need to worry.

'But if I told them there would be a reason for them to worry. Mothers being mothers and fathers being fathers they worry, so I didn't say to them that there was trouble around.'

Today, the military helicopters flying to and fro across the sky like giant bugs alert Kian to the other side of life in this territory.

'It doesn't bother me,' he shrugs.

'I don't go around thinking something is going to happen. It's like, every time I go for a drive in a car, I don't think I'm going to crash.

'You can't think like that. You put your trust in the people who have organised the event here and we have all this armed security around us, so it's OK.'

After the trouble-free concert, Mark is in an elated state. It's as if he'd been subconsciously expecting disaster to strike. It had felt strange staging a big showbiz event in the middle of a war zone, whether he wanted to admit it or not. But now he can see the justification for it as far as Westlife are concerned.

'It was such a nice feeling for me to be on stage and to see all the kids smiling,' he says earnestly.

'Personally that's rewarding that we can actually make them smile through the troubles. I know myself, if I'm feeling down, a certain song will cheer me up. Hopefully for the hour-and-a-half that we were out there we made them forget about whatever trouble they have to deal with in their lives.

Who knows, maybe we even gave them some hope for the future, if a pop group can do that?'

With Westlife and Five sharing the same hotel in Tel Aviv, the after-show celebrations turn into a boozy session.

Bryan is showing off a new tattoo he'd had etched on the base of his back by an Israeli tattooist earlier in the day. The adornment features five naked women making the peace sign, with Kerry's name etched above them.

'Kerry's going to love it,' he insists. 'She's got Winnie The Pooh tattooed on her bum.'

Despite media reports of bad blood between the two groups, they're like blood brothers tonight as they laugh and joke together. With copious amounts of drink being consumed, the banter gets more silly and laddish with every passing minute.

Kian, Shane, Mark, J, Richie and Abs all end up in Nicky's room where they're still partying at eleven o'clock the next morning.

Kian is disappointed.

Hanging on to the bar of a Jeep as it bounces along through the South African bush in the blazing heat of the morning sun, there are no lions to be observed in their natural habitat.

On the journey here, Kian had been anticipating the thrill of a safari and watching wild animals roam around in the wilderness, as he had seen so many times on TV wildlife programmes.

Westlife's tight schedule only allows time for a morning outing and the African guides on the trip have warned that it's too hot for the animals to come out. Being sensible beasts, they're sheltering in the shade somewhere in the undergrowth.

Kian's face fell when he heard this. He so wanted to see some of the more interesting species right there in the flesh.

But just in case of any surprises, one of the guides is sitting up front, armed with a gun.

There were some compensations. Over in the distance were elephants and zebras.

Kian's face brightens up when he sees about 50 monkeys trailing after each other.

'That's quite cute,' he says, pointing them out.

But what he really, really wanted was to confront the King of the Jungle.

Sadly, no lions today.

It's Westlife's first time in Africa, even though they've already been in the charts and sold 300,000 albums in this fascinating land. On this tour, the sold-out signs have gone up for their concerts in Capetown, Sun City and Johannesburg.

Fan-mania is at a peak. The hotel has been surrounded by girls and, at the opening concert in Capetown, the sizzling sun hasn't stopped the fans queuing all day long outside the venue. It's an amazing sight as the trail of young people stretches for a kilometre. Local promoters haven't seen such a fanatical reaction since Michael Jackson's last concert in the territory.

It's a two-hour drive from their concert in Sun City to their next show in Johannesburg, a journey along miles of open terrain. On the way out of the city there are families trying to eke out a living by selling souvenir ornaments at the roadside. Adults and little children are strolling barefoot through the dust tracks as Westlife pass by in a convoy of six Mercedes cars.

'What must those people be thinking,' Nicky remarks to no one in particular, as if suddenly overcome by a sense of guilt that he enjoys such good fortune.

During the trip, Nicky rings Georgina back home in Ireland on his mobile phone. The Westlife star is describing the scenes from the car and the contrasts between the dirt-poor shanty towns and the high-rise buildings and palatial homes that he's seen arriving by plane.

'You really are seeing the world,' Georgina remarks, as a comment rather than a hint of jealousy.

Westlife have come off this tour with a kaleidoscope of images and memories of unusual people, different cultures, strange food, hotel floors, war, poverty and the smiling faces of the thousands of fans who flocked to their concerts.

Kian lifts his baseball cap and scratches his head as he reflects on the whirlwind that has swept him through the last three years.

'This is what you dream about, but you never imagine actually doing it. And even when you do, it's still not in your brain that you're actually doing it. When you're not doing it, that's when it hits you. When you're sitting at home at four in the afternoon watching MTV and your video is played, that's when it hits you.

'One night before the tour I was in Sligo and I'd had a normal night out with friends, playing snooker. Later, when I got home, I was lying on my bed and I was staring up at the discs all over my wall.

I started thinking, "What the feck is this? What is going on?"'

Sometimes, if you think really deeply about it, it's hard to take it on board, but the main thing is, not to let it go to your head.'

Their elevation to the top of the pop ladder had been a baptism of fire for the individuals in Westlife. One day they were normal, anonymous young guys going to college and dreaming their dreams. A year later they were household names at home and abroad, being chased by girls, living away from home and struggling to keep up with a mad-dash schedule that didn't allow time for family and friends.

The stress of being a pop star 24/7 occasionally manifested itself in in-group friction and fighting. But with the benefit of three years experience of coping with all kinds of bizarre and tension-fuelled situations, the young Westlife men now have a healthy grasp of life in the pressure chamber and of each other's personalities and idiosyncrasies.

'Surprisingly, we don't seriously argue anymore,' Nicky says. 'I won't say we're grown up, but we know how to get around things now. We realise that we're all in the same boat and we're all doing a job. It's as hard for Kian, Shane, Bryan and Mark as it is for me.

'We have become so close and we are like brothers. We look out for each other like brothers and we fight like brothers. Tensions build up in every relationship and have to be released.

'Sometimes we might only have three or four hours sleep and when you wake up and you're feeling like shit, people annoy you. Someone might put on music or say something out of order. If there's an interview in one of the papers someone might say, "You shouldn't have said that!" and it's, "Shut up, don't tell me what to do. I'll say what I want!" It's just silly, silly arguments.

'There are occasional screaming matches, with lots of swear words, that might last for 20 seconds. But when it's out of the way you carry on as if things are normal. You've had your little bitch and that's the end of it. You don't have to say sorry because people know you're sorry.

'But at the end of the day we're so close. If I go to McDonald's and the others are back in the hotel, one might be on the phone, one is asleep, one is reading a book and one is on the phone to his sister, I will surprise them with a take-out. I'll arrive back at the hotel with bags of food and I'll know they're going to love it.'

Westlife haven't put a time limit on the future life of the group. Their ambition is to last longer than any other boy band. They know that they're going to have to confront all kinds of personal pressures along the way, but they've resolved to enjoy the rollercoaster ride while it's happening, although sometimes when they look back it's all a blur.

Nicky is humming the Take That tune, Never Forget.

'The lyrics in that song really sum up the life of a boy band,' he says. 'The opening line is, "We've come a long way, but we're not too sure where we've been."

That alone just says it all because we've been everywhere and yet we haven't a clue where we've been.

'If you asked me where I was in some of the months last year, I could list a load of places in America and Europe, but I couldn't be sure when I was there.

'I'll get flashbacks to funny things that happened along the way. Like the time in the restaurant when the waiter fell over and the food went all over Bryan. I'll remember those moments because they're priceless.'

And he wanders off singing, 'Never pretend it's unreal, someday this will be somebody else's dream and now its ours.'